A HIGHLAND LADY IN FRANCE

Elizabeth Grant
of Rothiemurchus

A Highland Lady
in France
1843–1845

Edited by
Patricia Pelly and Andrew Tod
With an Introduction by
Andrew Tod

TUCKWELL PRESS

First published in 1996 by
Tuckwell Press Ltd
The Mill House
Phantassie
East Linton
East Lothian EH40 3DG
Scotland

British Library Cataloguing-in-Publication Data
A Catalogue record for this book
is available on request from the
British Library

The publishers acknowledge subsidy from

THE SCOTTISH ARTS COUNCIL

towards the publication of this volume

Typeset by Hewer Text Composition Services, Edinburgh
Printed and bound by
Cromwell Press, Broughton Gifford, Melksham, Wiltshire

Contents

Introduction	vii
Dramatis Personae	xviii
1843	I
1844	67
1845	201
Index	247

Introduction

The 'Highland Lady' is the name affectionately bestowed on Elizabeth Grant of Rothiemurchus by her niece, Lady Strachey, who brought out the first edition of her writings, just over a century after her birth in 1797. The full title of her book is *Memoirs of a Highland Lady*, and in the following century it has been recognised as an acknowledged masterpiece portraying the life and times of the Grant family in the first thirty years of the nineteenth century. David Daiches' *The New Companion to Scottish Culture* (1993) may speak of it in seemingly guarded terms as 'one of the lesser Scottish Diaries of the second rank' but it is made clear that Boswell and Scott, the sole representatives in the premier class, are there by virtue of their world status. In any case, to be in the second rank means standing alongside such other works of genius as Henry Cockburn's *Memorials of His Own Time*, so there may not really be much difference of opinion with those succeeding generations who in the hundred years since its appearance have chosen to see this important series of memoirs as a true classic of nineteenth-century Scottish writing and an extremely valuable window into the past.

The Highland Lady (who, to be consistent with earlier editorial practice, is referred to in the introduction and footnotes as E.G.), however, also kept many journals throughout her long life, most significantly from 1840 to the mid-1850s and then more irregularly to the end of her life in 1885. By this time she had got married to Colonel Henry Smith of Baltiboys (the name of his 1,200 acre estate some twenty miles south of Dublin in Co. Wicklow) whom she met as she describes at the end of the *Memoirs*, when she accompanied her father, Sir John Peter Grant, to India on his retrieving the family's dismal fortunes by his appointment to a judgeship in India. The editors of this present volume, Patricia Pelly, who as one of the Highland Lady's great-great-grand-daughters is able to provide family insights into the workings of her remarkable ancestor's mind and Andrew Tod who produced the first complete edition of the *Memoirs* in 1988, worked on an edited version of most of the 1840s, which was published in 1991. It was made clear that the purpose of this edition was to trace the improvements made on the estate and chart the lives of family and tenantry as they faced the desperate challenges of the famine. However, in order to keep the book within manageable proportions, it was decided not to include any of a two-year spell from August 1843 to July 1845 when the whole Smith family, including their three surviving children, Janey, Annie and Jack, went to France. 'This seemed', the Introduction stated, 'to be a self-contained period that might well stand on its own as a separate publication.' We hope that our edited version of these two years measures up to the standards set by *The Highland Lady in Ireland* and that it is agreed that the quality of her writing, powers of vivid observation and sheer interest were in no way diminished when she crossed the Channel.

It would under the circumstances have been perfectly understandable if the journal had become a humdrum duty reluctantly to be squeezed into the busy schedule of her life in France. To understand this it is necessary to examine their reasons for taking this big decision. After all, on the surface it made much more sense to enjoy the sort of quiet but cultured country life they so appreciated on their fast-improving estate so close to Dublin and not impossibly far from family in Edinburgh or Rothiemurchus. This was certainly the reaction of their friends and neighbours in and around the market town of Blessington: people like their irascible, inveterate gossip of a Doctor, George Robinson, or the Earl and Countess of Milltown, whose high-handed effrontery had left Elizabeth Smith as almost the only person who was prepared to conduct a conversation with them. There was also astonishment expressed by the Doctor's brother, John Robinson who was the Agent, and the Steward, Tom Darker, both of whom were in a good position to assess the wisdom of their employers' decision.

However, there was the ever-present question of their health. Colonel Smith had chosen to accept early retirement soon after his marriage, although he had originally planned to stay on in India for three years because of the severity of his asthma attacks, and it was accepted he would be much more comfortable in a warmer climate where he should be able to lay the foundations of a healthier existence later when they returned to Ireland. But there was also the matter of E.G.'s health. Although she was only forty-six when they left and was only halfway through her long life, there are clearly many points when she was unwell and seriously doubted whether she would live to see her children reach adulthood. From the point of view of the whole family, it was decided that two years in France would be to everyone's advantage. She summarised their thoughts in what she called a 'little review' written in her Journal on Saturday, 14 May 1843:

> The last three winters have made a sad change in me the first passed as accidental derangement, the second staggered *me*, the third frightened *Hal*, and I am sure not causelessly. With Mary's example before our eyes it would be worse than folly to try a fourth; so no sentimental nonsense shall overset me, feeling our removal right, I will make it agreeable, so *couleur de rose* must brighten all.

A second consideration was the desirability of organising their finances so that the final stages of the improvements they wished to make to the house, the estate and the tenantry could be set in motion. Much had been achieved by 1843 and the Journals show clearly that advantage had been taken, for example, of the opportunities presented by government loans, but if all was to be done that the Smiths wanted to achieve at Baltiboys, then one way of doing this was to spend two years in what was perceived as being a cheaper country. Colonel Smith was in a somewhat fortunate position in that four times a year his London bankers, Cockburn's, received his pension from the East India Company, and that acted as a certainty in the somewhat problematical world of Co. Wicklow estate finances. Nevertheless, if the family could live a fulfilled existence in one of the many agreeable towns in France that hosted exiled communities from the British Isles, then the rents from Baltiboys could be left to accumulate to fund the projected improvements. All of this she explained in her Journal on 14 May:

> Having determined on going abroad for two years we have
> offered to let this house for that term, furnished, with the
> garden, orchard, and good stabling and for a good tenant
> might throw a cow's grass into the bargain asking £150 a
> year and the gardener's wages.

In her usual practical way everything had been organised. The
sale of the jaunting car, the harness and saddlery, and all the
riding horses would be sufficient to pay all the travelling expenses
to Pau. Living expenses there would be taken care of with the
Colonel's E.I.C. pay and the Baltiboys rent leaving 'the rents
of the Irish property to accumulate, as Tom Darker thinks
the profits of the farm should nearly pay all the unavoidable
expenses attending the estate'. Tickets had been organised on
the boat between Southampton and Bordeaux, the *Calpe;* Mary
had been written to so that the Smiths could rent their apartment
when the Gardiners moved; arrangements had even been made
to hire a cook and a footman.

It is important to emphasise something that emerges loud
and clear from the diaries that have been already published.
Elizabeth Grant of Rothiemurchus arrived in Ireland with
very clear ideas of what she regarded as the duties of a
landed proprietor, and as Elizabeth Smith of Baltiboys she
was determined to play her part in helping her husband to
carry these out to the best of her considerable ability. It has
been mentioned that she was an inveterate writer and she
had many articles published during the 1840s, principally
in Chambers' *Edinburgh Journal.* Most of these were written
with the specific aim of raising money to play her part in the
financing of the running of the estate and of course, once the
tragedy of the famine struck after the Smith family's return
from France, then every means of raising money was exploited.
One such article was published in Volume 14, Number 360 in
November 1850 and it is entitled quite simply 'Retrenchment'.
One short conversation between a landlord's wife (whom it is not
entirely fanciful to see as the Highland Lady) and her nephew
by marriage summarises the essence of what she regarded as the
all-important contributions that ought to be made by a resident
improving landlord concerned to retrench in the interests of all

resident on the estate:

> Mrs. W. Why did you not see what was going on and endeavour to set right all you thought was amiss?
>
> George. Just as if a man had nothing to do but to wander about among mud-cabins. When I was here, I came for the hunting: three times a week out with the hounds left little leisure for other things. There were my plantations for the idle days, and the new avenue and a number of improvements in short, which I am sure you and my uncle, as model landlords, ought to be pleased to hear of. Then Lucy gets low without society; we have always a good deal of company during the winter; and in the summer we were off somewhere; so I'm sure I don't know where you'd find time for all these inspections.
>
> Mrs. W. From not making time, you see, my dear nephew, what you have brought yourself to – not only yourself but all your neighbours, for we can't separate our individual interest from that of the community. One careless landlord affects the welfare of all. Many careless landlords cause ruin.

She was, therefore, well aware of what was involved in the whole concept of retrenchment in the context of landlord responsibility and there is no doubt that they were determined to return to Baltiboys with their finances in sound order to set about the tasks they believed necessary both for the improvement of the estate and for what she in particular, in her strong-minded and idiosyncratic manner, regarded as the moral and practical advancement of the condition of their tenantry.

But there was also a third reason why she wanted to be in France. Her youngest sister Mary was grievously ill and, with her husband Thomas Gardiner who had resigned from the East India Company in order to look after his ailing wife, and young family, shuffled from spa to spa in a vain search of that elusive combination of good health and social *bonhomie* to which, she felt, her comparative youth and privileged upbringing entitled her. As is clear from the Memoirs and the Journals, Mary the youngest was in many respects the favourite, and it must have been heart-rending for the rest of the family to know she was so ill and not to be able to play a part in her possible restoration to good health. This was therefore a third compelling reason directing the

Smith family towards Pau where the Gardiners with their family
were well established by the summer of 1843.

Such an ambitious expedition, no matter how well organised,
involved a frenzy of arrangements and there was still the question
of trying to say farewell to her mother, who was in Edinburgh,
and her favourite Aunt Mary (most commonly referred to by her
married name as Aunt Bourne), who was in Oxford. In the end,
mother agreed to rendezvous with E.G. and Jack in Oxford and
appropriate farewells were exchanged with this somewhat taxing
of women. When the travelling party assembled in Southampton,
the Smiths were joined by Colonel Litchfield, an old E.I.C. friend
who had decided to join them in their adventure, Miss Hart
the governess and Margaret Fyfe, who hailed originally from
Rothiemurchus and was the housekeeper at Baltiboys.

The voyage to Bordeaux took three days and three nights
and with plenty of time at her disposal she produced long and
interesting descriptions of their experiences. E.G., of course,
had travelled extensively before, notably to and from India, but
never to France. Neither of the Colonels spoke French, so she
had to play the leading role in any negotiations, not one with
which she was unfamiliar, both on the rest of the journey and
when they set about completing the organisation of their lives
in Pau.

There was quite a substantial colony of British residents. It is
estimated by Mrs. Ellis,[1] who seems to have been a reliable guide,
that the population of the town was about 14,000 with the British
colony numbering between three and four hundred at their peak
in the autumn, when those seeking a more benign climate for
their ailments tended to arrive for the winter. Naturally, this
was the social milieu within which the Gardiners and Smiths
were expected to take their place. This had certainly been true
of Mary but it was only partially an accurate description of the
society sought by the Smiths. E.G. was not mightily impressed by
what she saw and the relentless gossip bored her; in particular the

1. She wrote a book about Pau called *Summer and
   Winter in the Pyrenees* which had been published
   two years before in 1841; E.G. read it and
   thought it a very accurate and useful guide. See 5
   November 1843.

long-running saga in which two long-established doctors fought a vendetta against a third recently arrived, suspectly qualified medical practitioner which brought out, she felt, the worst in this close-knit community. Nevertheless, it is in her description of the details of everyday life and her fascination with recording in her Journal everything that interested her that the most vivid portions of her writing lie.

There was obviously great concern about the wretched condition of her sister. Most days saw a medical bulletin being confided to the Journal and it became increasingly clear that Mary's condition was steadily deteriorating. So, although there was much to rejoice about in the physical delights and natural advantages of their choice of abode on the Continent, the disadvantages of Pau society and her pessimism about the chances of Mary's recovery meant that there is a prevailingly resigned and sad tone to much of what she wrote. This is most obviously seen, perhaps, in her final entry for the year. She roundly condemns society in this backwater: 'as far as we have seen of it, far from being agreeable, judging from all we hear I should say the best is bad'. She is also uncharacteristically harsh on the English who made up the bulk of the British residents: 'they are just a little worse than the English at home and the most odious people on earth. We accustomed to Scotch or Irish never could get on with them, I am sure'. But the principal reason for her apparent disenchantment lay in the contrast between their lives at Baltiboys and at Pau:

> It is a stupid life [here] to those who have been used to the activity of a country life on their own property, for there is nothing to see here but the face of nature, nothing to do but such work as people can cut out for themselves, nor resources of any kind for the indolent or the idle.

When the Gardiners' restless spirits led them to consider leaving Pau and it was decided that a move to Avranches in Normandy would be best for Mary, it is hardly surprising that the Smiths were pleased to follow them north.

Mary and her family left first in the middle of May 1844, and before following them, E.G. organised a fortnight's tour through some of the beautiful parts of the neighbouring Pyrenees as recommended by the Mrs. Ellis she had been reading. Her memories of this expedition she was to use to good effect on her return to Ireland with a series of writings for William and Robert Chambers' *Edinburgh Journal.* 'Wintering in Pau' ('by a Lady') appeared in the autumn and winter of 1848, earning her fifteen pounds for five articles; two further ones next year, 'A Month among the Pyrenees' and 'A Few Weeks at Cauterets among the Pyrenees', earned three pounds. True as always to the responsibilities she consistently believed to be appropriate to her status, Chambers' records show that she left instructions for these payments to be sent direct to John Robinson the Agent to be used for the general benefit of the estate.

They left Pau and the Pyrenees, then, with pleasanter memories than would have been the case had they departed with Mary. E.G. had liked the basic situation of Pau ('Edinburgh in miniature') and she shared the view of an earlier traveller, J. Augustus St. John, about Avranches;[2] he wrote that its site was 'truly beautiful, raised upon a gentle hill and commanding on all sides the most rich, varied and extensive prospects' including the views across the bay to Mont St. Michel. However, as both he and E.G. were well aware, there were other factors that helped to explain the move:

> A great number of English, as many, it is asserted, as four hundred, reside here, on account of the beauty of the site as well as the cheapness of the provisions; and they are said to live in great harmony with the inhabitants, by whom they are highly respected.

Relationships were not as rosy between the Smiths and those with whom they had to deal when house-hunting, but such matters swiftly were relegated into obscurity when E.G. realised her sister was fast approaching the end, and indeed she died on the last day of July.

They decided to stick to their original plan of retrenching for a full two years. There is a naturally sombre spirit to much of E.G.'s Journal over the next year but she is still intrigued by all she sees around her and as ever she writes in an engaging, vigorous and enthusiastic style. They kept up to

2. He wrote a *Journal of a Residence in Normandy*
    (published in Edinburgh in 1831).

date with their newspapers and magazines; they subscribed to the *Scotsman* and the *Edinburgh Review* and they were sent their regular Irish journals like *Saunder's*. Letters were received from Agent, Steward and Doctor so that Blessington and Baltiboys developments were brought to their attention: best of all, George Robinson himself came to stay with them in April.

As a result, the Smiths were well informed about the political developments that took place in Ireland during their absence and E.G. gave her reactions to them in her Journal in terms that emphasise she was in no doubt about their significance. It has been thought best to give a commentary here in the Introduction on the central political issue of the years 1743–1845, rather than clutter up the text of her narrative with endless footnotes.

At the heart of all that happened was the intense personal and political rivalry that had existed between Sir Robert Peel (Prime Minister, 1841–1846) and Daniel O'Connell (1775–1847), the hero of Catholic Emancipation in 1829, universally known in Ireland as the Liberator.[3] E.G.'s French Journals have a full commentary on the movement launched by O'Connell for the repeal of the Act of Union. In spite of his popularity as Lord Mayor of Dublin 1841/1842, only eighteen M.P.s favouring repeal were returned in the General Election of 1841. Clearly a change of tactics was required and this took the form of a series of 'Monster Meetings' commented on in the Journals. Peel's tactics were to undermine this nationalist fervour by a series of reforms of which, as E.G. fully realised, the proposed trebling of the annual grant to the seminary at Maynooth together with a capital grant of £30,000 was the most controversial. However, when O'Connell planned to hold the last of the Monster Meetings at the hugely symbolic site of Clontarf before summoning the Council of Three Hundred to plan a bill for the repeal of the Act of Union, it was banned and a week later O'Connell was arrested on a charge of conspiracy to subvert and intimidate the lawful government.

3. For an accessible and readable account of the detailed events surrounding the complex relationship between these two arch-rivals, see *A New History of Ireland, Volume V: Ireland Under the Union I*, edited by W.E. Vaughan; particularly valuable are the two chapters by Oliver Macdonagh.

Oliver Macdonagh describes this as the climax of the 'political duel' between the two great protagonists.

The 'State Trials' as they are referred to in the Journals commenced on 15 January 1844 and it is interesting that from the very start E.G., somewhat in contrast one suspects to the line taken by her husband (who is several times described as being of the 'Orange persuasion'), believed that the trials should not have taken place. They lasted for twenty-five days; there were no Roman Catholics on the jury. O'Connell was found guilty but sentence was deferred. On 30 May he was given a twelve-month jail sentence, fined £2,000 and bound to keep the peace for seven years. When the news reached E.G. in the middle of her tour of the Pyrenees, she thought that the light sentence and comfortable conditions in prison were appropriate responses. However, O'Connell's appeal to the House of Lords was upheld and on 4 September the earlier judgement was reversed. Justice, she felt, had to be done but 'just as the country was forgetting him . . . the whole country thriving, here comes out the mischief-maker to put everything into confusion again' (11 September 1844).

And when ten months later the Smith family returned to Ireland, 'thriving' was exactly how they found everything. Public events suggested that Sir Robert's magisterial grip on the tiller of government was as sure as ever. Dublin had never given such a favourable impression of prosperity. And close inspection of Baltiboys showed that the encouraging and optimistic reports sent regularly by Tom Darker had indeed painted an accurate picture of an estate that lived up to its Blessington reputation. A fortnight before they had left for France two years before, one of the old women on the estate had remarked: 'Faix – were they all sich landlords as the Colonel, Mr. O'Connell might go whistle for repalers', upon which E.G.'s comment was simply: 'The old body has hit it'.

Finally, a word of explanation about the editorial practices. E.G.'s idiosyncratic, to our eyes, spelling has been retained (Punjaub, Blair Athole, and Hayti; plaister of Paris, Emperour and pacquet) and an attempt has been made to make it consistent. Brackets in the text are additional pieces of explanation not worth a footnote. The four sets of initials used in the Introduction and the footnotes are E.I.C. (East India Company), D.N.B.

(Dictionary of National Biography), O.E.D. (Oxford English Dictionary) and the S.N.D. (Scottish National Dictionary). Everything written in Elizabeth Grant or Elizabeth Smith's meticulous hand is a model of neatness and clarity; it is hard to recall anything that is crossed out or obviously the result of muddled thinking. However, she wrote in one continuous flow and the one major change that has been made to the text is the introduction of paragraphs. As with all our efforts, the intention has been to try and ensure that justice has been done to this wonderful diarist's unique and important contribution to a greater understanding of her life and times.

BIBLIOGRAPHY OF THE EDITIONS
OF THE WORKS OF E.G.

Memoirs of a Highland Lady, edited by Lady Strachey (John Murray, 1898)

Memoirs of a Highland Lady, second (smaller) edition, edited by Lady Strachey (John Murray, 1911)

Memoirs of a Highland Lady, edited by Angus Davidson (John Murray, Albemarle Library, 1950)

The Irish Journals of Elizabeth Smith, 1840–1850, edited by David Thomson with Moyra McGusty (Clarendon Press, Oxford, 1980)

Memoirs of a Highland Lady, edited and introduced by Andrew Tod (Canongate Classics, 1988)

The Highland Lady in Ireland, edited by Patricia Pelly and Andrew Tod (Canongate Classics, 1991)

Dramatis Personae

FAMILY

COLONEL HENRY SMITH inherited the estate of Baltiboys when he was in his fiftieth year on the death of his somewhat discreditable elder brother in 1830. His career had been with the armed forces of the East India Company and, as he suffered from acute asthma, he took this opportunity to resign and return to Ireland to restore the fortunes of a much run-down estate. By 1843, when the decision was taken to retrench in France, the estate was back on its feet and he calculated that two years away would be enough to save sufficient funds to enable a final programme of improvements to take place, leaving their family finances on a secure basis.

Before leaving India, he married ELIZABETH GRANT OF ROTHIEMURCHUS who had accompanied her father out to India when he had been appointed to a judgeship in Bombay. It is clear from her Journals how much she supported her husband in the many ventures that were undertaken to improve the condition of the estate and the lives of all who lived and worked on it. But it was not only economic reasons that took them to France. Her sister Mary was extremely ill and had been travelling restlessly for some years in a vain attempt to recover her health and Elizabeth wanted to be with her sister to help her face this crisis.

There is mention of:

Their surviving children JANEY (who was born in 1830), ANNIE (1832) and JACK/JOHNNY (1838)

Her parents SIR JOHN PETER GRANT (1774–1848), who was still a judge in India, and Jane née Ironside

Her brothers WILLIAM PATRICK (1798–1874) and JOHN PETER G.C.M.C. – K.C.B. (1807–1893) both of whom were educated at Eton and made their way in turn to employment in India William married SARAH SIDDONS (d.s.p.) and John Peter married HENRIETTA CHICHELE PLOWDEN and had four children

Her sisters JANE (1800–1863) and MARY FRANCES (1804–1844) were both married – Jane first to COLONEL GERVASE PENNINGTON and then to JAMES GIBSON CRAIG (d.s.p.), and Mary to THOMAS GEORGE GARDINER, who had retired from the East India Company

The GARDINER children THOMAS GEORGE (Tom), JOHN PETER (Johnny) and JANE (Janey)
Her mother's sister 'AUNT BOURNE' – MARY IRONSIDE who was a widow living in considerable comfort in Oxford

IRISH FRIENDS AND NEIGHBOURS:

EARL AND COUNTESS OF MILLTOWN OF RUSSBOROUGH HOUSE
JOHN HORNIDGE and his son RICHARD OF TULFARRIS
MARQUIS OF DOWNSHIRE
DR. GEORGE ROBINSON, the Blessington Doctor
JOHN ROBINSON, a Dublin grain merchant and the Baltiboys Agent
REV. WILLIAM OGLE MOORE, Rector of Kilbride
FATHER ARTHUR GERMAINE, Blackditches Priest
Baltiboys school-mistress, MISS GARDINER

Governesses referred to: –

MISS ELPHICK, the Grants' Governess at the Doune
JANE COOPER from Rothiemurchus who was the governess at Baltiboys
MISS HART who was the Smith children's governess at Pau but who was dismissed at Avranches

AT PAU: –

Residents in the Maison Puyoo . . . the Smith family plus their household
MARGARET FYFE, the Baltiboys housekeeper, originally from Rothiermurchus
JACQUES the manservant
ANTOINETTE the cook
MARQUESA DE NAVARRES
M. ET MME. DE COSTANO
Doctors . . .
DR. TAYLOR
DR. SMITH
MR. HAZLEWOOD the 'quack'
Chaplains . . .
REV. MR. KERR
REV. MR. HEDGES
REV. L.J. BUSCARLET, a French Protestant preacher

1843

Carle Vernet. *English Travellers*. c. 1820 (detail).

SATURDAY, AUGUST 26. Late in the evening reached Bordeaux, after a prosperous voyage. The sea was very rough in the Channel and on rounding into the Bay of Biscay and the first evening the rain was very heavy, in the night almost tropical filling the deck buckets in little more than an hour; the wind was so high one of the yards was broken right in two; the pitching was dreadful. Many on board had crossed the Atlantick, been to the Indies and back – none ever suffered so much as during this night in the Channel, for it blew a high west wind, rolling in the seas we were crossing in our small steamer the *Calpe* with a swell there was no supporting. How ill the people were! and my poor children! I was sick once myself. Next morning was fine, and those who were able refreshed themselves on deck; but the evening was rainy again and we were all sent down to that odious cabin, where eleven children – one of them an infant three weeks old, three maids, Miss Hart the governess dead sick and three ladies beside myself, were packed into those dreadful bed-boxes.

Friday and Saturday were beautiful and after passing the Isle of Ushant, the water became gradually smoother, till we entered the Gironde, after which we hardly felt any motion. One by one all crept on deck; the air, the scenery and the near close of our voyage diffusing cheerfulness among our whole party. Our passengers were, Mr. and Mrs. Valpy, five daughters, a niece, a son – all dreadfully sick, half of them nearly insensible while the rough sea lasted. When they recovered they appeared very nice people, children well brought up, papa and mama clever; he a Bengal civilian, knows my brother, John,[1] voted for him when he canvassed so successfully for the Treasurership or Secretaryship of some Literary or other fund, and had therefore plenty to say to me I was glad to hear. We think he must be son to the famous classical Valpy, the master of Reading School[2] and should have

1. Sir John Peter Grant (1807–1893) had a distinguished career in India (Lieutenant-General of Bengal) and the West Indies (Governor of Jamaica after the revolt of 1865).
2. Richard Valpy (1754–1836), the colourful Headmaster of Reading School for almost fifty years,

3

supposed his wife to be Sir Robert Peel's Mrs. Valpy, whose letter exculpating Lord Ellenborough from one of his many presumed absurdities so confounded the barking radicals of young England, for she seems clever and spirited enough, but she accompanied her husband home and therefore cannot be that heroine.[1] They are bound for Pau for the winter on account of her health and are guided on their way thither by a French courier, who with all the civility in the world looks like his caste, but what can they do? they can't speak French.

Mrs. Drysdale had her baby with her – a good little dolly on the whole, when it had not got the stomach ache from over-feeding. Her husband, a doctor in some regiment quartered in Ireland, a canny Scot, accompanied her on board and gave such particular directions about the gruel for his baby, was so pertinacious in his various requirements for the comfort of his wife, so long and so energetick on his leave-taking, that he amused, surprised and discomposed all beholders. They had never been separated before. He was refused leave and has to join his regiment at Templemore, while she was to proceed alone with her infant of three weeks old to pass the winter with her parents at Montauban, a climate better suited to her delicate health than the damp air of Ireland; the poor thing had been with him in the West Indies and very ill, and there she lost three boys in eight months – her all – I fear she will lose this fourth one too, unless she very much

had ten children by his second wife and wrote many best-selling text books; for the D.N.B. he 'inspired his pupils with an intense personal affection and had the reputation of being one of the hardest floggers of the day'.

1. This is clearly a reference to an obscure piece of political gossip involving Edward Law, Earl of Ellenborough, who was Governor-General of India from 1841 to 1844; it is worth mentioning that the Grants would have had little regard for him after his leaked comment to the *Times* in 1829, following the appointment of two servile judges to join her father on the bench in Bombay, that this was 'like a wild elephant between two tame ones'.

alters her management of it. By way of nursing, she nourishes
it herself only in the night. What can the milk be that is pent
up near sixteen hours! All day it is stuffed with gruel, great
doses each time and a dozen times in the day; and when it
hiccups with wind, they call it smiling. She a'n't a very wise
person, the poor, patient creature, but mild and ladylike and
grateful for very trifling kindness.

Our next on the list was a Mrs. Vaux from Sunderland with a
fine spoiled boy three years old, going to join her husband, the
Captain of a trader and to accompany him on a coasting voyage
to the east. No other female to be on board their vessel, for Lor!
she was never *hill*, so should not want one. She was a very pretty
woman and clever too, but so very queer a mixture of Wapping
and Sunderland, betwixt which places she has passed her life,
varied by a couple of trips across the Atlantick in the trader. A
Mr. Clark, a sensible merchant, a resident at Bordeaux, a very
obliging man, and a couple of handsome seamen, one of whom
was too ill to shew himself till quite in smooth water, completed
a party far too small to secure the Steward his expected profit,
though large enough for the accommodation.

During our progress up the Gironde there was nothing the
least attractive in the scenery – a wide, muddy *firth* with flat
banks – but at the junction of the Dordogne and the Garonne it
improved into beauty, and when we turned into the Garonne,
the whole way up was a succession of wooded banks and pretty
villages and many more neat country houses of some size than
we had expected. Amongst them the retreat of M. de Peronnet,
who shared the fate of the two de Polignacs and was at last
sent into exile here; he never quits his own grounds and is
but rarely seen.[1]

At the Lazaret [Quarantine Station] the Officer of Health

1. Jules de Polignac (1780–1847) and his brother
   Armand were the mainstays of the final ultra-
   conservative ministry of the last of the Bourbon
   monarchs, Charles X (1824–1830); the so-called
   bourgeois monarchy of his successor Louis Philippe
   enjoyed the reputation of treating its political
   opponents with generosity.

came on board accompanied by the doctor and all forms required were gone through. Our passports were taken from us, a list of passengers made out and given to the Guardship, which we passed a little higher up and two officials left with us as spies whose comments on our national peculiarities as they discoursed with the old skeleton of a pilot whom we had picked up some miles before entering the river was anything but flattering to us. Dinner was going on. I suppose they were hungry and nothing was offered them to eat. It was our Captain's first voyage to these parts. He is young and irritable and impatient, vexed by delays he did not anticipate and ignorant of the language in which all these vexatious forms were conveyed to him. Miss Hart and a cabin boy, Mr. Clark and I were the only interpreters on board. She and I heard all the murmured ill-humour with regret and mentioning it to Mrs. Drysdale, who is well acquainted with Captain Russell, she at once went up to him to enlighten him upon the gloomy looks. An invitation to partake of some refreshment immediately followed and our guards accepted with eagerness – no more moody looks on either side. We were all in agreeable humour, thanks to kind Mrs. Drysdale. 'Si l'on mange l'on paie,' said the Pilot in reply to some remark of our surly spy. 'Remplir le ventre . . . penser à d'autrui . . . c'est là leur caractère,' was part of the rejoinder, which had disturbed us as we caught the few words and the looks were so ferocious; but all was harmony after the feed. It is a pity the English are so ungracious, they make enemies actually for want of decent good breeding, as if they were naturally both ill-tempered and inhospitable, whereas they are merely impolite, in other words, selfish.

After coming to an anchor the whole scene was confusion. We lay amidst a crowd of shipping, with a fine old town on either hand, the deck covered with luggage, different officials arriving from time to time in little boats, a fleet of which surrounded the vessel waiting for hire; porters thronged on board and hotel keepers, thrusting their cards into every hand they could seize on. It was getting dark and we feared the Custom House Officers would either order us up to the Custom House or delay visiting us till the following morning, which would have detained us where we were all night, but at last they came and were very civil giving little trouble comparatively – perhaps because we had no reserve of manner nor anything contraband in our trunks. They overlooked the two or three first very carefully, were less diligent as they went on and quite laughed at my confession about a pack of playing cards. It was a long job too and very, very hot and very confusing, there was so much bustle. This part of the business fell to Margaret[1] and me. Colonel Smith and Miss Hart undertook the more fatigueing part of walking in the heat all the way to the hotels to choose among them and bargain for apartments. At length the deck was cleared. Mrs. Vaux and a dreadful sailor brother, mate of the husband's ship, who had come down the river with his perfect wig of curls to meet her, rowed off to their vessel. Mr. Clark took a bag in one hand and a box in the other and descended to the same boat which conveyed Mrs. Drysdale, her baby, her maid, her mother and her mother's maid to the hotel, where an apartment had been secured for her by her mother, who had come all the way from Montauban to receive her. The Courier with a deal of bustle collected all his flock. And we in one boat with our baggage in another made our way to the quay, where a coach was waiting. After a battle with the boatmen we gave them more than they should have had though much less than they wanted and proceeded to the Hotel de la Charrente [the cart] where we have two large and two small bedrooms and a sitting room all nicely furnished for twelve francs[2] a day with a balcony to look from and the theatre 'the finest theatre in the world' one of the principal objects to look at. A good cup of tea soon refreshed us. I had a violent nervous headache for an hour or more from the Custom House proceedings; laying on my back in the dark and then the tea quite cured it. Hal had

1. Margaret Fyfe, originally from Rothiemurchus, was the housekeeper at Baltiboys and accompanied the Smith family to France.
2. Her calculations (see 27 October 1843) were, like those of Mrs. Ellis during her earlier stay in Pau, based on an exchange rate of one franc equalling ten pennies (or nearly four pence decimal.).

no asthmatick feelings and we were all so tired that we went very early to bed. Jack quite done up.

27. Sunday. Last Sunday in dull, gloomy Oxford with my poor Mother and my sober Aunt in that dreary house and half-dead place. To-day in Bordeaux, how many hundred miles away, cheerfulness all round me, gaily furnished rooms, streets thronged with blythe-looking people, troops marching, bands playing, the obliging waiter smiling on every order, and for fear of all this excitement failing, the porters who brought our luggage and whom we had not paid last night on account of their having left a basket behind, brought with it this morning a determination not to take the five francs they had agreed to hire for. Mr. Valpy's Courier having given his fourteen, they would rather go before the Commissaire! but they did not – their courage failed them, and on giving an additional franc for the recovery of the basket, we got rid of them. Such a crew! Not worse than others of their sort elsewhere, though – London, Liverpool, Southampton, Dublin. These kind of chances are their harvest, and happening but seldom, they must make the most of them.

Colonel Litchfield[1] appeared at breakfast with swollen eyes and other unequivocal symptoms that his repose had been less sweet in his polished couch, surrounded by mirrours and gilding than it would have been in a simple English country Inn. Annie had suffered equally, so Miss Hart set out to buy spirits of lavender, which is said to banish disagreeable intruders. How strange that with such luxury in furniture, such excellent cooking, attention and civility, there should lurk dirt in every corner, vermin in every bed, and an odour upon the staircase from the disgusting impurity of an apartment, the cleanliness of which is of first-rate importance to British comfort, really sufficient to create typhus fever.

Our breakfast today was good – milk, coffee, plenty of bread, butter, radishes, pears, peaches and grapes. Our dinner – vegetable soup, excellent, then four plates containing a

1. He was a bachelor former E.I.C. colleague of
Colonel Smith's who accompanied the Smith family
throughout their two-year residence in France.

small kind of herring peculiar to the place, fried, a pâté of fowl and pigeon, the *bouilli* [boiled meat] with pickled cucumbers, fritters and potatoes in their skins, next came a morsel of roasted mutton, haricots, salad, custard puddings in cups, a dessert of fruit, including small hautboy strawberries high-flavoured and cheese, two bottles of small claret; all very neatly served, with an anxiety on the part of the waiter to oblige us, which indeed seems to be the manner of the people and is particularly agreeable.

All the early part of the morning the two Colonels with their interpreter, Miss Hart, were out about their passports, etc. Nothing could be done it being Sunday, Mr. James Maguire called with a note from Mr. Gardiner to Hal, kindly welcoming us and telling us all was ready at Pau. Mr. Maguire a handsome middle-aged Irishman, seemed delighted to meet a countryman for he sat I really think near two hours talking of our neighbours the Hornidges, with whom he had been at school and the places about Naas, near where he was born. He made himself very useful to us in every way, and will help us out of the scrape about our plate, which Mary had led us to suppose was admissible. In the meanwhile it is left on board in the steward's charge as part of his cabin stock.

28. Yesterday evening we strolled about this very fine old Town among crowds of the middle and lower ranks enjoying Sunday night either sauntering about the streets or sitting in small groups outside their doors. Not an uncivil word or rude action thought of. Some wine shops were full and in one were people playing at dominos. Ices were in request either at the confectioners' or under a large awning before the theatre, which was open and chairs and tables placed thickly, all filled. It was a curious crowd, reminding us something of Bombay from its variety and the dark complexion and the Indian style of head, worn by so many Portuguese-looking girls of the servant class, probably consisting of a gay-coloured handkerchief tyed with more or less care round the head. Generally speaking I should say that a very bad style of dress prevailed among the women and that very little beauty is found to counterbalance this; the men are extremely undersized, with fine eyes, good coats and *bright*

new hats – this particularly struck us. We saw no wonder
but the old Cathedral built as usual by the English of the
olden time and well worth a much more accurate survey
than the waning light permitted.[1] Our places being taken in
the diligence public stage coach for Tuesday morning, we got
all ready for travelling. Miss Hart and the Colonels went the
round of the Bureaus and each had to pay two francs for the
renewal of their passports. In the evening we paid our bill, the
porters came from the Diligence office for our trunks and the
facteur [transport agent] promised to call us by half after three
next morning.

29. I was up when the facteur came; he went from door to door
and roused us well. We had coffee before starting and Colonel
Smith being much pleased with the attention of the garçon,
gave him eight francs, which agreeably surprised him and
probably caused the landlord to charge us rather more for
our single dish of coffee and morsel of toast than he had
done for our good breakfasts of former mornings, or it might
be that he required a little extra for rising so very early to see us
off. The porters, too, on being offered three francs for carrying
our luggage mutinied in a body and demanded twenty. We
had given so much to the boatmen, so much to the other
porters, besides a franc to a man who brought my recovered
basket – they knew to a sou what we had spent among the
fraternity, and were quite noisy on the subject. Not the least
un-civil – we have met as yet with nothing approaching to
surliness. Miss Hart gave up the battle. I did not, I called the
conducteur, who awarded them six francs.

We were off before five and were some time in getting
through this large town which is beautiful and interesting,
and I should think thriving, as some new and really good
houses are being built in all directions and a great many
old ones in the act of being replaced by better. The country
was pretty for the first hour or two, merely from being well
wooded, for there was a great sameness in the flat scenery. No

1. The Romanesque Cathedral Church of St. André
   was begun in the eleventh century; Bordeaux was the
   most significant port in England's Angevin Empire
   from 1154 to 1453.

neatness anywhere – bad gates to fields, half-ruined fences, not a shrubbery or a garden or a flower plot to be seen – the tolerably sized houses, decent and that was all; the cabins in the country very Irish, in the Towns quite Indian, for there was a *side* open, all the family and all the wares on the floor within and without; no furniture, no finishings, and at night just such a wretched lamp with half-expiring flame as is used in an Indian hut. Were it rainy here, it would be Ireland – the same untidyness about the doors and everywhere else which passes in a fine climate for want of taste, but becomes wretchedness in a wet one. No cultivation of consequence anywhere. Vine-yards for the first forty miles exactly like hop gardens, a few fields of maize and Indian corn, a very little hay, no cattle, no farm-yards – that beautiful feature in English and Scotch scenery. As we got on we came to a great many patches of fir trees with fern, broom, copse oak and *heather* of two or three kinds, very brilliant in colour. The inns were very bad on the whole road. We stopped to breakfast at ten at a place not nearly so respectable as a publick house. The rooms were larger but miserable, more like a set of small barns. I don't know what the passengers got to eat, for we did not join them, having bought at the last post for half a franc a large basket of grapes, and having bread with us, we made that our meal. We of the *intérieur* at least. Colonel Smith and Colonel Litchfield, who were perched up in the Banquette [outside seats] we could not reach. At four we dined at Mont de Marsin, a good town in the Indian style with a decenter inn, and where those that joined the *table d'hôte* said they fared well. I was afraid of headache, so had bread and wine and water with Miss Hart and Margaret in a very tidy bedroom.

Here ended all comfortable travelling. We had hitherto gone briskly on changing horses every eight or ten miles; but from this place the stages were longer, the stoppages ditto, and the horses went slower. Between seven and eight o'clock we made a halt in earnest of more than two hours to rest our tired horses, who had then to take us on, for the whole road has been deranged by the fêtes at Pau in honour of the Duc de Montpensier, who had been there to erect a fine statue of

Henri IV,[1] and the crowds who assembled had made such a run upon the post horses that the poor creatures were fairly done up, though their brethren of the diligences had assisted. We were all the better, however, of the rest; the position in the inside of a narrow carriage is very cramped and with sleepy children, baskets, clokes and extraordinary heat, it had been very exhausting. We all got out and walked to a bridge over a good sized river and up and down the street of this perfectly quiet town, the residence of an archbishop too, small as it is, and I am sure this enabled us to bear better the remainder of this very disagreeable night. An intelligent Norman traveller, whom we found seated at the door of the post house had been waiting three hours for a seat in some other diligence detained by the same cause. He was not disposed either to admire the Duc de Montpensier – stupid young man – Duc de Nemours haughty – Joinville – Aumale – a shrug – the Duc d'Orleans alone had talents worthy of his father and manners agreeable to the nation.

30. Between six and seven in the morning reached Pau in a fog too thick for the Pyrénées to peep through. We had had a mile or two of hilly road, more trees than usual, a brook and shady banks – all telling of mountainous scenery, rows of clean stone houses next appeared, and we drove into a *parc* full of trees where were handsome barracks, and then into a new *Place*, open, airy, handsome, the Place Henri IV. Mr. Gardiner was eagerly watching for us and his dear little Janey. They had been walking there since three o'clock – the ordinary hour of arrival. I have seen Mary, went to her after breakfast, came home again to unpack, dined with the Gardiners at two, home again, back to them to tea, home and to bed by nine.

1. The Duc de Montpensier (1824–1890) was the fifth son of the sole Orleanist king of France, Louis Philippe (1830–1848); he had spent the previous year as a serving officer in the French army in the recently conquered colony of Algeria. Henry IV (1589–1610), whose reputation is secure as, perhaps, the person who more than most contributed to the end of the French Wars of Religion, came from Béarn and was the first of the Bourbon Kings of France.

31. We occupy the basement of Maison Puyoo and enter it by a handsome door from the covered pavement of the Place. A clean lobby leads on to the folding doors, which shut in our apartment; the stair to the higher stories is in this outer lobby and clean and spacious, like the stairs in our houses, not like the Edinburgh common stair. Our door opens on a small matted room with a good window, chairs and pegs for hanging hats, etc; a door on one side opens to our bedroom, on the other to the drawing-room, a very pretty room, nicely furnished, with pretty chairs of different kinds, sofa, bookcase, several tables – little and big – clock, etc., and three windows well draperied and very handsome paper and polished floor, through this is the dining-room, plainer but very comfortable, and the stairs to a lower story, for this row of houses, being built on a hill-side has a fine, airy rear. Our room is a very pleasant one, beyond a short passage, which has a water-closet on one side and a small room for Margaret on the other. Out of my room, which is a drawing-room with a bed in it and most nicely furnished with wardrobes, etc., is a small, light, washing closet, large enough for my trunks to remain in it and well fitted with pegs for gowns and a small dressing room for the Colonel with a bed in it for Jack. Downstairs Miss Hart and the girls have a large double-bedded room; Colonel Litchfield a bedroom and dressing-room; there is a manservant's room, the cook's room, a small parlour, kitchen and plenty of cupboards and closets all over the house, with good cellarage for wood, etc., below again.

SATURDAY, SEPTEMBER 2. The three trunks having arrived from Bordeaux, we unpacked them; then I went to sit a couple of hours with Mary. The pianoforte we had chosen came – a very good one, grand cabinet with all the new keys, quite new, a very pretty piece of furniture. Mr. Valpy called, they had just arrived and he was house hunting. This hotel being full, he went with the Colonel to look at the apartment above Mr. Gardiner, and found an old schoolfellow in our truly amiable brother-in-law.[1] The little girls went out in their

1. As employees of the East India Company, they had been educated at Haileybury and the I.C.S. (Indian Civil Service) School.

new French bonnets, which I had some trouble in keeping sober enough for my taste – they are Italian straw, very simply trimmed and very becoming.

3. First Sunday at Pau. We may consider ourselves settled for our things are all unpacked, we are all in our places, our arrangements made; still we are not quite at home. I don't exactly understand yet what our daily expenses are likely to be. Our own servants don't come to us till tomorrow. These are Mary's, new ones she has engaged to replace those who are only remaining with her till ours can quit their present services. The Inventory has yet to be taken. M. Puyoo and his housekeeper are both so much occupied with other apartments in the different hotels belonging to himself and his father that they put off from day to day attending to us. They must give us a few more little necessary comforts – more jugs and basins, some kitchen utensils, and enable Colonel Smith to get a little air into his dressing-room. I daresay it will take the best part of this next week before all is as it should be.

In the meanwhile our little party seems very happy. Dear Hal is perfectly well, no asthma, no cough, no headache, no dyspepsia – no wonder this novel feeling of perfect health should make him pleased with all around him. The air is very delightful, very soft and very balmy, though rather too warm for exercise and apt to have a closeness in it towards night, but after ten it becomes fresher – there is nothing like the Indian night, though the day reminds us of India sufficiently. Colonel Litchfield looks infinitely better already, his spirits are improving daily, he sleeps well, eats better, and if he would but leave off *half* of all the medicine he swallows, he would very soon be a different person. The little girls are delighted with everything. All is new and all is charming. These are their holiday hours, for as yet we have not thought of study. Their nice little cousin too they have taken to with all their hearts, so they have no regrets.

Miss Hart too is very cheerful in her ways, they like her and she likes them and I think she will bring them on nicely, for she is anxious about it, clever, well-informed and steady; but there are great drawbacks to our quite approving of her, particularly after quiet, ladylike Jane Cooper. Naturally of a gay disposition, she has been spoiled by the Gardiners and is noisy and boisterous and forward, chattering with vehemence, expressing very decided opinions, a manner in every respect unfeminine and ungraceful and unbecoming her station – it is only manner I hope, and I think it will subside. I think when the studies begin and she is less with us and more occupied in her own department, this excited style will give way to one more suited to us. I can quietly discourage all this offensive racket and by directing her thoughts to wiser things than seem latterly to have occupied them, I hope her own good sense will do the rest in time with patience, for her valuable qualities are many and not always to be met with united.

Unluckily the Colonel has a perfect horrour of this sort of manner – he can't endure it – it makes him quite uncomfortable, destroys the quiet happiness of his home, so unless poor Miss Hart sobers considerably, we shall have to look about for another Governess, and her warm heart and high principles and good talents will not easily be replaced. I must say that I much like her. She saves me every trouble, every expense in her power, puts up with anything, everything, consults with me in all her plans for her pupils, is much more easily accommodated than poor Miss Cooper, manages the servants better, makes the children happier and teaches them more agreeably. She will stitch and mend and help to dress them, and sit up at night to read something to introduce into conversation at proper moments next day, there is only this unfortunate manner to regret, perhaps it will cure, it is all good spirits – innocent good spirits – from youth, health and happiness. Jack don't take to her, though she is very kind to him. He is an odd child of the sensitive nature of his father, and I know it is her want of gentleness that repels him.

Poor, dear boy, he is not happy here; he longs, like his Mama, for his country home. He used to be so happy digging all day under the hedge which bounds my flower garden, or messing in the little pond, helping the labourers, out in the fresh air – neither hot nor weary – enjoying all his boyish plays. Here he has his short walk before breakfast with his Father or with Colonel Litchfield, his longer – and his hotter – walk at night – our state procession; but this is no pleasure to him, and all the weary day he has but my room or the passage to play in – no playthings, for he don't care much for toys; no companions – for Annie, once his best resource, is now quite occupied with her cousin, and poor Jack can only creep to me to be brightened by a talk of Baltiboys. He will find amusement soon in a degree, and so must I get the time over the most useful way I can; but as to enjoying life here with my habits, it is not possible. Not that I mean to be discontented, I have nothing to complain of, it is simply a mode of life not to my taste – perfectly uninteresting; but I will do my best to make the best of it, and as I do not feel ill, it will be less difficult. The Colonel thinks I am getting fatter, of course looking better. I sleep as well as at home, eat better, have neither cough nor headache, nor fever, nor do I suffer from the heat.

4. The little girls, Miss Hart and Colonel Smith went to Church yesterday; a prosy parson, no musick, but the psalms screamed by three or four ladies very untunably and the heat was great. In the evening it is the custom to assemble in the Place Royale to walk about to the musick of the Band, but we a'n't quite Puseyite[1] enough for that way of spending Sunday evening, so a quiet walk in the *parc* satisfied all but me and I passed the time by poor Mary's couch.

5. Four bullock carts loaded with wood, a better sort for parlour use, waked me at six. The noise made by the drivers and the porters in unloading and arranging the *billets* in the cellar was astounding, screaming away like the Hindus or frantick people. Mr. Gardiner ordered a *bouchet*[2] for us at the cost of 60 francs, for firing is very dear here. We paid 11 francs for sufficient wood faggots and charcoal to last the kitchen a fortnight only and we shall want more charcoal still. The washerwoman brought home our travelling clothes – merely

1. This is a reference to the 'High' section of the Anglican Church she so distrusted, often referred to as the 'Tractarians' or the 'Oxford Movement' and sometimes named after one of the founders, Edward Bouverie Pusey (1800–1882).
2. Billets are thick pieces of wood cut to a suitable length for fuel (O.E.D.); according to Larousse, a bouchet is defined as a .measure of firewood equalling three *stènes* or 3.06 cubic metres.

rough-dried and asked 15 francs for doing them – I gave her 7. Then came the woman to iron them; we shall have a scene, I suppose with her. Here is Mr. Valpy again to beg further assistance in arranging his family, and the cook with her marketing, which I must say I find quite dear enough. I spent the afternoon with Mary. Walking in these close evenings I find rather exhausting than refreshing.

6. Went to see Mary after breakfast. She had not passed a good night. Then Hal and Jack and I walked to the Rue de la Préfecture, the high street of the town, to buy spoons and forks of M. Montgrand. He received us as visitors, recognised me as Mrs. Gardiner's sister, paid her a great many compliments, said that the first winter she was here her beauty and her affable manners won all hearts, in short, that she shone as a star, that every one admired her, that the whole city was now in tears on account of her illness. The son then took up the discourse and he said he thought the two little Miss Janeys very much resembled each other, which is quite true. His Mother had been much struck by their likeness to each other, and he was equally struck with my likeness to my sister; on which the father came in again to add his having also seen this at the same time, conveying without the slightest rudeness, but rather indeed in a complimentary manner, that he did not think me quite so handsome. It was evident he said that we had been most carefully brought up. An English shopkeeper exhibiting in this way would be considered only fit for Bedlam. In fact the national manner would not admit of such a style at all; in this Frenchman it seemed mere matter of course, a polite way of serving a customer, and far from being disagreeable it was rather gratifying.

I recollect at General Robertson's[1] their excellent French servant, Prosper, coming into the drawing-room on a general search for keys; he approached his master with a peculiar smile and said in his broken English that he believed he must be

1. Colonel, later General, Henry Robertson, had been the Resident at Satara where Henry Smith commanded when E.G. visited with her father in 1829. In the early 1840s he was a member of the Council of the East India Company.

permitted to search in certain pockets where ordinarily such little matters were to be found, and there the keys were, in the General's waistcoat pocket. But could we fancy an English valet presuming on this sort of playful irony with his master? It would have been the height of insolence in George or Thomas. It was actually respectful in Prosper.

All the afternoon I sat with Mary. She was very, very ill. When I first saw her last Wednesday this day week the shock her appearance gave me was indescribable. Except her manner, there is not remaining one trace of beautiful Mary, her whole features are changed, lengthened, drawn, her eyes starting from her head, and they are dimmed and faded, her form wasted quite away, her skin thickened and darkened and wrinkled, her long, bony fingers make one shudder, then she is swelled with the dropsy to a most unnatural size. Still when made up for dinner she looked wonderfully pretty, the wreck of loveliness, but not the least like her former self. I should never have known her, for even her voice is changed. She was comparatively well this day. She has never been so well since and now that I have watched her for a week I think she has lost strength during the seven days and I fear the disease has gained upon her.

Last night it appeared as if her chest were becoming affected. She gasped for breath, called out for room and air and her head was evidently affected. I had one serious conversation with her Doctor, he gave no hopes, talked delicately of nothing being impossible, that all going well she might be kept tolerably easy by skill and care for some time longer, but that he must own he took a most gloomy view of her condition. Dropsy[1] is the fatal termination of many diseases – in her it results from *three*. It is difficult to cure when a complaint *per se*, nearly impossible when proceeding from other causes. Her heart is seriously affected, its action impaired, her lungs slightly, her liver very much, her stomach also greatly injured – this prevents her receiving sufficient nourishment, her digestion being weak, wind and heart-burn nearly exhausting her, and

1. A morbid condition characterised by the
   accumulation of watery. fluid in the serious cavities of
   the body, according to the O.E.D.

it has forced them to discontinue the only medicine which expels the water, for it was injuring the coats of the stomach. She suffers pain in the lower bowels, in the back, the loins, the chest and the great gut; she has piles to a great degree; and now an ulcer in the great gut, which is agony. Added to all this a frightful cough and little sleep except from opium. Can we wish her to live under such a complication of miseries – to be *palliated* only – for there is no cure. Dr. Taylor thinks worse of her than Dr. Smith does.

Our new cook seems to be a pleasanter servant than even obliging Marie and more economical and very clean. Jacques, the man, is also particularly nice and nice-looking. We are really very comfortable. I hope eleven or twelve francs a day will pay everything except tea, wine, wood and washing. Johnny is happier since he began his lessons and since Jacques came, who amuses him famously. We are obliged to have an old woman to draw the water, go messages[1] and wash up the dishes, 'tis the custom of the country – the cooks only market, cook and tidy, they would lose caste by more menial work. Jacques waits at table, cleans shoes, knives, etc., all pantry and valet work and part of the housemaid's, as he rubs all the floors, sweeps, dusts and cleans the grates. Margaret only makes the beds, empties the slops and arranges nick-nacks besides waiting on our toilettes; she will have to make the sweet things too, the French cooks understanding nothing of confectionery, and she must make up the muslin dresses and the fine linen. We walked last night the whole length of the Parc for the evening was very pleasantly cool and then I sat an hour with poor Mary.

7. Saw both Dr. Taylor and Dr. Smith. Nothing new – Mary's case is hopeless, her disease must encrease, the vital powers must decline. The water may at any moment fill the cavity of the heart or chest. She may live some time, she may be suddenly called away. She can recover never. We must only hope she may be prudent in her care of herself and that no unforeseen accident may hurry her end, for if her sufferings can be, as they say, alleviated, she might yet have

1. Scots: to get the shopping.

a degree of enjoyment in life. We are all loth to leave it, all loth to see those we love leave it. She looked better this morning, and she was better, not up, nor dressed though.

We went to call on the Valpys at the Hôtel de France, they leave it this day for the apartment *au second* just over the Gardiners'. Both Mrs. Valpy and the delicate daughter have been better since they came here; the place certainly works marvels on many. Colonel Litchfield is improved beyond belief; Colonel Smith never was better, though he had indeed a little feeling of asthma this morning about five o'clock – he had eaten plentifully at dinner of bean soup, which at home would have nearly put an end to him; he got off well here after such imprudence and it is to be hoped will not be tempted to renew it.

This is about as hot an afternoon as we have had. Ever since our arrival it has been very sultry – this month of September is reckoned the hottest in the year, there is a great want of air from about three or four in the afternoon to nine, after that a refreshing night and very pleasant morning follow; one can walk out to shop or visit without inconvenience from the sun, but it would not be either prudent or agreeable to take a good long walk. We have therefore seen little of the Town and nothing of the country, but such views as we catch from the Parc. The Town, an old and pretty large one, is well hung up and down many little hills; the streets are very narrow, very badly paved, yet full of good shops. There are two or three open spaces, squares filled with rows of trees. At the further end of one close to the prefecture stands the fine white marble statue of Henri IV lately erected with so much pomp by the Duc de Montpensier. The view of the river from a terrace at the end, with the bridge, wooded banks, pretty villages and the Pyrénnées behind must be quite as beautiful as anything in Switzerland. The market house is very handsome, our Place, Henri IV, looks well; but the jewel of the little town is the old castle on its rock with the river flowing round one side and the parc stretching along its bank for a mile beyond the Basse

Plante,[1] Edinburgh in miniature as to situation without those hideous barracks to spoil a picturesque old building.[2]

I am as well pleased with our apartments as with any we have yet seen – airy and cheerful, close to the old castle and the *parc*, in the way, yet out of the way and no stairs to mount on coming in tired. Noise seems to belong to the country – they are so fond of it that they are quite ingenious in their contrivances for encreasing it – the horses in the diligence, the bullocks in the heavy waggon are all hung with bells; advertisements are announced in the streets by the blowing of horns; a woman who runs races daily very nearly naked, blows her horn stoutly before her start; then they sing all day; a modiste [milliner] behind us sits at work beside her brother or her husband, a cobbler, as busy as herself, whooping in the most agonising manner. Occasionally some amateur friend accompanies her on a squeaking violin. The maid of Madame de Navarez plays the guitar in the garret above. Miss Emma Campbell and two sisters play and sing alternately just over us; our own girls have their practisings; and every evening merry, young men give us duetts and trios from a neighbouring coffee house; a musical instrument maker on the other side of the Place hires an artiste to perform on his organs, and several wandering guitars and a chorus of dogs complete the comfort of our soirées. At Bourdeaux there was such a racket of carriages all night that we were quite persuaded the people never went to bed or else they did it in watches so that the noise might never cease. Noise and glare together are rather much for the nervous.

M. Puyoo drank tea with us – a most tiresome man – I was in hopes I was neither young enough nor handsome

1. In her article 'Wintering in Pau' written for Chambers' Educational Journal in 1848, E.G. wrote: 'Those who for the first time climb the steep path to this beautiful natural terrace, little foresee the scene of enchantment awaiting them'.
2. This westerly portion of the familiar silhouette of Edinburgh Castle ruined the mediaeval building she so admired; she commented in equally uncomplimentary terms after her summer visits in 1842 and 1847 (see H.L. in I.)

enough to answer for a point of attraction for such a beau. At present unluckily there is no Englishwoman but myself in any of his houses who would do at all, Mrs. Campbell above us being near sixty and thin, poor Mrs. Valpy not élégante and speaking no French, so he really has no one else on whom to bestow his tediousness; he is very good-natured, but his visits are sadly frequent. I wonder how Mary ever could have been bothered with him.

8. Hal was not well last night, he therefore applied to his own box and his friend, Colonel Litchfield's bottle. At home he would have had a serious attack, here it has been nothing, for he had no sitting up nor cough, and he does look so well; certainly the climate suits him perfectly. I don't feel a bit stronger, but I have no cough – Jack don't bear the heat well, indeed they all look pale.

The people of the country have a fine clear brown skin, but no roses; they are short, neat, active and some of the young women pretty. All men and women have a good expression of countenance. We were quite surprised at the under-size of the soldiery, both here and at Bordeaux, they all look like little boys and one is quite amazed to see the moustaches on such little creatures. Colonel Smith says the same thing struck him years ago in Paris.[1] The officers are of a larger race, few of them fine looking though. There are 2,000 troops here with about 60 officers, out of which number not more than seven or eight are the least like gentlemen, so we *hear*, for we know none of them, but the report is very unlike the idea we had formed of French Officers, as is the diminutive corps they command quite opposed to all our notions of a fine soldiery; however, gallantry don't depend on size, and *endurance*, the quality most essential to the profession, is possessed in a double dose by the lighter made. The uniform I don't think handsome, blue long coat, long white belt, red trousers, and in full dress, a tall, frightful glazed cap; the funny bag with a tassel on the two top ends which they wear in undress is prettier.

The peasants wear our Lothian bonnet of different colours,

---

1. Colonel Smith had served with the allied army of occupation in France after Waterloo.

blue or brown the most general, and a short blouse. A few of the girls a large Swiss straw hat, all the rest, young and old, the eternal handkerchief – so do the Cooks and the under servants – the waiting-maids have neat caps; the better sort of shop girls their hair nicely arranged. None of this lower class are permitted to wear either bonnets or kid gloves or silk gowns. They don't dress as tidily as I expected, nor do they look nearly as neat or as smart as the same class in Flanders. The cooking is not particularly good to my mind, nor the washing either as far as I have seen; the marketing is not cheap, dress is extravagantly dear, furniture the same. Masters may be cheap, but they are few and by no means first-rate. We shall live cheaper than at home because our household is smaller, we shall see no company, and have no stable; otherwise economising here is nonsense, and there appears to be no getting into the French society if we were so disposed; and that it is best to avoid most of the English.

It is a bad place I think for girls, no quiet walks, too many idlers about and Janey Gardiner is in the habit of going out by herself to drink tea here and there and then walking out with her young friends and their elder brothers or cousins. 'I hope Janey won't fall in love with M. Antoine Le Gras,' said Mary last night. 'La,' replied Mr. Gardiner laughing, 'I am sure I hope not.' 'She is very susceptible,' added Mary, 'and I must say I hear of nothing but M. Antoine Le Gras.' Now Janey will not be fifteen till November; would it not have been more proper to have lived in a cheaper house, to have less expensive dress and a cook at lower wages, spare in any other way and keep a steady governess for a forward girl of this age very pretty and very clever and who will be very rich in French eyes, but this is not the Gardiner way. Poor Mary will spare nothing on herself, on her own peculiar luxuries and Mr. Gardiner never dreams of denying her a single whim, he spends nothing on himself, very little on Janey, as little as can be on his boys, and their income, which is not small – much more than ours – is all lavished upon her fancies and her doctors. Poor thing, *now* one can say nothing, but it never should have been.

10. The two Colonels and I dined with Mr. Gardiner, his dear little daughter and Dr. Taylor yesterday; he is a pleasant and

I should say a clever man. Mary rallied in the evening. He has begun the elaterium[1] again, some Miss Hart brought with her from England – two grains of which do better than eight of the French, affect her more gently, as effectually and without pain. Miss Hart and her children came to tea and, our hopes reviving about poor Mary, we really spent a pleasant evening. No view can exceed in beauty the prospect from the drawing-room window, the parc on the one side, the old castle on the other, a connecting bridge thrown over the road between them, a brook murmuring round the base of the little wooded rock on which the castle stands, and in front the rich plain of the Gave dotted with villages, skirted by vine-clad hills on which are pretty country houses, and in the distance the Pyrénnées various in height and picturesque in form. Mr. Gardiner confessed to me that adding to this beauty of scenery, the delicious climate of the country, he should feel himself rather uncomfortable in any other.

Mary passed a middling night, was going on well this morning. God send she may be safe for this time. I find myself constantly repeating this hope, though when I consider that her prolonged life can be but a succession of suffering, reason tells me to hope for nothing, to wait the Almighty's will in patience. We were at Church to-day, the neat chapel the good Duchess of Gordon[2] helped to build. Mary was prayed for. My heart rose to my throat and seemed near choking me. I thought of Kinrara, the Doune, other days and other climes;

1. This is the sediment from the juice of the Squirting Cucumber, whose bitter taste acts as a drastic purgative – this is the English elaterium as opposed to the less drastic French one produced by the evaporation of the juice.
2. Jane, the fourth Duchess of Gordon (1748–1812), appears in the Memoirs as one of the major influences in the H.L.'s upbringing; it is observed on 10 December 1843 that she had donated one thousand pounds towards the construction of an English Church in Pau. Mrs. Ellis (see 5 Nov 1843) believed she had purchased the ground around 1836 and that the building costs had been in part 'defrayed by her munificence.'

here at Pau, so changed that none would know her, lies on a most uneasy couch the wreck of Mary, with only, of all her kindred, me to watch her dying hours.

11. The afternoon set in so rainy we had to shut up all the windows. We had to keep the house till quite dark, when we got a few turns under the colonnade, brought newspapers back from Mr. Gardiner's. He gets the *Evening Chronicle* three times a week and the *Scotsman* once, both disagreeable, factious papers, but they give the news and one need not read their comments.

12. Our walk this morning has been delightful after the rain of yesterday. We went again to the country which is so beautiful, particularly on the river side, and we looked at a fine house with a little garden commanding a lovely view. The lady who showed it to us was queer looking enough and untidy enough and not over-clean, but she was very agreeable in manner; full of our Queen's visit to her King, delighted at these agreeable *relations* between our Sovereigns, surprised to find our Queen so pretty, so gracious, so well-dressed and speaking French like a native. M. Puyoo would not believe me when I told him she was far from plain, neither deformed nor awkward, etc. Surely this visit will soothe French feelings. It is a great step in advance for crowned heads, at least a British one, to begin to enjoy life like human beings, the State prisoner style is invaded. How our young queen will enjoy this visit. She has been received so warmly by the French nation, so affectionately by their Royal family and so much pains has been taken to render her abode at the Chateau d'Eu agreeable that she can hardly have been otherwise than happy.

13. There was a long letter from Jane from York Place written a week after her return from her happy Highland tour. She was in such spirits, radiant quite – a life all sunshine. I read it while watching poor Mary's uneasy slumber, the effect of opium, the pain and uneasiness she suffers, disturbing even her sleep, her poor wasted form showing only too plainly that I am here to soothe her deathbed. She who in the scenes of beauty Jane so well describes, among the many friends by whom she has just been welcomed, once shone the fairest, the loveliest, the dearest. And at Altyre, where all her young hopes were raised and crushed, Jane found the tomb of the

gifted and erring woman who had played so false a part to the innocent rival just about to follow her.[1] Why should we cling to a life in which there is so much misery?

We all walked in the park this morning, it was quite cool. A letter from Dr. George, who is dull enough, a long letter. They had beautiful weather, a fine harvest. Tom Darker doing well with the farm, new schoolroom roofed in. Mr. West, the Clergyman, would like Baltiboys from May next for two or three years certain; every body is well. My own dear home, how I do love you, how very dull is the life here comparatively. Yet Pau has advantages – Hal's perfect health, the improvement of the children, the arresting of disease in myself, the privilege of comforting the last days of dear Mary. Little do they think at home of the state she is reduced to, nor do they dream of the certainty of her death and the chance of its speedy approach.

14. Our little Queen has returned to Brighton accompanied by the Prince de Joinville. It is curious that in despotick countries much more familiar intercourse is permitted between the Sovereign and the people than is allowed in freer states; this must have struck our little Queen, who never goes about nodding her way through crowds at home. Our manners would not admit of her moving easily outside her own gardens – guards and suites and bands and bother must always keep her prisoner in publick. She could not take her parasol in one hand and her little daughter in the other and set out on a country walk like any other rational being. She is quite the Queen Bee kept up for State purposes, paid with pomp for want of power and want of freedom.

There is a very temperate and a very excellent letter from Mr. Sharmon Crawford,[2] on the relations of Landlord and

1. This is an oblique reference (one of several in her writings) to her father's scheme whereby Mary was to be betrothed to Alexander Cumming of Logie and E. G. to Sir William Gordon Cumming of Gordonstoun.
2. William Sharman Crawford (1781–1851), who owned 6,000 acres in Co.Down, was M.P. for Rochdale. He believed all rents should be fixed by arbitration and that, so long as these rents were paid, there should be absolute security of tenure.

Tenant in Ireland, published in all the papers explanatory of the Bill he had intended introducing into parliament and only withheld in the expectation of some such measure being introduced next Session by the Government. The Tenant under existing practice is certainly defenceless against the injustice of a Landlord. Where there is so much want of a proper education ill conduct on both parts must exist in a very great degree and any plan that could alleviate the bad effects necessarily ensuing from such a cause would be a real blessing to our distracted country. Whether this sort of enactment would be of use I know not – a lease for twenty-one years and compensation for improvements. I am rather inclined to think steam will do more than any legislative enactments; intercourse with a further advanced and more highly principled people will rouse the worthy and shame the profligate into a course conducive alike to their own best interests and the future prosperity of their country.

Went to the shoemaker's, M. La Croix, a most agreeable-looking fat man with such beautiful eyes, told me I had a very pretty foot, was very clever and had the air of a person of consideration, shewing I had been well brought up, etc. His shoes of course fitted, and he deserved they should for he took an infinity of pains about it, seeming to consider it a matter of the utmost moment worth any expense of time and trouble. The French do everything in earnest – no wonder they so seldom fail.

17. Janey Gardiner is not altogether so far advanced as our Janey, in some few things she is beyond her, in others not equal to her. I like our Janey's quiet manner and lower pitched voice and gentler mode of expression much better than the other little creature's very decided opinions, rapidly and loudly and energetically delivered in a squeaky, Cockney voice, utterly unmusical. Her attention has been directed to much that is frivolous, her habits are not domestick, her duties don't appear to have been pointed out to her. She has, to my mind, all to learn, and her own good sense, which I believe to be great, must be her only instructor, poor child, for she seems to be left to herself entirely. I cannot understand the practical morality of my brother-in-law and poor Mary, both religiously disposed, he in particular, rather remarkable for

what people agree to consider piety – they are in debt, they
borrow from all their friends, they accept presents of money
at all hands, and this is all spent, not on the education of their
children, the necessary requirements of an invalid, but on the
best, the handsomest lodgings in Pau, the utmost luxury of
accommodation for the personal indulgence of a fine lady; an
expensive cook for him who don't know the taste of one thing
from another, for her who can digest nothing beyond an egg
or broth, dress for her such as a Countess might be proud of –
not only robes, clokes, lace, hats and feathers that she can but
have worn but once or twice and never will wear again, poor
thing, but all her necessary linen of the most costly description
in such quantities that I sit by her in amaze [sic] wondering how
her mind can be constituted when laying upon satin cushions
in an embroidered cambrick nightcap, with every expensive
luxury that caprice can devise about her, she laments their
poverty obliging them to deprive Janey of her Governess and
only fit companion and to refuse her such or such a master,
and to see their boys but once a year, etc.

Would not a rightly disciplined mind and a rightly feeling
heart deprive *self* of something that husband and children
might be a little considered. She has no idea she is wrong,
no notion that she is failing in duty. When my Mother gave
the £100 to bring her here from Passy when no one thought
she would ever get here alive, little did she dream that it was
a heavy milliner's bill that had left them so destitute. Words
can't express what I felt when I found that it was at this crisis,
at this hurried return in the hope of saving for a while her life,
that she had burthened herself with these fantastical fooleries
out of money hardly her own. I don't wish to judge her harshly
– I neither know her temptations nor her power of resisting
them, but I think *he* might have directed her fine abilities
more profitably considering her naturally good dispositions.

The whole scene is to me so melancholy, past, present and
future that no comfort dawns on me when I think of it. I can't
comprehend knowing right and doing wrong. Many do very
very wrong because they don't know better; but nothing will
ever persuade me that either Mr. Gardiner or Mary don't know
they have been very wrong, the one so to spoil, the other to yield
to being so spoiled, and if as Miss Hart says neither is happy,

I am right in so believing, and what has it ended in? Mary's ill-health is of her own procuring; Mr. Gardiner's exile his own work – God knows they are both punished sufficiently. May their example be a sad warning to our children. The path of duty alone is the path of happiness – a little rub is easier born than the prick of conscience, and if there should be sometimes a little more self-sacrifice required than is exactly palateable at the time, the after feeling is purely pleasureable as if our God had communed with us in our hearts, saying: 'Well done, thou good and faithful servant.' [St. Mathew 15 verse 23]

22. Mary slept tolerably well. Yesterday evening she was quite exhausted from the effects of the elaterium – it brought away between seven and eight pints of water at the expense of the coats of the stomach which it injures fearfully, it all reduces her strength and when weakened her heart acts so little that the blood passes very irregularly into the lungs and she gets those fits of gasping and faintness so distressing to witness. I have taught myself to look upon her death as certain and I only pray God that it may please Him to allow her to pass away without further suffering.

There was a grand inspection of the troops going on all day, which kept the Colonels very busy; Jack and his sisters must attend it also, though the sun was very hot. The poor little soldiers were under arms four hours and a half, they made a very creditable appearance. The prettiest part of the show was the little band of suttlers,[1] respectable women as I understand, for they give out the wine, attend the hospitals, wash and mend, they are all dressed alike in red trowsers strapped down under their boots, blue jackets made à la militaire to fit like wax, blue petticoats very short, white

1. Persons living in garrison towns supplying soldiers with food and drink (O.E.D.). In her 1848 Chambers' Educational Journal article E.G. wrote about those she termed the 'soldier ladies . . . a little row of vivandières, six or seven little women, smart, active, gay little creatures as military as dress and air could make them; they are considered to be respectable women in their military way'.

aprons with pockets, shirt bosoms plaited beautifully, black
stocks, neat caps frilled and small leather hats over them, the
neatly painted keg of wine at their backs. They attend all
parades, march with the men, wait at the repasts, in short,
like true Eves act the helpmeets for the French soldiery, and
are represented to be really decent, quite a distinct class from
the dreadful Camp followers of our army.

24. Certainly the congregation at our little chapel is like anything
in the world but an assemblage of ladies and gentlemen. A
queerer set of respectables could hardly well be collected.
And we had a bad sermon, good bits in it, text always well
chosen by Mr. Carr the thrice that I have heard him, but
his doctrine is so disagreeable that I don't like his preaching.
We have not yet called on him nor on the French protestant
clergyman who has service twice a day in the same chapel
and is I hear an agreeable man and a fine preacher.

Some people have waived the etiquette of the place and
called on us – Mr. and Mrs. Campbell and Miss Emma, their
daughter, who lodge just over our heads. Above them are a
M. and Madame de Costano or some such name – natives –
up again the Marquesa de Navarres, a Spanish lady of rank,
and once a great beauty, the reigning belle of Paris for more
than one season, of whom the Duke of Orleans was reported
to be the lover, now incurably ill, poor woman and still young.
Her husband is in Spain trying to keep his property together
these times of trouble. A Colonel and Mrs. Percy Douglas
have also called; they are from Calcutta, where they had seen
my father.

I am quite uncomfortable about Miss Hart, her manner is
so disagreeable to Colonel Smith that he actually dislikes her
on account of it. The poor girl has not a thought of ill, she
has no 'retiring delicacy' most certainly, but I am not the
least afraid of her pupils copying her loud voice and eternal
chatter and boisterous style altogether – they see it and dislike
it, and she has no other serious fault. Mary has encouraged a
love of gossipping which I suppose entertained her, but as the
doings of the little clique of underbred British to be found in
this remote corner don't interest us, this frivolous habit will
die away. However, if Colonel Smith can't keep his temper
with her he must not be teased by her presence in his family.

It will be very unpleasant to have to tell her to go and it will fret poor, sick Mary and I am sure I don't know how or where to replace her and I like her very well and think she will rather do the children good than otherwise for there is good temper, cleverness, cheerfulness, warmth of heart, and sound principles to counterbalance the *fearless* manner. She is fond of the children and they are very happy with her. It all vexes me very much, and added to Mary's condition makes me find full as many cares at Pau as ever worried me at home. I suppose one need never expect to be free from annoyance of some kind.

Then as to health – I have no cough certainly, the chest is free and the throat well, but I am not one bit stronger, one bit more fit for exercise or fatigue or worry than at home; in some respects I am not altogether so strong as I was there latterly and the place having a tropical climate, most wretched society, no masters, and not being cheap, I can't see that it possesses one single advantage. Colonel Smith is perfectly well here while he is prudent – so he is anywhere else. He expected he might be imprudent here, but he finds he can't, for he is really asthmatick now – has been this fortnight – not very ill, but certainly sufficiently punished for his indiscretions. So that I should say we had no inducement to remain here after our year is out, nor reason either, except the expense of another move. My opinion may change when I know the place better though I have no idea that it will, but one can be happy anywhere, so I will make the best of Pau.

26. We could have no coffee for breakfast, the milk having broke on the fire. It is brought but once a day, though the cows are milked twice; they mix the night and the morning's milk when they can, so in a hot day it will not keep. The cows are worked too, and there are no dairies – a peasant has one or two or three cows as it may be, he sells what he don't want, not caring to please his customers being quite sure of that another should one fail, not meaning to encrease his store. None of them have any ambition, they succeeding to the lot in life of their parents without ever dreaming of raising themselves. No more milk was to be had, so we had to take tea with the small quantity of milk intended for the two who generally drink it divided among seven.

A great noise of thrashing draw me to the window. M. Puyoo's servants were remaking a mattress; it had been ripped, the ticking washed, and they were beating the dust out of the wool and hair which were spread on separate raised frames in the yard, two men with long wands thumping with all their might. Another frame on which lay the under part of the ticking Mlle. Toutine presided over: she received the stuffing as it was ready and shook it equally on the tick till she had it the proper thickness, the wool below in the larger quantity, a thin layer of hair at top. This is done every year, and is certainly very cleanly; but 'tis strange to see it done in the streets. The Chemist next door has all his family with their mattresses on the terrace in front of the houses. The wife of a coach-maker in the lane round the corner has just spread a quantity of maize on a long cloth laid on the bit of smooth pavement before her shop and has seated herself, with her knitting on a chair beside it very near a raised stone which a good woman yesterday found a convenient resting-place while putting on her shoes, her stockings and her garters, hindered rather than helped by a stout man in a blouse who stood beside her with a basket talking loud enough for me to have heard every word he said had I understood the ugly sounding mixture of patois, French and Spanish which goes by the name of the Béarnèse language. A little beyond this pair stood the wife of a horse-dealer at the gate of her yard, first feeding and then fondling her pig, scratching it, brushing it, tickling it, kissing it, putting its head in her lap, and between every caress coaxing another morsel into its hideous mouth. Pork is said to be very fine here – nasty woman, she whips her children for ever; affection lavished on them would bring her no money. In general they seem to be a gentle people, kind to every living thing, polite and obliging – we never hear an angry word, though there is plenty of wine drunk.

27. The water is a great plague here – only one fountain in the middle of the town supplies it good enough for drinking. We have all to send there twice or thrice a day and bring what we require home in earthenware jars on a woman's head. Common water is to be had from pumps and wells here and there close at hand, but we have to send in the same way to fetch it, none being brought into the houses. The

convenience which M. Puyoo and his English tenants think so much of has its small reservoir filled by the hand. Our poor old fille de cuisine has four or five weary journies up and down stairs between my passage and the fountain in the yard every morning. Besides fetching the water, these women clean the kitchens and other demeaning work. Neither cooks, valets nor chambermaids will condescend to perform certain parts of their several employments considered in this country debasing; we therefore have to give eight francs a month and her dinner to an old woman who comes every morning and every afternoon to save Antoinette's dignity, who merely markets and cooks, the rest of her time appears to be spent in chattering with anybody she can get near, and in sewing a little, hemming her rubbers. She made her own aprons and Jacques', which made Mrs. Gardiner wonder – Jacques and Margaret complete our establishment, twenty-five and thirty-five francs a month the wages of the two French. They live in an odd way according to our ideas – up very early, before six, and take a cup of coffee, milk coffee with a slice of bread, before they set about anything. At eleven they breakfast on *onions* stewed up with meat and bread or sometimes they take the meat and onions cold. They dine after us on any dishes the Cook don't mean to keep over to the next day, and I know of no meal following this, though they sit up rather late – till eleven always. If they drink wine they provide it for themselves – their bread is the common household bread of the country, not very white and very sour, being made with leaven. We can't eat it, so pay high for rolls, called here, English bread.

I am keeping Antoinette's book to about ten francs a day. I will set down this day's as a fair sample, though it comes to nearly twelve: rolls 1 franc, eggs, two dozen, 1 franc, flour 60 cents, veal for cutlets 1 franc 80 cents, a gigot for to-morrow 2 francs 70 cents. Duck 1 franc 50, Sugar 1 lb., 80 cents, Ham 40 cents, vegetables 60 cents, fruit for three days 1 franc, spices 40 cents. Jacques had an account against me too, a bottle of blacking 40 cents, two bottles of beer 80 cents. Cakes for tea last night 1 franc – altogether nearly 14 francs, or 11s, about £4 a week for everything but tea, wine, candles and firing – £200 a year, £100 for those extras, £100 for rent, £100 for personal expenses, should do it all very well, and Colonel Litchfield's proportion will come in for fear of accidents. Hal says he would be unhappy if he did not contribute, in fact would not remain with us and as he could not possibly live as cheaply anywhere else and as he has plenty and we have not, I am content.

I must learn two things here – how to make coffee and how to manage the pot au feu – this last furnishes the daily soup and the foundation of every sauce and no expense, for nothing but odds and ends goes into it; and the pound of coffee lasts four days – Colonel Smith, Jack and I having each a cup when we wake, three servants and six upstairs breakfasting on it daily and good and strong too. They are heavy on sugar – about a pound a day for everything. Tea is good at six francs a pound, green eight; butter dear and horridly nasty; firing high, one franc 40 cents every week for charcoal, eight or nine francs as may be every fortnight for wood for the kitchen alone. We have ordered four *bouchet* for the drawing-room against winter at fifty-five francs each and the cutting up and packing in the cellar will cost about three francs each more. I think four bullock carts will bring a *bouchet* home, if of a good size, but some of the primitive carts of this country hold little, they are the rudest machines with such wheels, such rickety axle-trees, such putting together. It is surprising that the two patient *cows* who drag at a snail's pace these mishaped vehicles can get them and their burdens along in safety. A great deal is brought to the market in packs on the merry little horses, the owner sometimes leading, sometimes merely accompanying – often, when the load is light, riding, the women quite as numerous as the men sitting astride, man fashion, with a couple of aprons one to each leg, set on to a band fastened round the waist for decency. And a gay sight it is on a market day to follow the crowded road for a mile or so, or to elbow along the streets filled like the market house with goods and stalls and people and ponies and carts and sacks, etc., so many different costumes, so much gesticulation, real business once a week for a few hours; all the other days are dull, nothing doing, shops empty, at night neither them nor the streets lighted nor any one almost out; but there may be more stir when the Prefêt and the magistrates and the advocates and other big people return from the waters of the

Pyrénées and the sea bathing at Biaritz near Bayonne, where they all flock during the months of September and October, the only holidays they have throughout the year.

We walked last night through the village of Jurançon and round by the foot of the vine-covered hills beyond it, Mr. Gardiner and Janey with us. Miss Hart sat with Mrs. Gardiner while her husband got this rare bit of exercise. It is a lovely country. It was in this direction a week ago that I saw two very old women in different places, each with the same beautiful cap, a stiff starched clear muslin, neat narrow full quilled frills close to their wrinkled faces, and a round large crown standing up like a drum above their heads, they tell me it is a very old fashion not followed now, it is a very picturesque one, something in the style of the Rochelle fish-women we saw with oysters at Bordeaux, only they had extravaganted the thing, wearing actually pillow-cases on their heads stiffened into buckram,[1] the two top ends pinned half way down so oddly. I am beginning to like the coloured handkerchief if the faces were only a little prettier, but there is no beauty here, nor any grace. A good clear dark skin, placid expression and features in general rather unobjectionable than interesting, stature low, a slovenly walk, clothes ill put on, badly made, neither very clean nor very well selected either as to colour or fabrick. They make a pretty crowd with their baskets and pitchers on their heads, their bullock carts and their ponies, their stalls, their freedom of manner in their sunny climate and pretty old town or beautiful way-sides. Individually they don't reward inspection. Hal and I went out about one on business first to M. Brus to order tea, he charges five francs for a much smaller bottle of sherry than we get at home for 3/ –.

Then to the post office to enquire the cause of the strange uncertainty of the rate of postage. We were all informed at home that a uniform rate of 10d. or 1 franc payable at will either beforehand or not had been agreed on between the two governments and our English part has been honestly fulfilled. We at home never paid more either on prepaying letters or on receiving those which had not been prepaid. But here it appears to be perfectly arbitrary. Sometimes those prepaid in

1. Coarse linen or cloth stiffened with gum or paste.

England come to us for nothing more. Sometimes they add ten sous to them, no difference in the weight either. And all those we prepay here they charge us 32 sous for. They could give us no reasons, promise us no redress, only exhibited a little bit of passion, talked of railroads, Havre and Calais and said we must keep to shew them the next letters so charged that we received. Colonel Smith thinks Lord Cowley's Secretary[1] should be written, he fancies the passionate clerk knows more about these overcharges than any one else and that to us perhaps they will occur no more.

We then went to Madame Jacob to get some buttons for a waistcoat – there were none – her shopman, however, would not let us off, he tried to entice some custom by unfolding all the bargains in the shop, and when I told him we wanted nothing and much regretted his giving himself so much trouble he replied it was on the contrary a pleasure to attend on Mrs. Gardiner's sister, that charming woman now so ill. 'How did you know I was Mrs. Gardiner's sister?' – a shrug of great meaning – 'We heard Madame was expected: there could be no mistaking her.' We then tried M. L'Alouette for the buttons, not in the least suspecting he was the great tailor of the place; he had them, took great trouble in suiting them to the waistcoat, and would take no payment, though he had never seen us before. 'Oh, no! no! we don't sell such trifles as that.' The shoemaker is equally gentlemanly. M. Lacroix mends all our shoes for nothing, even those he has not made. If he has the custom of the family, he asks quite enough for the new shoes to cover all cobbling of the old.

28. On my way to Mary passed all my neighbours, the wife of the horse-dealer, ditto of the coachmaker, the hair-dresser, the nasty pig woman, etc. seated on chairs in the middle of the streets, in a knot together, mending their family linen. It began to rain before I turned into the Basse Plante; a girl I had never before seen ran up and offered her umbrella, my silk dress would be ruined, she said: real, genuine good heart this shews, total absence

1. Henry Wellesley, first Lord Cowley, and nephew to the Iron Duke, was Ambassador to Paris from 1841 until his death in 1846.

of selfishness. I am getting quite fond of these obliging people.

Mary was wonderfully well. Her household in great confusion: Sarah, who has long looked wretched, fairly laid up in bed with fever; Julia, forced to confess to an abscess in the knee, extended on a sofa, useless. I staid till dinner and then sent Miss Hart down and took the afternoon studies myself. They were reading the history of England, Lingard's,[1] and working, and their remarks, which they have been encouraged to make freely, shew that their young minds are opening considerably, they understand perfectly what they are doing. Janey shewed me a journal Miss Hart has advised her keeping in this new country – not at all bad, and a plan of giving them words, which they are to apply properly in sentences of their own construction, amuses them much and will give them a very accurate knowledge of their language. Altogether Miss Hart's plan with her pupils very much pleases me, their writing is considerably improved, too.

30. Hal and I were up this morning and out by eight and have had a very nice walk on the Bayonne road for near a couple of miles; then we turned into a lane leading to the river and walked over a sort of common to the *parc*, having so fine a view of the mountains the whole way back, with their ragged summits covered with snow, that we were quite sorry to turn into the shaded alleys. We passed two rude enough mills: one for flour, where there is no machinery for sifting, the other a saw-mill of infinitely ruder construction than any of the very oldest set once scattered through the Rothiemurchus forest, decaying in my childhood, replaced twice within my memory by still-improving works. I have Antoinette's book to settle, my first business after my Journal every morning after breakfast, and then I generally go down and sit with Mary till the 'singing hour,' taking my needlework with me. The snow on the Pyrénnées has cooled the air of the valley

1. John Lingard's Catholic 'History of England' was
   published in eight volumes between 1819 and 1830;
   Leo XIII granted him an audience on his visit to
   Rome in 1827 and was so impressed that he made
   him (an admittedly verbal) offer of a Cardinal's hat.

to a fit temperature for exercise, it is very delightful. We all took to a blanket last night and we had a fire after tea in the drawing-room.

SUNDAY, OCTOBER 1. Mary continues easy, her maid is really very alarmingly ill: the poor creature has a brain fever, they have had to get a nurse for her, Doctor three times a day, ice blisters, leeches. All the world will say she was killed nursing Mary, while we who know the truth think she barely did her duty. She was never yet kept up a night, never called up during the night except on one or two very rare occasions. She attended in the sick-room during the day, but her task was shared by others; Julie ran all the errands. Sarah is an odious, noisy, vulgar woman, quite unfit for such a situation, rude and ill-tempered and coarse; she worried her mistress to death and really made so much bustle that she was the worst possible person to be about any one so weak as Mary; one is sorry for the poor woman now she is suffering, but I am very glad to have her out of the way, the sick-room is so quiet without her.

2. In our evening walk – saw some cats scampering out of the way at such a rate as put me in mind of the information Jacques gave us the other morning at breakfast. The children had been up half the night hunting mice – they had had them on their beds, on their pillows even – I told Jacques not only to set a trap, but to get us a cat if possible. 'For what use?' said he, 'it would be stolen.' 'Who would steal it?' said I. 'What would they steal it for?' 'To eat,' said he. 'They eat cats in this country – they say they are very good.' 'Oh, yes,' said Miss Hart, 'the traiteurs [caterers] use them constantly. Mrs. Gardiner once got her dinners from a traiteur, and we could not make out what funny little bones were in some of the dishes. At Bagnères the people are very glad to get them, they have bad markets there.' Why indeed should not cats be as good as many other creatures which prey on what has life – or, may be, worse – ducks, pigs, fish.

6. I have seen those little soldier women and I never saw anything so pretty. Just now, when I was at Mary's, I heard first the musick and then the tramping of troops, and looking out of the window there was the street filled with them, all in marching order, knapsacks, etc., turning round the corner

and marching along into the country to exercise; immediately after the band marched these suttlers, their little kegs of wine slung on their shoulders, their neat waists rising above the innumerable plaits of the full petticoat, smart feet – the tidy boot and strapped pantaloon setting off the ankles – and the coquettish air of the broad-brimmed, glazed hat, set on one side over the quilled cap, with a tassel dangling from it, and the clean white collar and their military bearing, good firm step out; altogether it is quite as pretty as any procession at a play. The little women did not move so gaily on their return nearly five hours after. It was a weary move up the paved hilly street.

8.   A letter from Mr. Cockburn [the Colonel's Banker] announces the safety of our plate returned in the *Calpe*. A fine harvest in Britain, and fine weather till quite latterly, but there people could not well undress as I have done to-night by an open window – it is open still – the moonlight streaming into the room, the old Castle standing well out before me when I went to look out from it. We have never had a fire but the one evening, nor is the blanket necessary, though having put it on during the few cold, rainy days, we did not like to throw it off again. A Sunday in this part of France has nothing to distinguish it much from other days, the people are rather better dressed, cleaner looking, and in the evening the *parc* is full of the tradespeople walking quietly there with their families, but there is no gaiety among them; they seem to be a very sober race. In the morning there is a market as usual, shops open, women at their needles, men at their trades. I don't think our servants go to Mass, Antoinette may perhaps go to early prayers. Jacques certainly goes to nothing, too much of a gentleman; four times in the year, on some very particular days, it is etiquette for men to shew themselves at church; the women are regular in their attendance.

9.   Mr. Gardiner told me that the women I so much admire really do belong to the regiments, being the wives of the few soldiers who are permitted to marry. It is difficult for the men to obtain this leave, it cannot be granted by their Colonel, they must go to the commanding officer of the district. When they do marry, the wife is regularly adopted into the corps, clothed and fed, and her children also; the little boys dressed as little

soldiers may be often seen exercising with their parents, and they frequently march with them, a little pretty band just in front of their mothers; the girls are dressed like their mothers, all are educated and provided for, the boys in the line, the girls portioned and generally married to soldiers. This must be all Napoleon, I should think, like all his enactments, so suited to the temper of the people he governed. We have met these last few days a good many of the *gens d'armes* walking about – very superiour-looking men to the regiment in garrison here, these are tall, large, fine soldierly persons in a very unbecoming dress.

12. A letter from Tom Darker – such a good one, and so full of all we wish to hear. Work all getting on well, people all doing well, weather fine, harvest plentiful. Mr. and Mrs. Fraser expected about the 20th. I have read it all over and over again, and while pacing up and down under the shade of the old trees in the Basse Plante, where Johnny was running along with his hoop, instead of the old town of Pau, with its bridge and peaked roofs and the Gave and the vine-clad coteaux and the rugged Pyrénnées, I saw only the Liffy, our young plantations, our green meadows, the rookery, my garden and the Wicklow hills. In sunshine, what can be more beautiful, and with what delight shall we return to scenes so dear when our work is over here, Hal's health and mine re-established and dear Mary at rest. I cannot write all I feel; I have a hard task to get through, and he who loves me best, I am sure without intending it, makes it harder. I do all I can for all of them, yet fail to please. This unfortunate dislike to poor Miss Hart, whom I would gladly improve if I could, or change if I could, poisons our comfort. What a treasure to a woman is the use of her needle! And my two naughty girls have yet to acquire a love for it.

13. Dissatisfied with myself, because Hal was displeased with me; and although I cannot accuse myself of any intentional fault, something must be wrong when he is annoyed with me. Few reasonable people *commit* errours – glaring errours – but they *omit*, they don't forbear, they are impatient, or they tease, or some way or other irritate, and as it is the woman's part to submit, she is in errour when, as a wife, she vexes her husband. At the same time I really very much wish my husband would

be so good as not to get vexed, for he worries both himself and me for no reason. A long visit from Dr. Smythe this morning, who rated me well for not taking more kindly to Pau, when the climate agrees so perfectly both with my Colonel and myself. Hal is certainly without a complaint, so am I, and also I now feel a very great deal stronger, and I am getting fat.

14. On going with Jack to the terrace this morning was much amused by the mode of breaking horses, a young, hitherto untried, thin-looking creature was popt into the middle of the trio which leads the diligence, a steady companion on either side of him, an honest plodding couple behind, a man at every head, a dozen all shouting around frightened the poor animal more even than his novel situation, kicking, floundering, foaming, he made four steps and as many fresh starts, while I kept sight of him; then when weary with the fight he had his poste of so many leagues before him. The crowd which was accompanying this essay returned before Johnny had run his hoop many times up and down, and a by-stander told me the affair was finished, the poor beast would give no more trouble, that the diligence being heavily laden was in no danger of an overturn and that the passengers in it were accustomed to these scenes occasionally. So we turned to look at a basket-maker busy in the open street making substantial baskets for holding wood of slender twigs, which he was weaving very neatly. Colonel Douglas joined me and we discussed all the troubles in Europe of all sorts in all countries till Colonel Litchfield carried me off in search of good bread, which we found where we had been directed at Pauchon's. Nicolai, the Valpys' Courier, purveys admirably for them. Unconnected with the place, he has neither friends to fear nor acquaintance to serve, he hunts about till he finds good things and he lets nothing bad enter the house. Our breakfast was quite a treat. I shall now take the butter under my care and endeavour to get some that is *tasteless* at any rate.

15. Such commotion in Ireland. Mr. O'Connell having arranged a perfect monster meeting for last Sunday at Clontarf, which was to be attended from all parts of the country, far and near, a meeting of certain Protestants was held to draw up a petition to the Lord Mayor to put a stop to such a desecration of the Sabbath and to set forth their alarm at such an assemblage.

The Lord Mayor remonstrated with Mr. O'Connell, who yielded so far that he delayed the hour of meeting till after two o'clock and promised that none of the processions to it should pass any Church during the service. This did not satisfy the petitioners, who applied then to Government – just I suppose what the Government wanted and has waited for with such patience. On the Saturday a proclamation was issued forbidding the meeting; early on Sunday the Military took possession of the ground, the police turned all back who were approaching, and though there was much surliness on the part of the disappointed multitudes, weary and excited as all were, there was no mischief.

That extraordinary O'Connell within a quarter of an hour of the appearance of the Government proclamation issued one of his own, in the same Royal style, 'Whereas' this, that and the other and a few skits at the grammar and the intention of the Authorities, he counsels all who love him and their country to respect their rulers; he gives up the meeting, urges his mob to disperse, and despatches all the pacificators here there and everywhere to calm all his subjects upon his unforeseen crush to their hopes. What a melancholy farce it all is. He has opened his arbitration courts, which are to supersede all law everywhere and there at a green table, neatly railed in, sit Mr. John O'Connell and I don't know who more settling the various disputes of the quarrelsome Irish. Is he not a wonderful man? What can be done with him?

Janey has caught cold and could not go to Church. We had really a fine sermon from Mr. Kerr in which there was much matter for serious reflexion, though I never can subscribe to these puritan doctrines. There is a want of true religion in all the penance style of that narrow school. It is best at once to go into monasteries and give up this sunny world in good earnest if one must walk through it in sack-cloth and ashes to ensure heaven at the end of it, the very *form* of godliness that Christ preached against, these affected Christians insist on as the one thing needful, and instead of letting no man see them fast, they put on their extra sanctity in the market-place, and shrink from the innocent gaiety God has made every creature to enjoy. Mr. Kerr has an ugly, narrow head, no room for much intellect in it, and not a fine expression of countenance either, quite the contrary. Neither Lavater nor the skull man,[1] whose name I forget, would make a good subject of him. I always pity the poor little children in those houses.

16. Yesterday evening Hal and I got a long walk in the mud along the Eaux Bonnes road, and we found the publick houses very full and very noisy in consequence, we supposed, of the wet. There was no quarrelling, a good deal of singing and in one barn sort of place very merry dancing – twenty or thirty fat and lean, young and old going gaily through a Contredanse to very decent musick. On our return the ball-room was empty of all company save three or four quiet cows. Our garrison is departing for St. Jean de Luz and other frontier towns on the Spanish side, which they are strengthening, these unquiet times. Two detachments have already gone, quite in the gray of the morning, band playing, making believe that the soldier's is a merry life; the outgoing is gayer than the incoming. I hope the next regiment will be as well-conducted as this, we have never had a disturbance of any sort among these little bodies, nor seen one drunken man.

Mr. Gardiner has just called in with another letter, from Jane to Mary, and one from John to Mr. Gardiner, both containing much the same news. Henrietta has a fat little daughter, born at Inverness the first day of the Northern Meeting, which gathering of the great and gay was attended by grander people than have of late years honoured our happy annual assemblages, the Dukes of Richmond, Marlborough and their belongings, Marquis and beautiful Marchioness of Douro, and ever so many more with, for climax, Prince something of the Netherlands.

The riots in Ross-shire prevented many attending, the seceding ministers have so grossly misconducted themselves, misled and perverted and infuriated their ignorant flocks that the military have had to be sent down to disperse the mobs which with sticks and stones assailed the new ministers and

---

1. Lavater and Spurzhein (see 20 March 1844) were two of the three founding fathers of phrenology. E.G., as is clear from her journal, knew the third, George Combe (1788–1858), well from her Edinburgh days.

all who supported them.[1] One of the Seceders cautioned any of his former flock from attending in their old parish church, from which, he said, he had carried away the Bible and all else that was holy, leaving behind only the Devil. The Duchess of Bedford has been giving a dance at the Doune, at which appeared uninvited a queer set of rude people, who turned out to be Lord and Lady Abercorn, Mr. Landseer, etc., dressed up and acting to perfection; no one knew them.[2] Margaret tells me that old Peggy McKenzie, my Mother's trusty house-keeper at the Doune, who has been the plague of the Duchess and of Henrietta, and of everybody who has ever had anything to do with her, has at last been convicted of a long continued system of dishonesty which will cover her old age with shame.

18. A letter from the doctor, he is very dull, sadly out of sorts without us he can't be duller than I am or poor Jack, who is really home-sick; the child is pining for Baltiboys, it is most curious; we must try and amuse him and alter his food, he may have had too much meat which he is not accustomed to. He is not ill, sleeps well, a good tongue, but he has no appetite, is chilly, yet feels hot, is getting very pale and very thin and very dull. I have watched him narrowly yet can make out nothing particular that ails him; still he certainly is not well, and it is quite odd his sleep should be so sound, so still and calm, quite undisturbed, while he looks so languid. A few days of a perfectly bland diet may bring him round: he was too much out in the sun with Colonel Litchfield and the walks they took were too long. The Doctor tells us there is no excitement about repeal left, the people were just as satisfied to have the meetings put a stop to as to have them settled. The good harvest I suppose is occupying them and they are

1. E.G. was totally out of sympathy with the seceding one third of the ministry of the Church of Scotland who left to form the Free Church in 1843.
2. Georgina, the youngest daughter of the fourth Duke of Gordon, married the sixth Duke of Bedford who rented the Doune from the Grant family. Edwin Landseer the artist, who was the father of her ninth and tenth children (born in 1821 and 1823), had his proposal of marriage rejected after the Duke's death in 1839.

in these improving times beginning to weary of travelling all over the country to hear speeches ending in nothing. Perhaps it will all blow quietly over – they are dreadfully frightened of the soldiery when they find them in earnest.

The peasants here should be no richer than with us, yet how much more comfortable they look. Too placid to take the least interest in anything beyond their immediate business, instead of flying about half mad in rags to make mischief, they spend their quiet lives in habits of the strictest industry – the painter might prefer the wild, bright-eye and rugged countenance, the thin, active figure, the rags and the tatters and the picturesque misery of the Irish cotter, but the philanthropist must dwell with far higher feeling on the comely features of the Béarnais, plump, contented, well-dressed, well fed, occupied. I have not seen a rag or tatter since I came, no men out at knees and elbows, no curious collection of bits hung together by some miracle as a covering; all garments here are good and whole, sometimes well patched, but never ragged, and the industry of all is untiring – every little body at a stall has her knitting or her needle-work; the girls going for water, the wives coming to market, the old women driving a pig or heading a cow, each has her stocking or her seam or, more primitive still, her distaff and spindle, which engage her busily while she walks. The *Morning Herald* is perfectly right, what is most wanted in Ireland among all classes is the habit of industry – idleness is the mother of mischief indeed.

21. Such a walk as Colonel Litchfield took Hal and me yesterday – about eight miles, I find from M. La Croix, who has been here measuring me for a pair of boots fit for mountain roads. Nothing could be more beautiful, up the river, through pretty lanes a mile and a half beyond the hara, then we turned to the hills, up a very steep zigzag road, through a wood of sweet chestnuts, past two or three fine country houses and all among vineyards where of course we regaled ourselves while resting. I brought a nosegay of wild flowers home, composed of above twenty different sorts of very pretty little things, many of them unknown to me. To-day we have had another not quite so long a walk, about five miles, to Perpignan on the next hill to Gandalous, a long, steep ascent, but such a view to repay our trouble of the mountains on one side, plains and hills

and dells and glens below them, Pau on the other with the Gave, its rich meadows and its lanes and fields and woods, vineyards all round us. A large handsome house, real well laid out gardens, greenhouse, shrubbery, avenue and lovely flowers. Mr. Cole has taken it for the winter.

22. Mr. O'Connell, his son, John, three or four priests and other agitators, ten or a dozen, held to bail in heavy sums for their appearance to answer a prosecution for sedition; I hope the Government is sure of convicting them, otherwise . . . Mr. O'Connell still preaches peace. After exciting the mob by every conceivable means and defying the Government, which, if it aggressed, he was to resist to the death, they were to trample on his corpse, he was to hurl at them – I forget what – only his tongue, it seems, for he is to have no more meetings, it is all to be perfect obedience ending in a parliament in College Green. What can it mean? Is he frightened? Is he glad of the excuse? Has the agitation grown beyond him? Is there anything under all we know not of? Time will decipher much that is at present little better than a riddle. I am glad we are here.

23. A most busy day. The modiste has received her winter fashions from Paris, and we had two loads from her magazine sent down to Mrs. Gardiner's, to which place I followed. We thought it would amuse her to see all the things, and that we should be benefitted by her good taste in assisting our choice. The model bonnets were most curious to my British eyes, the shapes quiet, very little trimming – so far so well – but the colours! One is pink satin and pink velvet with hot-house flowers, the other lemon coloured velvet, trimmed with bright red pomegranates inside and out. I also had Mlle. La Rose with me settling colours for new frocks, and then we walked to M. Vigerie to order a detachment of dresses down to Mrs. Gardiner's in the morning. She is wonderfully well really.

That odious Sarah has begun to plague them in every possible way, but this time she has overdone the business, both master and mistress are so thoroughly weary of her that they have arranged to board her with a Mrs. Alcock till she is strong enough to be sent back to England. I never heard of such a series of impertinences as her whole conduct seems to have been. She was far too low a person to have in such a situation; the lower English are very little above the brute part of creation, and this coarse woman was from the dross.

24. A letter from Dr. Robinson: Mr. West will take Baltiboys even for a year, hoping, I suppose, to get it on. I know very well they will never let me go home again, and surely I am very little better here – this place is as much too hot as Ireland is too damp for me. Repeal he says is over.

28. In spite of a dull drizzling rain, set off with five or six Valpys, Mr. Gardiner and M. Puyoo to spend the morning at Gandalos. We went first to La Tisnère to see the wine made, not so amusing, nor one-half so troublesome as brewing beer, and hardly worth looking at this year, so little is making – three or four barrels instead of 160. A blight early in the season destroyed all the fruit on one side of the hills. It was too wet to walk through the vineyards, we went through the house instead and looked long from the window of the drawing-room up the beautiful little valley. We went on in the heavy rain to Gandalos, which even in this dreary weather looked charming. The house is altering into a truly comfortable and very handsome English Country-house, every kitchen convenience, five or six good bedrooms, delightful drawing-rooms with such a view; then the grounds are so pretty, so many little flower-gardens and bits of shrubbery and walks in woods – we fell quite in love with it, and half think of taking it; we elders so much dislike town and love the country. A nice wood fire was blazing, fruit cake and wine set out on round tables, plenty of arm-chairs to lounge in. We made a long rest of it, then walked merrily home – mud, rain and all.

29. Pau is filling very fast, large families arriving daily – all the Hunter Blairs I hear, and a Captain and Mrs. Strattan, friends of the Bilton Freres, Lord and Lady Cavan, and I don't know how many more, but Dr. Taylor does, he regularly counts noses, for he can catalogue the whole colony – 'tis a pity the place is so cut up by faction. Each Doctor has his set, each clergyman and each leading lady. We are wise not to visit. Party spirit may do good perhaps, but it certainly is evil.

It disgusts one to read the radical press on the present times. Unable to falsify facts they account for them falsely, they are forced to acknowledge O'Connell put down, repeal over, agitation frightened into calm, but they won't allow the

Government credit for the wisdom which has produced this quiet. It is anything or everything but that which did it. My fear is lest the Conspirators should not be convicted; they would hardly venture on the prosecution one should hope without good grounds for believing in its success.

31. We walked out shopping with Mr. and Mrs. Valpy – very funny people, particularly the gentleman. They seem to be quite happy here among a set of the Elect, who fraternise in the most amicable manner. They have prayer meetings and hymning meetings and Dorcas meetings[1] after the American fashion, where those that are not Elect say that all manner of scandal is hatched – the little Valpys are entered to all.

We have as little turn for this kind of dissipation as for any other, and as we have therefore small inducement to remain shut up in the town, we are seriously thinking of removing to the country, of taking Gandalos as soon as it is ready. The house is large, commodious, cheerful, the situation airy, close to the most charming walks in every direction. Now we have a long walk before getting to our walk, and a disagreeable one through a long dusty street. Our great pleasure is rambling about this beautiful country. It will be a little dearer as to rent, but I think will quite be met in other ways, besides that it must be more healthy. The two Colonels seem quite keen for the scheme; so am I as far as my own wishes are concerned; there are some things to be considered, and we must well consider them before encumbering ourselves with such a house for two years.

Agitation altered in tone, lowered several pegs, yet still fluttering on. Mr. Smith O'Brien has been so foolish as to join the repealers in their death throes – one respectable name among this mob of folly.[2] I am really glad we are here out of

1. A Dorcas Society (named after a woman mentioned in Acts chapter IX) is a ladies association in a church set up to make and provide clothes for the poor. (O.E.D.)

2. A land-owning repealer and M.P. for Limerick from 1835 until his conviction for high treason in 1849 after a farcical attempt at armed insurrection. She variously refers to him in her journals as 'an audacious broiler', 'mad' and 'a noble goose'.

the way of this melancholy nonsense. The pot must boil over soon, and then it will soon be settled.

WEDNESDAY, NOVEMBER I. A curious first of November, bright sun, no fires, leaves on the trees. Hunter Blairs all come, not Sir David, however, but the Colonel who was long in India and is well known in many ways, as [is] his once beautiful wife.

2. The last two or three days having been teased by a slight cold I took a French cure to get rid of it – Last night bathed my feet in hot water full of wood ashes and drank a tumbler of boiling water and brandy in bed, laid in bed half a day, and am well.

3. Astonished as Mr. Valpy said I should be on seeing Monsieur Buscarlet,[1] young, graceful, very handsome, very interesting, he stood beside his old red-haired bustling housekeeper-looking wife the most perfect contrast ever brought together. Mary says he is an enthusiast full of zeal, his wife a bigot full of spite. Between them they do little in the way of improving the character of the Huguenots which by no means ranks high in these parts, very few of the upper class have remained in the purer faith. Yet this is Béarn where the doctrines of the reformation first took root in France. A people so little speculative or reflective as the French never can be expected to be spiritually enough minded to take in good earnest the *Christian* code of morals, pagan they and the Irish are and will be till more of the Saxon mingle with the Celt; yet the highlanders hate popery in feathers, though they cling to it in sackcloth – materialize their feelings. Now off to Gandalos after this bit of philosophy.

4. Gandalos delightful, house, grounds, situation, but alas! we shall not get it. The Messrs Puyoo have too keen an eye to their own interests to carry their extreme politeness of manner into any matters of business. We had hoped that the uncertainty of letting a country house at this season and the certainty of letting this convenient apartment to some of the many arrivals who find it so difficult to suit themselves, would have inclined our landlords to transfer us, we paying the difference, but no, we must be responsible for the rent and the furniture of this

---

1. For Mrs. Ellis, the Rev. L.J. Buscarlet was 'the truly pious and benevolant French pastor'.

place though we may sublet it if we like, and we must pay for the other from the first of September last, as well. An absurd proposition which has put an end to all negotiations between us. We must therefore stay where we are till May, then take ourselves off somewhere for the hot weather and if we remain another winter here, look out for a house that will suit us better.

Mrs. Kerr and Mr. Gurney came riding up on two ponies, and half Pau followed in the same direction Monsieur Puyoo fils told us in the evening. We met him at Mary's where the two Colonels and I went for a couple of hours to play whist. He was dressed for a ball given by the Colonel of the regiment to all his officers and their wives and was in great force, very sorry to leave our quiet party for his dance. We had very funny whist, Janey Gardiner sometimes playing. Those nasty little French cards are so ridiculous I can't play with them. I can't make them out, they are so badly printed, nor hold them they are so thin. I shall never play again with such absurdities, it makes it all quite disagreeable. How glad I am that we have three or four packs of good honest British cards with us for our own fireside amusement.

5. The news-papers fighting away, for party purposes, the countries becoming quieter. We at Pau have nearly forgotten the British dangers in the excitement of local politicks. It has been determined by the extreme gauche to turn Monsieur Puyoo out of the command of the National guard to which he has been re-elected annually for the last dozen years. The reason of this insurrectionary movement is to vex the Mayor whose staunch friend Monsieur Puyoo is. The Mayor is a very loyal man, the Commandant of the National Guard has by right of office a seat at the Council Board and it is a bold stroke of the Liberal party this attempt to replace a firm supporter of the Government by a man who will oppose every plan brought forward on proper opposition grounds. They have been successful in some subordinate changes and therefore confidently expect to carry this point also. The guard being never called out now, and his uniform having become too tight for him, Monsieur Puyoo is philosophically leaving the affair to providence. The little girls and Miss Hart who drank tea at Mary's found him there in high spirits. The two Colonels

and I kept the fire warm at home, I read Mrs. Ellis,[1] she gives a perfectly candid account of Pau and the Pyrénnées, judging of what I don't know by what I do, and her little book is very interesting, making allowance for her missionary zeal. I shall recommend it to my mother and my Aunt.

6. I had a letter from Jane in the morning. Extracts from my father's last despatch with a postcript of her own, rather in the low vein. My father has convinced us all that Lord Ellenborough[2] is insane upon military matters, he made a speech the other evening in reply to his health being drank in connection with the Indian army, thoroughly cracky, talked of victories to come, greener laurels yet to reap, vanquishing Asia, governing by the sword!! raised his voice, flushed his cheeks, thumped the table, harangued for two hours in this 'Ercles' vein to the dismay of the whole company. 'Tis said he affects Napoleon, particularly in the proclamation department, with a dash of Alexander the Great. Heaven help India.

My father and William and Sally were in sight of Point de Galle having gone to Ceylon in the steamer with the intention of spending the long vacation there, a very nice place, one I almost envy them for I very much like Ceylon. I shall never forget its 'spicy gales' as they reached us on the deck of the Mounstewart Elphinstone, nor the extasy of the few hours we spent on shore at Point de Galle after nearly five months

1. The wife of William Ellis, Secretary of the London Missionary Society with experience in the field in Polynesia, wrote both under her married name and her maiden name of Sarah Stickney. The D.N.B. describes her as 'a lady who acquired considerable literary fame' with books on temperance and the family. Her most successful book was probably 'The Women of England, their social duties and domestic habits' which went to twenty editions. Her guide with which E.G. was so impressed entitled 'Summer and Winter in the Pyrenees' had been published in 1841.
2. Whilst Governor-General of India (1841–1844), the D.N.B. believed 'the whole of his time of office was occupied in wars . . . of vengeance, annexation and conquest'.

of sea. When Colonel Smith and I were on our return home
we spent three weeks at Columbo with Campbell Riddell,
enjoyed the climate, the scenery, the ease of the life there,
and much wondered at the very extraordinary habits of Sir
Edward and Lady Barnes and the half crazy domestick circle
which surrounded them, poor Mrs. Churchill among them.
I think he is dead too, but am not sure, dreadful people. Sir
Edward died long since also.[1]

9. Thursday is a halfholiday in this part of France which we are
reminded of by generally meeting a large party of the young
men of the Academy on the afternoon of this day in their
very neat uniform, guarded by a master and followed by a
cake boy with his tray basket, all on their way out to the
country. A few fortunate enough to have friends at hand may
be occasionally seen forming parts of separate family groups,
or even, as to-day, riding on ponies. They are all healthy happy
looking young men evidently of respectable parentage, their
dress always in good order gives them a better air as a whole
than we commonly find among the little mob scouring over
the play-ground of an English school. The dress is dark blue
cloth trowsers and single breasted frock coat closely buttoned,
black hat, black stock, boots and gloves. What they learn I
don't exactly know.

We dined at the Valpys to meet the Messrs Puyoo, father
and son, and Mr. Gardiner, he and I were to act interpreters
and we found our office particularly entertaining. The dinner
was excellent with good wines. The old man looked quite like
an old gentleman. The French never are ridiculous because
they never affect anything. Neither father nor son pretend to
any station beyond their own, they neither shrink from their
humble birth nor parade it, simply when necessary they allude
to it. Someone complimenting the old man on his taste for
laying out houses, grounds and roads, 'C'est mon état', said

---

1. These recollections of her earlier years are typical of
    the memories that prompted her to write about them
    for her children in what came to be known as the
    Memoirs of a Highland Lady. The Ceylon episodes
    for example are to be found in Chapter 29. See also
    8 June 1845.

he quietly, as a reason for his skill. The young man knows himself to be a little higher in position and he takes his proper place with the same ease, only he don't allude to Waterloo often for he commanded a small detachment of Artillery on that great day, and on the subject of age he is less simple, equally natural perhaps.

12. Hal none the worse of his walk, nor of his *dinner*, nor of his *bottle* of claret, nay he had mulled wine at night again with the rest of us, and he slept in bed the whole night for the first time for near a fortnight. Cold day but very pleasant. We have our stove again and are making ourselves comfortable round it, for the draughts in the pretty drawing-room are insupportable. On our way to and from church we pass the house, a very small one, in which Bernadotte[1] was born. To judge by consequences about the greatest of the many great men in which our age has abounded, he has not filled the world with wholesale slaughter, he has only quieted a distracted kingdom and governed it in peace these many years. He is judiciously kind to his connexions here, neither quartering them upon the Swedes, nor raising them out of their own station, but he makes them comfortable in it in their native country.

Walking home again we found the whole town in commotion, filled as if by magick with such a crowd. A number of stalls full of various merchandise were laid out in the Rue de la Préfecture, around the *halle*, and along the bridge leading to our Place Henri IV., for the people don't mind cold here, they continue sitting in the open air at their works as if it were summer and our opposite neighbours never close their windows and sit at them knitting away without seeming to feel it. The Haute Plante was crowded with horses, mules, ponies, and other livestock, and a great many of the Spaniards who are to be the purchasers are already arrived and add not a little to the picturesque interest of the scene, from their commanding air and figure and the dignity of their peculiar costume, dirty though they be on near approach.

1. Jean-Baptiste-Jules, one of Napoleon's most celebrated marshals, was elected Crown Prince of Sweden in 1810 and reigned from 1818 to 1844.

Talking of our opposite neighbours, in the narrow street on one side, I may just note down that one of them is an Officer belonging to the regiment here, with his wife. They occupy a single room in the *entresol* [mezzanine] floor next to the pig woman with whom the wife appears to be very intimate for they frequently sit at work together. She knits a good deal, irons the clothes etc. and merely wears a handkerchief on her head while within. Last year an officer lived in this room who employed all his leisure in embroidering slippers for sale. All this is accounted for by the construction of the French army which obliges every man to enter the ranks and to rise from thence by his own merit, of course the noble class very soon deserve distinction, a week or two suffices for many steps, this is understood and not murmured at, for comparatively few of that higher class now enter the army and the promotion of the common soldiers is so justly regulated that all are satisfied. It is thus a distinction, a mark of merit, to become *sous lieutenant*, a very great distinction not easily attained to be more. Whether the middle class thus created be an advantage in point of discipline must be left to military opinion.

I have been buying some Bagnères knitting, a very little, for we did not come here to spend money, seven francs upon it and thirteen on some Valenciennes edging is the extent of my contribution to French industry. The knitting is very curious from the trouble it must take to make garlands of flowers and figures of animals and even people with such materials, and very beautiful from the rich bright colours and fine texture of the soft wool, the blankets plainly wove are however, far superior in utility and I even think in beauty. We have nothing like them at home, the Barèges fabricks in wool are likewise pretty, soft and thin and light, not cheap though, nothing is very cheap here, still we shall live very comfortably for less than we spent at home, for we have fewer servants and no stable, and the *luxuries* when we happen to want them really do cost less here, the necessaries are much about the same as in Ireland. It is ladies' clothing that is so very very dear, gentlemens' is cheaper. Take one thing with another and probably living may be a little cheaper altogether here. We shall be better judges by New Year's day.

Colonel and Mrs. Hunter Blair have called. She was once

a great Bombay beauty, now but the remains of a handsome woman more from bad health than age for she is young looking of her years. When Mary and I sailed for India with my father and mother and my brother John 1827, September, we had a little black woman for our maid who had lived long with Mrs. Blair and her sister Mrs. Baker, she half worshipped them both and talked to us incessantly of them. Still farther back Forbes Blair who died a few years ago, and left his large fortune to his brother Colonel Blair was in 1817 a beau of mine, whom I thought a great deal too old to take the trouble of *listening* to, he was beyond *dancing*. I wish we had the power of showing some nice people to our girls, time enough I daresay, we must contrive to do it by and bye for it is the better part of education and was certainly of more use to us in our youth than any thing else that was done for us with the exception of my father's unfailing polish of manner, his conversation, and the true wisdom he took every opportunity of storing our minds with.

By the way as wisdom and folly go hand in hand according to the fable, I see that Lord Ellenboroughs vapouring came from the Punjaub [sic], though people did not know at the time that our troops would so soon be employed there. Rajahs have been murdered at a great rate, different factions as they got uppermost deposing and murdering the conquered with all their wives and poor innocent children. We must put them all down and take their country and pay our expenses with their treasure, of which 'tis said they've plenty, and the country will flourish under our rule, and the people will be safe and happy, which they never can be under their own rulers, and Lord Ellenborough can have another glorious! campaign with as many proclamations as he pleases à la Buonaparte.

16. Hal less feverish, coughing still but no asthma. I am in rude health, a wonder to myself and all who knew me in my former winters of suffering, the children quite as well as myself. The Grand Jury have returned a true bill against Messrs. O'Connell and Tail, one Juror protested, one of the set I suppose. Dublin perfectly quiet, so is the country generally, rents all paying in a style quite extraordinary, no excitement anywhere. And reports of a strong case for the Government supported by witnesses gone over from the rebel crew. It is a thing not to

be explained by the rules of common sense how the opposition press has all of a sudden turned staunch supporters and great admirers of this the most contemptible set of disturbers of the publick peace that ever in any time tried to make mischief. But so it is, they are taking the whole agitation by the hand, laugh at the blunders of the copying clerks, nay chuckle at them as a good joke likely to be of use to these their new idols. Are scandalised at troops being sent into a country so *peaceably* engaged in measures of improvement, anticipate with transport the defeat of the prosecution, in short show themselves fit to be indicted for sedition themselves, only that it would make those little Editor bodies of too much consequence. And all their efforts are useless, the spell is broken by which O'Connell governed Ireland, he is accused, arraigned, him whom his mob thought too *cute* for law to touch, and in a moment he has sunk with them never to rise again. Neither will the return of two radicals in the room of deceased Conservatives unseat a ministry which has the good opinion of all practical men. The weaker party may triumph at an unexpected victory, they may bluster, and they may crow, but they won't be one bit nearer to Downing Street. Mr. Gardiner is quite absurd in his politicks, I have no sort of patience with him.

19. Mr. Kerr, who has been ill must have had his head affected I think, for he gave us such a John Knox sermon upon Sabbath breaking for which we are all to be judged at the last day and most unmercifully punished by eternal damnation if we either read the newspapers, or a magazine, or any other profane book, or speak of worldly things, or visit a friend, or acknowledge an acquaintance on leaving church, or miss a service, or take a walk etc. His text of course was from the Old Testament, his studies must also have been confined to Jewish history, for of the Christian tenets he is in profound ignorance, the message has yet to come to him.

20. The English part of Pau quite occupied with the arrival of a Captain Carey R.N. – brother to Lord Falkland whom no one expected ever to return, except really a very pretty girl about twenty, Selina Fox. Four years ago he fell in love with her. She was too young, he was too poor, the relations on neither side approved, he went away, staid away, wrote to Mrs. Fox, was

again rejected, to Selina, she must obey her mother. Selina then got ill, was carried to all the waters, got worse. Mrs. Fox had it conveyed to some mutual friend that of the two evils she would prefer giving her daughter to Captain Carey than to the grave, but Captain Carey was going to sea, his ship was to be his mistress, he had forsworn all pretty girls. At the Cape he somehow heard that Selina had refused a rich marriage, had been near dying of inflammation of the chest and was looking wretched, he returned home and just as we arrived here some people said Miss Selina Fox had received a letter from Captain Carey, it must have been from him because the post mark was Aix la Chapelle and he had an invalid Aunt living there. Other people said it was all nonsense. Miss Fox had no letter from Aix la Chapelle, Captain Carey had been highly offended and was never to be seen again. Nevertheless, Selina got better, began to walk out again and yesterday sat in the seat before us in chapel, only separated by her mother from Captain Carey, all looking so happy. It is quite a romance and would make a pretty novel, particularly if it be true that the invalid Aunt has been amicable, and I may add wise enough to settle three, or four hundred a year on her godson, she having, luckily, sufficient funds at her disposal.

21. The Law officers of the Crown seem to be thoroughly mismanaging the State trials in Dublin. They seem to have made all sorts of mistakes, to have committed every kind of blunder, to have done their utmost to make the whole business, not only useless, but ridiculous.

22. Went to mass, in honour of St. Cecilia, a good sized church St. Martin's, very plain, handsome altars only, not very crowded, the plan of chairs which each person takes on paying a sou or at most two sous is infinitely preferable to our pews which spoil the look of our churches and are too exclusive to be proper in a place where wordly distinctions should be in abeyance at least for the time, and too costly besides. In our little chapel we pay a franc for a chance seat, twenty francs for a seat by the year, and then come all sorts of books, the regular clergyman, the assistant etc. for repairs, for an organ, for the schools, and what not. A heavy tax when it is considered that most of us leave these very same sort of expenses behind us. There was very good musick for the saint,

a very good orchestra composed of the tradesmen of the town assisted by the military band. The organ is fine, the organist very good and the Priest who chanted part of the service had a beautiful bass voice, the Priest who kept dipping up and down in front of the altar, mumbling bad latin and acting a kind of pantomime in dumb show was quite undignified as were his four acolytes.

24. Went down last night to see Mary and in came Monsieur Puyoo. It is really too tiresome, he is never out of the house, morning noon and night this most good-natured piece of stupidity is perpetually there, he talks an immensity about nothing, and of course all must speak French in his presence as he don't understand I think, for the other day when she dined with us in he came and we had him for two hours very tender, he had been at a *déjeuner de campagne* and he has not a strong head. Last night he had sent in before him a small round Japan table as a birthday present and a bouquet of lovely flowers so he came to be thanked. The poor Italian master sent a bouquet tied with three coloured ribbons, and a copy of verses which though we rendered into English we could not make sense of.

29. Walking this slippery day and meeting heavily laden carts pressing so heavily in the steep descent upon the two poor patient bullocks which yoked together only by the heads had the utmost difficulty in keeping themselves upon their feet and the heavy cart from crushing them, we could not help wondering for the thousandth time at the small progress yet made in these parts in all the civil arts of life. Every day some rude machine or ruder habit strikes with surprise those who come from more enlightened countries, yet are they so happy in their ignorance it hardly seems right to wish them to be wiser.

30. I forgot to mention under its proper date a Concert which Hal took his little girls to. Monsieur Puyoo was so good as ask for the tickets for them from a Committee which has the direction of this really Amateur Society. The orchestra is as it was at the church, the trades people of the town, the principal performers are those ladies and gentlemen who feel themselves possessed of sufficient talent to give pleasure by their performances. The pianoforte was extremely good, Mme. Le Chartier on the harp very fine, her husband an admirable comick singer. Altogether

the Concert was very fair. The women all ill-dressed and ugly beyond idea. Mr. Valpy and Ellen came in a vinaigrette[1] here and took our party up, they had to go early as there are but few vinaigrettes and plenty of people wanting them. Six years ago there was but one. Twenty years ago none and old Mrs. Hay having to dine at the Préfecture one dreadful rainy day had to be set down by the Tarbes Diligence. English money has done not a little for the capital of the Basses Pyrenees.

SATURDAY, DECEMBER 2. Mrs. Taylor and Miss Hay have kindly invited us to parties next week, which we have declined; Hal don't seem inclined for company. I am always best pleased to be at home, and in these wintry evenings it would hardly be very safe for invalids to trot half over the town in those vinaigrettes after hours of such very hot rooms. There is very little self-denial in this resolution, for the society is none of the best – not of a high grade in any way and the gossipping and the evil speaking and the division into so many little parties, each as bitter as wormwood to all the rest, makes it good policy to have as little to do as possible with any of them.

We spent a very agreeable hour this morning in the old Castle, which contains more rooms, and those much more magnificent both as to size and to decorations, than the defaced appearance of the outside would lead any one to suppose. It dates from three eras; an old tower, and shaky-looking bit attached to it, is supposed to have been built in the tenth century either by the Moors or for protection against them – no matter which – Gaston de Foix, one of dear old Froissart's heroes, in thirteen hundred and something built the principal part of the remainder – his arms are still attached to the corners of the Cornices and the ends of the groined roofing of the royal apartment, which Jeanne d'Albret[2] altered, improved and added to.

1. A small two-wheeled carriage that can be drawn or pushed.
2. She was Henri IV's mother; it is likely that one of the principal aims of this frenzy of restoration was to stress the continuity between the Bourbon and Orleans dynasties after the July Revolution of 1830 brought Louis Philippe to the throne.

Louis Philippe has undertaken its entire repair; out and in, it is being put into thorough order. Below, on the ground floor entering from the Court-yard, is a very large dining-room made out of several smaller rooms, a stable, etc is newly fitted up in the oldest style, with dark oak, highly polished, and gilded mouldings, ceiling, and all large windows have been struck out looking on to a stone balcony running along the whole side. The walls are hung with fine tapestry, Offices of all sorts for the service of the dining-hall adjoin it. Very large stone stairs lead up to corridors, passages, anterooms, guardrooms, all handsome, with fine, groined ceilings, polished floors, carved chairs, crimson and green velvet, etc. There is a very large *salon de compagnie*, a small, comfortable, salon de famille, a bedroom the Duc de Montpensier[1] slept in, with Jeanne d'Albret's bed in it. The real bed and the bedroom furniture belonging to Henry IV himself at the Louvre, or wherever he lived, all sent here by Louis Philippe together with an old Chest, most handsomely mounted in gold, that belonged to St. Louis, some handsome old furniture from the private room of Louis XIV at Versailles, several marble tables and vases of Sèvres china, quite splendid, and such tapestry – real Gobelins, framed, the size of good pictures, and so beautifully worked, no one on earth would know them from paintings. Then there is a fine painted window in the little chapel; two tables and two immense vases of Swedish marble and workmanship sent by Bernadotte, and the identical turtle shell used for Henri's cradle, laid on purple velvet cushions, embroidered in gold by the Duchesse d'Angoulême and over-shadowed by pennone and javelins and other war-like trophies. A statue of the king done in his lifetime stands in the reception room; he is a little man, sturdily made and handsome.

The modern antique is admirably done in all the repairs and decorations; some of the carved ceilings struck me so much I spoke to the *officier de service* about the artist. They are all plaister of Paris stained and varnished. Is this only a French makeshift or is it known in England; how many fine old English country-houses might be restored to

1. See footnote p. 10.

their ancient beauty by this economical method of perfectly repairing them.

3. A cold Sunday; not having felt well the last few days did not go to church. The Mr. Medlicott, who preached the very good sermon we all liked so much, called yesterday with a subscription paper he is getting well filled by the charitable English, for with all our faults as a nation we open our purses liberally at the call of distress. An officer of the British Army who died near 60, only a lieutenant: has left four daughters and a son penniless; he had brought them up at Montauban in respectability on £120 a year without a debt. The boy has enlisted as a private soldier. The eldest daughter some lady has taken as a governess; the youngest, Colonel Tovey has brought home to his own house; the other two the respectable mistress of a school at Bordeaux has offered to take and educate and clothe and afterwards get them situations as governesses for £20 a year each. This is the sum Mr. Medlicott is trying to raise – 1000 francs for this first year; they say there are between 2 and 300 English in Pau, so it should be easily managed, for some have given very handsomely. These things are managed better in France; first no officer is permitted to marry unless he or his wife have a small independence; secondly, their sons are always provided for in the army if necessary. Our poor lieutenant should not have made a foolish marriage; his sin has been visited upon his children and to generations, for they have fallen low and their children must fall lower. But a Government should always have a commission for the son of a good soldier.

12. Janey, poor child, how she is spoiled; leading a selfish useless life, misspending precious time for she merely wastes it; it is most lamentable to contemplate the utter folly of Mr. Gardiner in all that relates to wife or daughter. What has it brought the one to? What will it bring the other to? Well, all I can make of it is to take it as a warning. Annie I have no fears for. She is the most amiable little creature breathing, clever and bright and gentle and tractable; but my dear Janey, whom I love as dearly as I do my Annie and who has many valuable qualities, a kind, affectionate disposition among them, is a little impracticable on the score of temper; a little indisposed to exertion, a little unwilling so far to controul herself as to do cheerfully what

is right instead of what is pleasant. Idle-minded she requires to be amused, makes few efforts on her own part, is easily discouraged, and then gives all up, don't buffet with the wave the least.

My very dear girl, when you read this the memory of the mother who now supports you and encourages you and counsels you will be all of her remaining to you. I shall not be by either to console you or to revive you, but you can recollect the time when I was always beside you; you can remember my words, the smile, the laugh, the reasoning which did not *then* convince, recall them now as you are reading, and believe me that our duties in the world I shall have left, are active, to assist others is our work, to consider ourselves *last* our obligation, to employ ourselves *usefully* our principal chance of happiness. And to this, my own dear child, that for a *woman* her *home* is the sphere chosen for her to shine in. To make home happy is woman's business here on earth, and most amply is it repaid her. The woman who looks abroad for happiness can never find it. What is she to the world? *Nothing* when no longer wanted in it. When her beauty, her spirits, her purse fail she will be left alone with her regrets, while the domestick daughter or wife or mother always employed in encreasing the comforts of those who *love her* will find herself under every circumstance the object of care and kindness. There will be no mortifications for her who is never thinking about herself, no dull hours to her who is always usefully employed, no petty vexations for her who has raised herself above them, by setting her mind *not* on the things which perish. Religion, dearest children, does not consist in long prayers, lectures on difficult texts, making Sunday dismal, or catching cold by going to church in the rain, etc. Religion consists in the perfect controul of our hearts, minds, tempers and manners, the endeavour to make ourselves as like to him who came for our example as is consistent with the infirmities of humanity. What has your poor Aunt Mary done? What is the consequence? And her Janey will fall into the same mistake unless she fall into wiser hands than her kind misjudging father's. The whole management of matters in that unfortunate family would go near to break one's heart.

15. Mary dined late yesterday and made a good dinner and slept a

good deal and woke up cheerful. I came home at nine leaving
Janey there to return with Miss Hart who went down then
and I found little Annie so dull at being alone to undress
while others were merry that I bundled her up in shawls
and sent her to join them. M. Daret, the dancing master,
whom Hal and I went to engage yesterday, has come this
morning to arrange his hours. A most vulgar looking man,
but they say a good master: he had been out shooting, had a
good gun – boasted of his dogs – lives in one double bedded
room. I should say quite à la française.

20. Rather milder though a thick fog rendered the day disagreeable. We go on with our long walks which seems to agree
with the whole family. What a stupid life some people would
think we lead. As soon as I am bathed and dressed have read
a little, I do my business with Antoinette, Margaret and
Jacques, then write in this queer journal. It is then eleven
and off we go calling in at Mary's to hear how she passed
the night. We are never home till after two at the earliest.
Talk a little bit with Mary who is then dressed and home
to dinner. Work, read or write till six, when the little girls
come up for their drawing-tea, musick generally with work
perhaps till the children go to bed, then help out the piquet,
the Colonels by that time being very tired of playing together.
Chocolate at ten, bed soon after. We think it a great bore to
break in on this routine to make calls now and then or go
shopping, it is really curious that we should be so happy. It
is the young people that make us so, their animal spirits keep
us gay, and their improvement occupies us and in a family
party where no evil spirit enters, the routine of daily business
is actual happiness.

23. I read the *Scotsman* while Mary slept, and was rewarded by
finding extracts from the notes Lord Jeffrey has appended
to the edition of the principal of his contributions to the
Edinburgh Review, and an admirable summary of the first
of Mr. Simpson's[1] series of lectures to the operatives of
Edinburgh. Janey Gardiner returned at ten radiant with

1. Two of the distinguished luminaries of Edinburgh's
   'Golden Age' she had known since childhood (see
   Memoirs and H.L. in I.)

happiness and I went home to a pair of moody Colonels at piquet, they must just learn to do now and then without their attendant for others have claims as well as those two spoiled bodies. We had a letter in the morning from John Robinson, all well, the tenants have paid pretty well considering the times, several of them owe more than they ought but we must put up with it while Ireland is in this very excited state. Tom Kelly has had a low fever that will nigh put an end to him, his recovery was mainly owing to his excellent wife's extreme care. Pat Fitzpatrick has lost his wife, Dempsey's strange uncouth daughter. She died of erysipelas[1], leaving a baby five months old. The girl's school is filling again, the boy's schoolroom is finished, no master ready according to promise, nor funds to pay him, nor books, nor desks, nor help of any sort, the funds are not sufficient for present expenses therefore no new demands can be complied with this year. They talk of an increased grant from Parliament etc. In the meanwhile we must wait.

25. A dark Xmas day. The children of both houses have all gone to church together, Jack insisting on accompanying his cousins. Our house is decorated with mistletoe, holly etc. and the church, they tell me, is beautiful. Miss Hart and the three girls having superintended the old porteress and gone themselves to Gandalos for the mistletoe. It is by no means cold, but it is cheerless, in short I hate Xmas. Perhaps all these young happy creatures may reconcile me a little to a season which has long since ceased to be mirthful to me. The changes and the losses of lengthening years render all anniversaries melancholy in time. The young who have no recollections can alone enjoy such.

31. The last day of an eventful year, not an unhappy one for how can we be unhappy while we are left all together, but a great change has come over us during its course; we have left our own weeping climate for the sunny skies of the South and we are here in a foreign land, without occupation, among strangers, for an indefinite time. We are getting used to it by degrees as one always does, become reconciled even to disagreeable

---

1. A local, febrile disease known also as St. Anthony's Fire.

things in time, and here, where there is so much that is pleasant we should the sooner manage this. The climate, though very far from perfect, is very delightful, rather too variable, rather too hot in the powerful sun, but proper precautions prevent any ill effects from these causes. The scenery is exquisite and when it is not too warm for exercise the walks up among the hills are quite charming, drives or rides could be taken all the year round, always in beautiful directions; were we living in one of those pretty country houses with our comfortable home establishment about us, we could be a very great deal better accommodated than where we are. The town is colder in the winter, much hotter in the summer than the country round it. And it would be worth while in preparing for a residence of any length to make such alterations as would secure us from cold draughts of air at one season and the vertical rays of a burning sun at the other. Comfort could be increased and I should think expenses would be lessened by this change, though a little more trouble would have to be taken. Cheap this place is not, not cheaper than Dublin I think.

So cheap as Baltiboys it undoubtedly is not, though we spend less here having fewer servants, no stable, no company, and our friend Colonel Litchfield is with us who pays a proportion of the housekeeping. It is a stupid life to those who have been used to the activity of a country life on their own property, for there is nothing to see here but the face of nature, nothing to do but such work as people can cut out for themselves, nor resources of any kind for the indolent or the idle. Society as far as we have seen of it very far from being agreeable, judging from all we hear I should say the best is bad. French provincial society is always considered martyrdom. Exile to a country town the severest punishment possible to be inflicted on a Parisien.

And the English abroad are just a little worse than the English at home and the most odious people on earth, taken in the aggregate. We, accustomed to Scotch or Irish never could get on with them I am sure. My recollections of my mother's Durham relations, my Aunt Lissy's law society in London, my sister Jane's neighbours at Malshanger, Mrs. Need's Nottingham acquaintance which by the bye were about the best of the whole, all relate to a class of persons so infinitely below any I had ever been accustomed to in my Scotch youth or have latterly lived among in my Irish age that I know well I never could get on with these with whom I should not have one feeling in common. Therefore Pau would be just as stupid to me as I have always found a watering place in England. I suppose it is extremely pleasant to those who form its gaieties, though Mme. de Navarez looks actually desolate when she calls it '*triste*.' Such as we who live for our selves very selfishly find every place agreeable where we have health, and both of us being better here than we have been anywhere else, the children thriving, Hal's best friend with us and poor Mary, her husband and nice children at hand, we are quite content for the present, independant of every thing.

1844

Jules Dupré. *Grazing in the Limousin.* 1835 (detail).

MONDAY, JANUARY 1st. Last night we were sitting quietly round the fire reading a little, talking now and then, the three children, Colonel Litchfield, Hal and I, for Miss Hart was dining with her first pupils – the door opened and M. Puyoo entered with pretty boxes full of bonbons and his good wishes for a happy New Year. This, it seems, is a custom in France – people spend a fortune on these *étrennes* –[1] relations and intimate friends make really handsome presents to one another, the next in degree give bonbons in cases more or less pretty; acquaintance call. Outside of every door today is placed a basket into which the visitors throw their cards, or indeed they may be sent by the servants as no one is asked for except there be relationship or great friendship between the parties. In the evening all these cards will be sorted and cards returned to every person leaving one in the course of to-morrow; this proceeds for three days, and then a week is allowed for actual visits, everyone making the grand round in person. Such a country for etiquette – placing a little chair instead of an armchair for a guest is mortal offence in most cases. M. Puyoo had hardly retired before a large basket arrived from Mary with three chocolate cups and saucers of Sèvres china for the two Colonels and me. This completed our gettings with the exception of some toys for Johnny, and we gave nothing except ten francs apiece to our own servants, five francs to each of our own children: toys to the two Johnnys and books to the four elder children. There is kindness in the custom but it is a great tax, the calling may keep acquaintance together, but I hardly think it worth the trouble if there be no other reason for continuing an intercourse. The children went down to drink hot pint with their Aunt which gave them all headaches. I read 'Thorpe Combe' to the Colonels, by that inimitable Mrs. Trollope, and we thought one in the morning struck full soon.

4. Been at my accounts and find December to have half ruined us. I can't think how we got through so much money, for there is nothing in the world to show for it. Setting the quarter's rent and the cask of wine out of the question, we have spent

1. Traditional New Year's Day gifts to family and friends.

a great deal, and not in housekeeping. The ménage is much the same, the young ladies' dresses and their shoes and the tailor and Mama's caps and the pianoforte have added many a heavy item to numerous et ceteras. Money has wings, I really believe, for it flies away like thistle-down.

6. Mr. Gardiner very happy at having made an arrangement with Mr. Scott to take his boys for three hours daily, from 9 to 12. Mr. Scott is a gentlemanly Oxford man, speaks pure English, is clever, has been for the last few years private tutor and Mr. Gardiner thinks he will bring Tom on; at school he has latterly been doing little. Johnny being but nine his studies are of little importance; however he will be a pupil too and they are to learn much more than mere Latin and Greek. Still they are none of them sufficiently anxious about the sciences and the modern languages to suit my practical ideas. And Janey Gardiner writing Greek exercises when she can neither dress her own hair nor mend her own clothes is to my notions very ridiculous. One good thing of this new arrangement will be the stirring her up out of her bed before nine o'clock of a morning for she must now be dressed by eight to make her brothers' breakfast. I have no early risers in my own household unluckily being at this season always late myself so of course all in a degree follow my bad example.

The two Doctors have at last caught the Pau mania and are in full fight, talking, writing, accusing, and employing the whole English society in the quarrel. How very wise we are to live alone. The gossipping is worse than the quarrelling almost; the English maids carry it from house to house of course improving it by the way, and all finds reception in poor Mary's sickroom, who seems quite amused with the little evilspeaking her Sarah utters about people most of whom are nearly strangers to her. I think I and my journal are having a fine dose this morning which it will be just as respectable to be done with that wiser employment may follow.

7. A thoroughly rainy Sunday – quite a downpour. None of us thought of church. The little girls came to ask about going, we told them certainly not, but we would read prayers at home. I was therefore a little surprised to find Miss Hart had gone – left her three pupils to the care of chance, for the Colonel and I seldom quit our rooms now before noon.

The real fact is that Miss Hart is quite unfit for a Governess – has no notion of the duties of the very serious station – did not learn them with the Gardiners – was originally ill-educated and born and bred in too low a class of life to have them inherent. For very young children she never could have been fit, for elder girls she will be equally unfit, for boys quite incapable. I like her, and I am aware of her many valuable qualities, and I think she has in some respects very much improved Janey and Annie, brought their intellect forward, she keeps them very happy too, and always busy; but she is coarse, boisterous, indelicate, uncontrouled, untidy, and very much taken up with herself and very independent in her proceedings concerning herself; fond of handsome men and no ways shy in flirting with them. We shall rub on very well for the present and take the first opportunity of getting rid of this clever, good-humoured annoyance.

I found Mary's opinion of her so very nearly to coincide with mine that I can't but wonder how she ever could recommend her to us. I am persuaded she was anxious to be rid of her herself, though really liking her as no one can fail to do. She thinks we have improved her, and I make no doubt she would be still further improveable were she away from Pau and did the want of a better render the trouble worth taking.

9. Fine bright morning. Delighted yesterday with Mr. Simpson's third lecture to the working classes. Also in the *Scotsman* were some extracts of a very able article in the *Edinburgh Review* on the condition of Ireland, not altogether correct as to facts, nor practicable as to remedies, yet much in it worthy of attention. The baths for the lower orders are progressing, probably the fever which has been scourging the abodes of poverty has frightened all classes into the attempt of bettering the condition of the operatives in Edinburgh.

10. In the Irish paper is the death of Mr. Alley in Blesinton on Christmas Day; poor man, at last, after his reformation and just becoming comfortable in consequence; six little children left with nothing. The poor mother is active and careful and will do her best for them, and she has relations who may help her. She ran away with him and has, God knows, suffered for it, though he might have been where other less talented physicians are having been born and bred a

gentleman, gone through College and given a gentleman's profession. Dissipation ruined all his prospects; anguish of mind confirmed habits of drunkenness and after years of misery, in poverty almost abject through which his well-born wife watched him and worked for him and cheered him, he suddenly gave up every evil habit and ended his once promising life as a village schoolmaster and apothecary. It is a moral tale worth studying. [Dr] George Robinson has the merit of the poor man's reformation. A brain fever gave him the opportunity of saving both his life and his reason, but there was considerable character in the person who would bear reproof and listen to argument and *keep* his promise of amendment – faithfully. George will look after the poor widow, I feel sure, and [the Rev.] Mr. and Mrs. Moore will attend to her.

Did not feel quite well enough for a walk so went down to sit with Mary, called also on Mrs. Valpy to explain my leaving her so early the night before. Mary was sleeping as usual. She don't rightly wake up till three or four o'clock in the day so that her sleepless nights cannot be wondered at. I am lending Mr. Gardiner Mr. Chambers' Educational Course and reading each little book myself again before sending them to him. All the mighty of the earth sink into insignificance by comparison with these two humble brothers and such men as Mr. Simpson, Dr. Combe, etc. In return, Mr. Gardiner has lent me an American work, 'Fireside Education,' which is admirable so far as I have yet gone. I sat reading it the greater part of the evening while the six cousins, the two Colonels and Miss Hart were playing vingt un [sic] with laughing accompaniments.

11. Our Irish paper of this morning says little. All appears to be very quiet everywhere except the pens of the 'outs' which are endeavouring with all their zeal to write their party 'in,' and the less chance of success they feel attend their efforts the more they flourish; repeal seems quite over – trade reviving – the new [Devon] Commission very busy – Ireland more comfortable than England where Mr. Cobden[1] and Co. are making a

1. Richard Cobden, M.P. for Stockton 1841–1847, was, with John Bright, the founding father of, and leading influence on, the Anti Corn Law League; it was in

great fuss; these troublesome people do good however by indirect means. There is an able article it seems in the last *Quarterly Review* upon our two monster Universities, Oxford and Cambridge, setting forth their frightful moral abuses and the very scanty information to be got in them. The writer might have proceeded to the publick schools – families are impoverished by the scandalous expenses of both school and college, and the best, the purest, the most promising young man must leave either contaminated, probably borne down by debt, crushed by evil secrets he dare impart to no one. My brother John left Eton at fifteen owing near £100.; had our kind Uncle Frere not coaxed this secret out of him and paid the money, what a millstone round John's neck would not this serious sum for one so young have proved through life. John Frere went to Cambridge, where his Uncle William Frere was head of Downing College, with an allowance of £400 a year, I think. His bills to his amazement amounted to £500 more. Tradesmen giving credit to any amount and money lenders being plenty, College rules set at nought, college care being unknown. The Gardiners thought of sending Tommy to Harrow for a couple of years, the Freres being all so anxious for it. So Mary wrote to enquire from Dr. Wordsworth the smallest expense at which it could be done. £200 a year.

It is time for a better system of education. Keeping boys by their mother's apron strings, if the Mother be a fool, may probably be as bad as sending them to these sinks of vice. But such homes as educated people now have to shelter their children in, combined with the publick instructions of Cheltenham or Edinburgh, have a better chance of rearing upright, actively industrious, and well informed pupils, than the old Latin Grammar, birch rod, fighting, drinking, and squandering system, and people with small means half ruined themselves to whole ruin their sons by means of it. The world is getting a little wiser, slowly.

large part due to their efforts that these laws were repealed by Sir Robert Peel shortly after the Smiths' return to Ireland. The Devon Commission had been set up in 1843 'to inquire into the law and practice with regard to the occupation of land in Ireland'.

Called on Mrs. Lyon to find the world as silly as ever. Found Mr. Gurney there quite excited, the lady ditto; they had been disputing about this schism among the doctors. I of course had to hear it all which took near an hour; then in came Captain Lyon to give it all over again with a great many additional particulars. Pau is in a ferment. 'Where on earth do you live, my dear Mrs. Smith, that you are so ignorant of all that is going on.' The answer is very ready. At my own fireside where we never admit either envy, hatred, malice or uncharitableness.

16. Mary had another of these spasms in the night. She slept none till morning, but is dozing on now as she has latterly done. All the children, the Colonels and I went to Gandalos, Miss Hart staid by Mary. I see less of her poor soul, than I should wish, but I don't know how to manage otherwise. She sleeps on till nearly two o'clock. It don't suit either any of the children or the Colonels to walk till one; the young have their various masters and studies – the old the reading room and their billiards; then we are out till nearly four when we dine, and after dinner the Colonel will not suffer me to move, partly on account of the cold, partly because he don't like to be left. By and bye however when the weather is better I can run down while he takes his nap. I shall not have her long to look after.

No one would think this was the carnival, there is nothing in the world going on, more like Lent; what then will Lent be? This part of France was so long Protestant that very little of the pageantry of popery remains here.

18. Dr. Smith called early to catch me in and tell all his grievances – no particular compliment for he has confided his sorrows pretty impartially to all who would listen. From his story he has reason professionally to complain of Dr. Taylor who neither acted fairly nor *truthfully* as has been proved. Whether Dr. Smith were right in noticing this at all, or in the method he took to express his dissatisfaction I can hardly say without hearing the other side. He says his communication was private and that the publication of the quarrel, for such it has become, was all Dr. Taylor's own doing. I suspect both have been to blame in this part of the business.

I don't myself trust Dr. Taylor. I don't feel him to be candid.

I know him to be jealous, and I am not sure that he is skilful further than natural abilities and considerable experience may render him so. I can't believe that he has had any education professionally or otherwise, except what he has scraped together one way or another, and that the consciousness of this makes him so very sore – all quick, as some one said.

Then Dr. Smith is evidently hot-tempered, anxious for practice, a little unduly vain of his College honours and touchy upon his medical reputation and sore at having been deceived on one or two occasions and made use of on one or two others without proper acknowledgment, so that he has every disposition to find as much fault as possible with the other party; his letter declining ever again to act professionally with Dr. Taylor he did not shew me, some friend to whom it was lent not having returned it. Dr. Taylor's reply, three long pages, is a very impertinent one – slanderous on a few individuals – contemptuous towards the English society here generally – insolent to Dr. Smith – and refuting none of the allegations brought against him. A soft answer would have turned away wrath. However I am judging without having seen the provocation.

20. A letter from Dr. George in low enough spirits; he is lonely and dull in his unfinished house, evidently unable to supply the place of the friends whose family formed his home and whom he well knows so truly valued him. The weather was beautiful, the country quiet, no excitement about these Trials which by the bye have begun. Dinner parties with champaign at Ballyward, fevers in other houses. Mr. West at Ardinode was so ill in one for three weeks that the Doctor could not get any holidays. The Milltowns have been reconciled after sad quarrels beginning but not ending with the Italian boy.[1]

1. Lord Milltown had three natural children who had been brought up and educated by their mother in Italy. The boy had arrived in England to make something of his life (or, to be more precise, his father's contacts: 'Moi, je suis Milor', E.G. reported him as explaining). Colonel and Mrs. Smith heartily disapproved of their neighbour's choice of surname, Fitzleeson, but nevertheless attempted to find a position for him in the East India Company (see 24 February 1845).

And poor Alley had resumed his ill habits and we fear that beside drinking he had been breaking trust for the loan fund books of which he had the keeping were found saturated with turpentine, on fire, and the schoolroom in danger of being burned down by means of them. Hal's £30 is gone for all vouchers of all sorts are destroyed.[1] All the children of both houses spent this evening together here, dancing very happily.

21. We had to walk in the park on account of the very dirty roads. I don't like it much on any day but I dislike it on Sunday on account of the crowd. Yet it gave us the opportunity of seeing all classes of the natives as well as many of the English. The men of the higher classes among the French are well-dressed, and well looking, clear and clean and gentlemanly, but such a set of little ugly, airless, awkward, ill-dressed women as the '*femelles de ces mâles*' I don't suppose is to be met with in any other land. The Bourgeoises are rather decenter – some of the girls in caps and handkerchiefs very pretty. The children beautiful; I don't know that I ever anywhere saw such lovely infants with such bright eyes and such fat cheeks and so very bright and healthy looking.

Spent the evening in reading 'Little Nell' dipping in here and there as the philosophy of the subjects struck me. Better than any sermon, almost as lovely as the words of inspiration is the whole detail of the death of that most beautiful creation of a pure imagination, that most angelick child. All the feelings, all the principles, all the ideas expressed are but so many exemplifications of the Christian doctrines – not the faith of the English Church or the Latin Church or any church of human device constituted for human purposes – not the doctrine of any priest – nor the adoption of any creed – merely the fulfilling of the Law Christ taught us – to love the Lord our God with all our heart and our neighbour as ourself.

1. The details of this local scandal are to be found
   in the minutes of the County Kildare Poor Law
   Guardians' meetings; Colonel Smith was one of
   their elected number before and after his two years'
   absence in France.

22. Hal passed an agreeable evening and a pleasant night. Asthma – the consequence of misconduct. Everything he sees he must taste – no matter what – no matter when – all the improper dishes he dines on; if they are not there he talks of mean dinners, disrespect to Colonel Litchfield, who never touches but the plainest food, and instead of the climate of Pau having operated as a mollifier of this quick spirit, I never knew him so irritable in my life. He takes fire even without combustibles. One dare not *hint* that he is doing wrong or is mistaken. I think him at times half cracky – most of his countrymen are whole cracky, so he is an improvement upon the species. Little Jack is to be a degree more placid still. To see him now, complaining of perpetual ill-fortune at his game of spillikins, throwing down his hook, leaving the table determined to play no more, – anyone but his mother would die of laughing, but I shall take care that he shall practise all games till he can win or lose with equal good humour – lose with tranquillity, win without being elated. Self-controul, invaluable possession – so much wanted by the Celtick race, I invoke you to descend upon my three children! as the only solid foundation of their hopes of happiness.

23. Sir Hudson Lowe is dead – a man forgotten these many years – once the theme of every tongue and very undeservedly censured for merely obeying his instructions. I can recollect the publishing of the 'Voice from St. Helena' by Mr. O'Meara, an Irish Army surgeon, a shrewd man of little principle he afterwards proved to be, anxious to make himself a name, flattered of course by the confidence of the great man and swayed to a one-sided view of all relating to him as everyone always was that ever was about him. Napoleon ill in mind and body was in no humour to receive any treatment with philosophy. An unconscious wish perhaps still to create an interest in the world from which he was for ever separated, together with an habitual disregard of truth common to all his country, dictated much of the miseries of his condition. The large party of opposition to all but what themselves originate, took up the 'Voice' as that of an oracle and echoed through the world the cruelties of Napoleon's jailor. Colonel Pennington [H.L.'s sister Jane's first husband] saw the poor man enter a club one day every member of which turned his back on him,

his bow was unacknowledged, his words unanswered; he sat down near a table at which Colonel Pennington was reading, and on my brother-in-law moving a candle nearer to him Sir Hudson became quite nervous and told him afterwards it was the first civility since his return to England that had been paid him by a stranger.

I remember fancying him to be rude in manner, rough in temper, a large coarse soldier, hoping I might never encounter him, sure he must be a monster whom I never could be brought to endure. I was a girl at this time in the Highlands where we were too apt to be shewn but one side of the picture and to take up our opinions rather strongly. After I married, on our voyage home we touched at Ceylon and while our Captain was loading his vessel with spices we spent very nearly three most happy weeks with an old friend and dancing beau of mine, Campbell Riddell, who was there in some special situation – Commissioner of enquiry into abuses or something – he gave a dinner to introduce us to the society; we had all the great people of Columbo and I was taken to dinner by a military man, a General Officer covered with orders, a little pale elderly person, very quiet, very gentlemanly and very agreeable; he had been everywhere, knew everybody. I thought him very pleasant for our conversation was becoming very interesting when I was startled by some one asking 'Sir Hudson Lowe' to do him the honour to take wine. It was a lesson in morals; he might be strict in interpreting orders, an enforcer of discipline for all I know, but I much question his having been discourteous.[1]

24. Made quite dull by seeing from Mary's windows the procession of the conscripts towards headquarters, nearly 500 very young men, the contribution, I suppose, of this department to the requirements of still uncivilised states. They marched in double file with a few drums before them and a few soldiers behind looking dull enough; some with a neat knapsack strapped upon their shoulders, others with only a red or blue cotton handkerchief held in the hand containing to all appearance a very small supply of necessaries. What

1. A full account of their visit to St. Helena can be found in the Memoirs 11, p. 288ff.

must it have been in the Emperour's day, when the call was more frequent, the number greater, the age so much less; and when they marched from home and all its simple pleasures to certain death. They now send them as soon as they are drilled to Algiers where the climate soon thins out the weakly, and it is strange that they like being sent there. Generally they make them sing to make believe they are happy; however to-day the silence was mournful. If the service were voluntary it would be all right enough as nations are still barbarous enough to require the *appearance* of armies at any rate, but this forced levy, this tax on life, it is like the victims in pagan countries offered up living sacrifices to the evil deities.

25. State Trials in Ireland begun. The Attorney General has opened the proceedings, very temperately, very fully, not very forcibly. There is no excitement among the mob. The Traversers did their best to excite, going down to the Courts the first day in a procession of several carriages, the Radical Lord Mayor and several aldermen accompanying them in their robes. Very few of the ragged unwashed attended them and those few shewed no enthusiasm. The next day O'Connell drove unaccompanied by sound or sight; his carriage for the first time for years had not even a beggar beside it. What a strange people. Repeal seems to be dead and buried.

The Pau world is all convulsed by a poem on the Doctors come by the post from Bayonne yesterday, printed and broadly distributed, quizzing both sides properly, and very cleverly, and very amusingly. Hits at the vanity of the Irish side, the jealousy of the Scotch, the folly of both; the leaning is towards Dr. Smith personally without doubt. Oh these ballads! Satire in verse, enthusiasm in verse, what a powerful engine when wielded with skill.

26. Mary is considerably better. Sleeping better. She was in the dining-room again yesterday. The Coles were calling there and we had great fun talking of this clever poem, taxing Mr. Cole with being the authour. He shifted the merit of it to Mr. Atkinson, a very clever roué here. Still Mr. Cole possesses the only private printing press in the place; perhaps both had a hand in it. I only hope it may have the effect of

restoring harmony to our little society; these sort of quarrels are so particularly unpleasant.

SATURDAY, FEBRUARY 3. The State Trials go on rather more rapidly than was expected. Great temper on the part of the Government; none whatever on the part of the Traversers. Mr. Shiel opened the defence with a long speech in parts very eloquent – two or three passages very fine but not affecting the subject the least, they might be cut out without being missed and would do for any other occasion; there is no reasoning, no argument, no attempt at answering a single allegation.[1] Very little excitement in Dublin; very little crowding in the Court House. Two of the Repeal Wardens have peached [turned informer] and much discomfited the conspirators. Still I continue to my first opinion that it would have been better not to have had the trials.

11. My dear sweet Johnny's birthday – six years completed this morning. And he is growing up mind and body hitherto as the most anxious parent could wish; the principal failing I can perceive in his disposition is a timidity he will require to overcome or it might degenerate into weakness; it is accompanied at present with a sensitiveness that sets him right; he has a tender conscience and an honesty of purpose resembling the perfect uprightness of his father, so that I do not fear his shyness leading him into vice – it may induce him to blush for doing right. Loviet and Vivian at different stages of his youth must be his study; he has a busy head at present and has made great intellectual strides during the last few months.

Mary is very well – better since she gave up so much wine and avoided ale entirely; really the quantity of strong drink she had got to swallow during the four and twenty hours surpassed all necessity. I am convinced that all her excitement and more than half her exhaustion was caused by the immoderate use of what in small quantities might be necessary. I was unaware of her excesses till quite lately and though I quite excuse them

1. Richard Lalor Sheil (1791–1851), lawyer, M.P. and dramatist, was counsel for the 'Liberator's son, John O'Connell; the D.N.B.. believes this was 'the most brilliant of his forensic speeches'.

and can comprehend the wish of momentary ease making her fly to any apparent relief I can't account for her being allowed to go the round of five or six different liquors one after the other with little intermission. Such a system of nursing, I suppose, was never pursued before except in poor Uncle Edward's [Ironside] sickroom where the same noise and bustle and confusion and commotion and irregularity and improper eating and excessive drinking horrified everyone that entered it. There is no use in speaking in this unhappy case of poor dear Mary's. She will only do just what the whim of the moment suggests; to this her husband always yields and as her principal disease is organick and incurable why tease them? Alas! all I can do is to assist in her moments passing agreeably. Naturally she is in every respect charming. She has had several serious conversations with me of late in which more of her heart and mind has been opened to me than I had ever suspected. And so pure and so good and so humble are all her feelings that she causes me both to love and to respect her more than I had believed she merited – dear as she has always been to me.

On Thursday Mr. Hedges came to give her the sacrament. Mr. Gardiner and I took it with her. He addressed us both before and after, evidently preparing her for a release from all suffering in so kind yet searching a manner that the impression he made I shall not easily forget; he took, too, all the sting from death and left us in a frame of mind resigned and tranquil. Good little man, his is the perfect love that casteth out fear and she feels with him though clinging still to life as human nature is formed to do. Who that has husband and children to leave could quit them without grief – the husband and his solitary home, in peril, her smile of encouragement, her support, her shield. Alas! little do they know, poor pets, how *cold* existence will be to them without her.

14. The English political world has been quite alive since the meeting of parliament. And all matters going as one would wish, the ministry stronger than ever. Sir Robert Peel assuming a higher position, a more assured tone than even during the last session while his moderation of temper appears to be strengthened. The Ministers meet the parliament with the composure of men who have well performed their duty.

We are at peace with all the world. Our relations with the sovereigns of Europe are all friendly, the disputes with America settled, the wars in the East successfully terminated, our Colonies recovering, our commerce extending, our home manufactures reviving, the state of the labouring poor much improved, and the revenue for the year considerably greater than the expenditure.

To set against this agreeable array there is nothing but Mr. O'Connell, for to talk of the 'State of Ireland' the present war cry of the restless outs is ridiculous – the only state that Ireland is in is that of gradual and very rapid improvement – landlords awakening to their true interests, intelligence dawning upon the people, comfort ready to rise on every side as soon as the country is delivered from the agitations of what Lord Brougham[1] so justly names as a gang of impostors.

The state trials are nearly closed; the Solicitor-General is replying – in the ablest speech by far among the many that have been made. No denouncings, no flashes of wit or eloquence, no poetical paintings, nor irrelevant appeals. The Traversers and their clever Counsel might have been pleading for some case in the moon for anything their very exciting and in some parts really fine speeches had to do with the subject on hand. Mr. Greene coolly, quietly, calmly, divests the case of all extraneous matter and keeps to the fact of these persons convulsing the country by illegal means for an illegal purpose, and so close and so sound is his argument that I should be very much surprised indeed if it did not convince the Jury. The conviction will produce no tumult – the Government are wisely guarding against evil by sending more troops with artillery to Dublin, but in spite of the most disgusting efforts of the radical press to keep alive the spirit of disaffection and to exalt these people into victims or heroes, the enthusiasm

1. He was one of E.G.'s father's political cronies in the Whig circles in which they both moved in the 1820s. Although Lord Chancellor at the time of the Great Reform Act, his posthumous general reputation is probably as much derived from the carriage named after him and his part in the development of Cannes as a summer retreat for the rich of northern Europe.

they once roused is nearly over. And O'Connell seems to feel it, his spirits are much lowered, his speech was very bad – a failure quite, and is so considered by all sides; his great power only lasted while he was thought to be invulnerable; his mob is now frightened and unless I have quite mistaken the character of the Irish O'Connell when a prisoner will be forgotten.

15. M. Puyoo had a fine luncheon at Gandalos the other day – Monday – a gentlemen's party with all sorts of good things to eat and stupid enough. Sixteen were invited, twelve assembled, and something like an hostile collision took place between Mr. Campbell and Captain Lyon on the never dying quarrel of the doctors: notes have swelled into a volume, words and speeches and reports succeed in rapid fury while blame seems to gather on every tongue and quiet to have fled for ever. Really a little town full of inferiour English is a perfect hot-bed of detraction.

16. I have been reading Madame de Genlis' 'Les Veillées du Château'[1] and have been quite surprised and quite delighted. She certainly was the founder of the improved plan of education, and how successful has been both her theory and her practice, Louis Philippe and his admirable sister yet live to shew. As some one replied to a person who was undervaluing her works and her character, 'the proof of both is on the throne of France'. Her French too is so beautiful. It was quite a *rest* to read it after M. Balzac whom it is the fashion to call vigorous, original, etc. I think his style coarse, vulgar and uneven; his new coined words, half of which are not to be found in any dictionary, are less agreeable than the known ones he discards, and his story of 'Eugenie Grandet'[2]

1. The Comtesse de Genlis (1746–1830) wrote this book in 1784 whilst she was tutoring the future king, Louis Philippe, the son of Louis XVI's cousin, Philippe 'Egalité' (who was also her lover). Napoleon was to be much impressed by her 'improved plan of education'; he made her 'Dame Inspectrice des Ecoles Primaires'.

2. Honoré de Balzac's reputation has perhaps survived better; this novel (1833) was one of a trilogy on the history of society in France.

is so uninteresting both as to actors and plot that I can't see the great merit of faithful pictures of stupidity; it quite disappointed me. The carnival here has been the dullest thing possible. I have seen no show whatever except a few fat cattle driven about in pairs with green boughs on their heads and the butchers who are to kill them walking in front with red sash and coloured sticks. Also a wretched bear and half a dozen dogs to bait him wander through the empty streets.

18. We were three hours yesterday evening, finishing the Solicitor-General's admirable reply and the Chief Justice's very careful charge of which I don't altogether approve. So glaring had been the illegality of repeal proceedings no one could expect but that the leaning should be against the Traversers; but the warmth of expression was beyond what was seemly in a Judge. I am sure all these matters prove beyond controversy that Irishmen are totally unfit for power. A nice mess they would have their country in were the mad schemes of the millions to succeed. With such uncontrouled tempers all their wonderful talent is mischievous rather than useful. The Jury were many hours considering their verdict and at last brought it in defective from not exactly comprehending how to deal with the various counts. They have to be locked up till nine o'clock on Monday last, the trial having unluckily finished on Saturday. It is 'Guilty' however with some reservations for one or two of the gang. Mr. O'Connell has not been in Court since he delivered his defence and is said to be ill, disspirited and failing.

21. The day before yesterday, Monday, Miss Selina Fox was married to Captain Carey, first at three o'clock at the Mayor's, Mr. Gardiner being one of the two English witnesses, besides which four French are necessary to make the ceremony legal. At five Mr. Hedges performed the religious part. The Bride behaved pretty well; yet at the solemn promise she has to swear to of loving, honouring, obeying, etc. the man whom she forsakes all home ties to give herself to for ever, this giddy, lively, rather forward girl was quite overcome and had to be allowed several minutes to recover her voice proving that deep feelings can be concealed by a foolish manner.

The rest of the service passed off well. Janey Gardiner went to tea to take leave of the Bride, before she drove to Billères

where they can remain but a day as the rich Mr. Beaumont
has taken it for a month or two, so they have to proceed to
Bagnères. Mr. Gardiner was to have brought her home when
he had to go to Mrs. Campbell's ball. Mrs. Campbell had
invited Janey but Mary had declined for her; however at the
marriage she was so much pressed to go by Miss Campbell,
the bridesmaid, and others that she actually *cried* herself sick
nor could she be composed till her mother gave a reluctant
consent, the first tear having quite softened her father. I was not
a little amazed certainly on entering the ball-room to see the
happy monkey perched up beside Mrs. Taylor, her chaperone,
to whom she gave very little trouble for she danced the whole
night and staid to the end – four in the morning – when the
older part of the Company had to help out the Boulangère,
Mr. Gardiner dancing with Mrs. –. Mr. Gardiner was in high
spirits, enjoyed the evening fully as much as his daughter and
when on our coming down to our own apartment about twelve
Miss Hart asked in sad accents how he seemed to bear being in
the rooms where his then beautiful wife had given her brilliant
fête only three years before, it gave me a pang to have to answer
that I did not believe any recollection of a melancholy kind had
once crossed his thoughts. It is a happy disposition for himself
and will make his happiness with his next wife the more certain.
She will be for her time equal perfection to him, he will be as
kind to her as he has been to Mary and every other woman he
has had anything to do with; and he really is good, unselfish
and amiable; but his way of feeling is strange to me.

Mrs. Campbell had very kindly invited our girls – of course
we did not let them go – no small sacrifice for our parental
vanity as they look particularly well when dressed and dance
so beautifully. Living in the same hotel I had no excuse for
declining on the score of health, and as Mr. Gardiner is out
every night we could not make poor Mary's illness a reason
for not going. I was glad too to have an opportunity of taking
a peep at the people and Mary herself was most anxious for
me to see and be seen, and what trouble she took to have me
dressed nicely. I went down to drink tea with her and she
made Sarah dress my hair, held the candle herself, went to
her wardrobe for beads to twist in it as I meant to wear pearls;
and she did look so ill, so worn, so suffering, it felt to me the

most wretched mockery of dressing ever gone through, but she was quite happy, quite occupied about it, and so charmed when I told her the modiste on receiving her instructions for the trimming of Brussels Point which was to be prepared for the black velvet dress and the coiffure of lace and paddy bird feathers[1] to suit, had promised to exert her utmost skill as 'Madame' must expect to be very much looked at, very much scrutinised 'étant soeur de *Madame Gardiner* qui se mettait si bien, avait les manières si gracieuses, etc,' and I really believe she was right and it was quite fortunate for the reputation of the family that the one sister was considered to be worthy of the other in matters of the toilette, according to M. Puyoo and our cook who respectively recorded the opinions of their several societies.

24. We are much engaged with the newspapers, all publick matters being just now very interesting. The Attorney General don't bring the conspirators up for judgement until next term and they are still at large some of them cutting new capers. The Repeal Association has met again – a very subdued tone of speaking, preparations evidently making for remodelling or even dissolving it, and the convicted newspaper editors have sent in their registrations – a farce – for they will just do as much mischief as ever and be fully as much belonging to the plot as when their names were registered amongst repealers. Mr. O'Connell has written a letter to all Ireland setting forth that the result of the trials has been highly satisfactory to him, that the cause of repeal has been considerably forwarded by them, that if the people but remain quiet which he implores them to do they may be certain of having the parliament in College Green in six months at farthest. The country is perfectly quiet, that is one thing very certain, the repeal rent small, and Mr. O'Connell off to London to resume his seat in Parliament; partially cheered on entering the House of Commons, warmly shaken by the hand by a small gang of allies. Extraordinary man, he is a complete puzzle to all his kind.

1. According to the O.E.D. these might be the feathers from the Java Sparrow, the White Egret or the Sheathbill.

Lord John Russell has made his motion on the state of Ireland and has got nothing by it; his speech is called a clever opposition speech the meaning of which appears to be that it is perfectly uncandid. He is followed by Lord Howick, good, but wild; Sir George Grey mistating facts; Serjeant Murphy mad;[1] Mr. Sharmon Crawford unluckily for his set letting out the truth that it is in truth a struggle for the ascendancy of popery. A great good has been the result of this long and still adjourned debate. It shews the Opposition to be as before to *men* and not to *measures*, to be as much divided into sects as ever, differing so widely from one another that it is matter of amazement how they ever gather so many of these little splits able to vote together; they are therefore quite innoxious except in so far as they take up time uselessly in making long speeches full of falsehoods which it is mere form to prove so as there seems to be one line of disaffection got by heart by the whole of them, repeated in turn with the addition of such rhetorical flourishes as each orator considers himself to shine in, the corrected misstatement of one merely setting on another to reiterate the same silly series. As for their press it is actually disgusting. In the midst of all this froth and frenzy appears the ministry, firmer, stronger, calmer than ever, shortly and quietly stating the truth, composedly appealing to the regular improvement of the country, seen and uncontroverted. Sir James Graham makes a calm businesslike speech which must be quite convincing to all who are unprejudiced. Lord Stanley is a little more angry, his birch rod is smart enough administered well yet with discretion and had effect.

28. Such a trial in the papers! Such a set of ill-conducted people exposed to the publick. Mr. Frazer who published our highland effusions, his wife one of the Vivians, and a set of acquaintance suited to their scale of morality. Mr. Frazer consequently cannot get rid of his fury of a wife nor does he

---

1. Representative of her views on the Whigs. When Russell became Prime Minister in 1846 he selected the well respected Grey as Home Secretary; Charles Grey, Viscount Howick, came from the same political stock; Francis Stock Murphy (M.P. for Cork) was, however, according to the D.N.B., noted for his wit.

deserve it. I had heard from Mrs. Macpherson that it had turned out a miserable marriage nor did I wonder. We knew all those Vivians when children, little ugly, stumpy, black girls with tempers, Mary Anne's the worst. She came out to Bombay under very extraordinary circumstances while I was there to marry her first husband Mr. Blair; her conduct was very extraordinary during the very short time he lived, and her second marriage took place within the year of widowhood. Mr. Frazer married her for her money. In my quality of authour he behaved very well to me so that I was inclined to like him; he was dear Belleville's friend too, and William Clarke's, yet I neither thought him handsome nor attractive; he is a half caste; when I knew him he had been little in good society, and he had been very carelessly educated. It was probably through William Clarke he had got acquainted with Mrs. Blair, for Miss Blair is William Clarke's wife; that is not a happy marriage either, I fear.

What really handsome men those Clarkes of Dalnavert were and what novels might not be woven out of their adventures. I should have made use of some of them in my 'Painter' or my other sketches had not India been a better stop to all our troubles. As it was Mary and I made upwards of £100 in a very few months by our scribbling when we were hardly doing more than trying our skill – Belleville our confidant, this wicked little Mr. Frazer our agent, and my poor mother's comfort our incentive to the work, and we were really very happy. In that ruined house with few servants, few comforts, no money and every post bringing some addition to our difficulties, youth, health, sanguine tempers carried us through a time of trial. We were busy all day either amusing and attending my mother or in assisting the business of the household, mending, making, tidying, storeroom and stillroom and the nicer parts of cooking even; the poultry yard and the garden and the schools were our pastimes; then in our walks we gathered the faggots which were to eke out our private fire and we stole from sleep the hours necessary for keeping faith with Mr. Frazer.[1]

1. This account of how their girlish writings provided
   almost the Grant family's only disposable income
   during the debt-ridden years before his fortuitous

He did not know our names, though perhaps he guessed. I shall never forget my mother reading from the *Literary Gazette* a criticism on a new periodical '*The Inspector*' in which our contributions appeared and were named as *the best*; how merrily we passed the evening; the tea we had bought tasted so good; the wine for my mother's negus was perfection! and when afterwards we bought some fat wedders we laughed so on concluding the bargain that I really believe that mutton digested better than any other. My mother was in our confidence and I suppose she afterwards told my father but he never spoke of our authourship to us. We did not envy Jane and Malshanger[1] while strolling through the forest of Rothiemurchus imagining some story with a lake before us, the sky overhead, tall pines all round, and a brook and a rock and heather and bog myrtle and wild thyme and chirping birds, and buz, and hum, but no human sound near us. It was not bad education.

29. The last day of February and all looking bright except the sky. Winter here is not at all a pleasant season, very rainy, very dreary. Mary is pretty comfortable; the children have all colds and my Janey does not thrive here somehow; she looks very pale. The great debate is over, ended by Sir Robert Peel in a fine speech, tranquil, liberal, firm, immeasurably above all low party feeling. No triumph in the tone of the man whose wisdom has redeemed his country, restored her commerce, revived her trade, put an end to war abroad and strife at home, *stopt agitation* and *annihilated opposition*. The majority without any trouble taken was 99, and in spite of three or four brilliant speeches this attempt has but further weakened a really contemptible set of little factions.

FRIDAY, MARCH 1. All to be seen in the newspapers to-day is the taking of an Island in the South Seas [Tahiti.] by the

appointment to be a Puisne Judge in Bombay is well described in the Memoirs. 'Fraser's Magazine for Town and Country' lasted until 1838 but there were only ever four numbers of 'The Inspector'.
1. Sister Jane and her elderly husband Colonel Pennington lived here when the rest of the family were facing these difficulties back at Rothiemurchus.

French Admiral who has deposed the black queen Pomaré. 'Tis said this is unsanctioned by his Government, but as this royal personage was under British protection there is rather a sore feeling upon the subject. Ireland perfectly quiet. A little while ago our neighbour Mr. Tynte had his pack of harriers burned poor things in their kennel; now, his haggard has been set on fire – oats and a mare and foal destroyed but owing to the exertions of his Tenants, labourers, etc. the premises are saved; private malice must be the cause of so vile a piece of spite; he has probably exercised some of the 'rights' of property in a way unpleasant to some ill-disposed character.

I am in great distress about a whim Mary has taken into her head with so much determination that nothing will avail to turn her from a plan so impossible of being carried out without the greatest risk. She is resolved to remove to Honfleur. She has a fancy that Pau is killing her, that Honfleur will cure her. She got well there before on leaving Bath wretchedly ill. She forgets what progress the disease of the heart has made in these four years. She tries to believe there is little the matter with her but the liver; poor thing, clinging to life as her chance of living diminishes, for no human being can look more deplorable than she has looked the last few weeks. She is to travel by land, in the diligences and set out about the middle of next month!!

Mr. Gardiner says if she *will* go she *must*, and he must borrow the money for the journey and to settle her there and to pay up everything here, and he will have to pay a higher rent for this apartment keeping it only one year, and what is to be done with all the quantity of property she has gathered – clothes, books, china, furniture, nicknacks, finery? And his boys taken from their English school and just settled with Mr. Scott, who must live here for his health and who will not endure the confinement of having them entirely under his care. And what are *we* to do? Travelling is not so cheap that a large family with small means can afford to move here and there at will. We must go sometime certainly; still we were not prepared to go now. And when we do move towards home, we should prefer a cheaper residence than Honfleur. Perhaps we shall none of us be called on for such experiments

– six weeks is a long time for one in her condition to look forward to.

2. Nothing particular. Have been reading *Nicholas Nickleby* with more delight than ever, and a Treatise by Mr. Bickersteth on Prayer[1] in which are many good reflexions, though to the principle of praying all day for and about everything I can't subscribe, nor indeed do I like any of their evangelical doctrines, declining society, dancing a sin, cards a vice, conversation always to be turned to religious subjects, etc. – nonsense.

4. Mary very unwell – wretchedly ill indeed – severe pain in her head, bloodshot eyes, general lassitude, etc. etc. Had to send for Dr. Taylor who ordered ice to the head and talked of bleeding to relieve the circulation; he then gave her all the particulars of his persecution of that poor dying Mr. Hazelwood which he has most successfully carried out, for what purpose it would be hard to say except it be to throw the chief practice here into the hands of the rival he is so very jealous of, Dr. Smythe, which it will most assuredly do. Mr. Hazelwood not only had no degree but most reprehensibly pretended to have one and this being proved he is deprived of the royal ordonnance and banished. His numerous patients who half worship him will never employ the man that has ruined him he may depend on it; and whether this strange rancour is becoming in the half educated man who *found him here*, or decent in any sense, or Christian, we may safely leave to the judgment of impartial people. All I have to do with it is to regret that these evil passions should be intruded into a sick room where excitement is very dangerous, and a charitable frame of mind of some consequence to the dying. They all opened upon me like a set of maniacks clapping their

1. Edward Bickersteth (1786–1850), an evangelical divine, wrote extensively and controversially; his 'Treatise on Prayer', for example, went through eighteen editions. His polemical energies were seriously diminished after an accident five years before his death when he was thrown from his carriage and run over by a cart transporting materials for the construction of a Roman Catholic chapel in Liverpool.

hands with delight at the result as if some kind action had restored the peace of hundreds, instead of one erring, sickly man having been dishonoured, ruined, for the satisfaction of another. I waited till their joy was over and then changed the subject, for really I was shocked.

12. A discovery that the wood merchant has cheated us of nearly a fourth part of our wood. At least we have every reason to suppose so, from our supply not having lasted so long by some weeks as we had calculated on, and Captain Lyon suspecting from the same cause in his consumption that something was wrong ordered two more *bouchets*, stacked them and measured them and found a large deficiency; so he made over the rogue to the proper authorities by whom he has been heavily fined after restitution of missing wood. The people of the country have not the slightest idea of probity in their dealings with the English. From the highest tradesman down to the market higglers[1] they cheat us at all hands. This and the squabbles and the bad climate will do up Pau; few that are here this season mean to return for another except such as cannot help it.

The quarrels are, we hear, raging more fiercely than ever. Dr. Taylor has lost ground in every way by this unfortunate persecution of the *quack*. And Mr. Gardiner has very foolishly mixed himself up with all this nonsense in his usual violent manner and is bustling furiously about with a minority of five or six against all Pau; he is really very silly in many respects and makes great mistakes from his party eagerness. There is no truth in the conviction or banishment of Mr. Hazelwood; here he is and here he is likely to stay, without any diploma certainly but with the royal ordonnance, and a clever Counsel from Paris arrived to help him to defend his remaining; the clapping of hands was therefore premature.

15. All quiet everywhere. Government stronger day by day. It has been a great victory in India, or rather two great victories – at some expense of human life, alas! A perfect carnage among the enemy, who being brave, well disciplined by French and Portuguese and half caste officers, and having

---

1. To higgle is to try and gain the advantage in bargaining (O.E.D.).

Russian artillery, fought like foes worth conquering. We lost between killed and wounded upwards of 800 men, of whom about sixty were officers – seven or eight are dead. General Churchill behaved gallantly; he was severely wounded, had his leg cut off after the action and died in a few hours; a handsome polished agreeable man.

It is fourteen years since we passed those merry three weeks at the Isle of France – merry fortnight at Ceylon, I mean, when he gave his wife to our care on her voyage home in the *Childe Harold*, and poor thing, she is dead, and Louisa married. Poor Mrs. Churchill, I liked her with all her errours. Her life had been one of much temptation in every way and she had no defence against it. He was thoroughly unprincipled, I believe, yet he was likeable too. Captain Somerset is severely wounded. We saw a good deal of him at the Hospital the Spring the Gardiners were in Dublin with the Blakenays, a very fine young man, a son of Lord Fitzroy Somerset's.

Lord Ellenborough was in the midst of the hottest of the fight going about among the wounded soldiers with oranges and gold mohrs! A second Napoleon! There are to be medals and trophies and a column in Calcutta, etc. And there have been three enormously long proclamations! Sir Hugh Gough after allowing himself to be surprised like a fool, fought like a hero – of old – only – there was none of the greatness of the *Commander* in his half crazy personal bravery.[1]

16. We observe in our morning walks in the Parc that almost all the tradespeople of the Town contrive to get an hour's exercise there with their families, while in the afternoons crowds of the shopboy and dressmaker's apprentice class gather for the same purpose; how much kinder and wiser is this than our British way of overworking ourselves and all depending on us, causing discontent, ill-health, early death, and avarice; neither will the time be lost in a business sense by this judicious break in the working hours. An overtasked frame is slow and feeble.

1. This was the Battle of Maharajpur, which won
control of the state of Agra the previous December.
Field Marshal Sir Hugh Gough, who originated
from a landed background in Co. Limerick, was
Commander-in-Chief in India from 1843 to 1849.

17. Sunday, St. Patrick's day. Who will give all our poor little children at home old ribbons to make their crosses of? I have read this week Tod's *Sunday School Teacher* from which I have gleaned many useful hints though it is absurd as a guide from being first unnecessary and secondly impracticable. Yet these enthusiasts do good.

Dear Mary has quite got over her little jealousy. She has for long allowed her good feelings full play. She is quite fond of her nieces, allows their perfections, likes their society and Jack is quite their amusement down there. I thought it would be so. I never forced them on her, never talked of them or of their acquirements, nor ever made any comparisons. I showed myself as I really was, much interested in her own children and I trusted to time to make her just to mine.

They are all like one family now. Each child has its own peculiar character, its own peculiar bias, its own peculiar merit; they form a most interesting little party with their dawning accomplishments, their little failings, their young fresh feelings, and their simple dispositions; they are now much attached to each other and perfectly happy together; and we are happy with them and in them for they are all truly amiable. I should not say from present appearances that there will be any remarkable degree of talent in any of them, but I hope they will all be superiour to the ordinary run of our kind, useful in their generation, doing their duty faithfully from right motives in an agreeable way; each the centre of an improving circle, spreading knowledge and kindness and happiness and comfort around them. How much the humblest among us may do – how little the most gifted have done; the way is better understood in these times; thousands with the best intentions really have rendered the progress of the millions slow, from narrow sectarian views the results of which failed to enlighten. Now we are all becoming more liberal, more really Christian, and in a better spirit the better educated work with better success.

20. Mr. Gardiner had lent me Tod's *Student's Guide* so excellent a work that I must remember to buy it, and also to mark it, for it is full of absurdity, in many of its tenets quite objectionable, mistaking the truth or rather not comprehending it in its fulness. Spurzheim [the phrenologist] says there is a bump

of *piety* in all heads which may be developed into religion, the distinction is well worth deep consideration. The necessity for venerating some ideal object added to the feeling of contrition which must belong to conscientious self examination, will degenerate into bigotted enthusiasm if there is not sufficient strength of character to raise it into true enlightened devotion. This accounts for Mr. Kerr and his school, the spirit of popery, or human nature, pride perhaps assisting to butter these poor people all over with self righteousness. The melancholy part of the business is the poor children, the reaction in their after life will probably hurry them down into the vice with which their parents had set out and which in most cases where the heart is good has produced this puritanism, now daily spreading.

21. Mary taken so ill yesterday there was hardly a hope of her living through the night, but she has Dr. Taylor with her three times; mustard poultices to her feet and stomach; hot water; cordials, etc. and when revived a blister. She went to sleep at two in the morning and she is, I hear, pretty comfortable. Dr. Taylor let nobody see her last night after her fit but her husband. I waited till near eleven to see him after she was arranged for the night; she had taken some gruel and was easy. I hardly expected to hear so good an account of her this morning. Dr. Taylor was seriously alarmed, not only for the present but the consequences must be very hurtful to so shattered a frame. I have seen her and she is better – lying like a creature but half alive, sleeping heavily under the influence of opium; how long her misery is to last there is no conjecturing. Between her complaints and the dreadful medicines necessary to alleviate them her strength appears to be now nearly exhausted. She must have had a wonderful constitution to bear up so long.

23. I should think this must be about the most changeable climate in the world – no two days alike for weeks back. Spring very late too. It was delightful all this long day in the Parc after the torrents of yesterday. A bright cheerful Sunday with a cool air, making exercise delightful. No appearance of leaves as yet anywhere though a few of the early flowers are appearing. Church was not crowded. Many people are gone, more will now be constantly going. It seems the quarrels here are annual.

Some such divisions among the English take place regularly –
part of the diversions of the season. Dr. Taylor began his attack
on Mr. Hazelwood three years ago; it raged one year in fury;
the next the Duchess of Gordon and Lord Newark pacified
the combatants, but this third season it seems to be war to the
knife. As I collect from this gentleman's friends who or what
he was originally he don't appear to be the least anxious to
say; he was one of the common herd of Edinburgh medical
students for some time; then in the 'Spanish Legion' during
part of the war; he came here in a very *seedy* condition, made
his own way, procured for himself a rich and a well connected
wife, and then commenced his campaign against the poor
doctor he found here and who had been settled here fully
twenty years, with permission from the French Government
to practise who is really half worshipped by his patients and
they have battled well for him.

Dr. Taylor says he considers himself on publick grounds
obliged to unmask an impostor; this friendly office would
have been at least better performed by any publick spirited
individual *non medical*. We impartial *spectators* think it would
have been best let alone. That University which was aggrieved
by the mysterious bargain concerning its diploma might have
proceeded against the purchaser of its purloined honours,
had its learned members deemed the affair of sufficient
consequence to be so noticed. As to any private person
taking up the cudgels it seems to be quite unnecessary.
So thinks the Préfêt whose letter in answer to the Taylor
remonstrance must be anything but satisfactory to the small
clique of somewhat a smaller Council than 10 who were
so occupied for near a month in framing it. So thinks the
Minister of the Interieur, according to his Secretary; and
our Ambassador Lord Cowley, whose letter to Lord Newark
settles the question.

I wish Mr. Gardiner had not so identified himself with such
absurd pretentions, but he is always violent, easily prejudiced
and not over sensible. His little daughter told Colonel Smith
that gross injustice had been done but should not be submitted
to, that it should be made a political question both in England
and France, this ridiculous jealousy of an obscure provincial
doctor! through the opposition in both countries. M. Thiers

and Mr. Wakley should each be furnished with full particulars and then let M. Guizot and Sir Robert Peel look to the consequences.[1] Quizzing being in fashion here, I thought he was amusing me. Not at all; it was all as true as that good Lord Ashley having carried an amendment to Sir James Graham's factory bill limiting the hours of female labour to ten instead of twelve. He had a majority of nine. Whether the result will be good may be doubted.

25. We went up to Perpignan to-day to call on the Coles. It was intensely hot, so I hired a poor little donkey to carry me up the hill and Jack rode on it to the foot. He and his sisters and Miss Hart remained under the chestnut trees till I had ascended and sent the donkey back to them when they took turns on its back home. We found Captain and Mrs. Elliot, their son, Dr. and Mrs. Taylor, and Captain, I mean Colonel Douglas all up there, and Captain and Mrs. Carey had just been there. Colonel Smith had a game at billiards; I had plenty of conversation, and my beautiful new bonnet was much admired. What will be the fashion, dear children, in *your* day, when you are reading this. My gown of to-day was a shot tabbinet orange and blue, striped and figured, with three deep tucks headed with guimp,[2] very full in the skirt, very long in the waist, and peaked, tight body, tight sleeves, ruffles, worked cambric collar, tan gloves, Indian shawl, the white one, bonnet of white velours épinglé [uncut vêtret] small close shape, with a trimming of white satin ribbon, and one long white willow feather. All this on the top of the donkey must have looked appropriate. Perpignan was

---

1. Adolphe Thiers (reforming journalist involved in the Paris revolutions of 1830 and 1848) was in opposition in the 1840s to the ministry of François Guizot (educational reforms); equally celebrated in this respect on this side of the Channel were Thomas Wakley (who founded the *Lancet* in 1823) and, perhaps, the greatest reformer of them all, E.G.'s hero Peel.

2. Guimp is a silk twist with a cord or wire running through it; tabinet is watered fabric of silk and wool, chiefly associated with Ireland according to the O.E.D.

beautiful; the view on every side so fine, the place so very pretty in itself. If there were less rain in this country it would be truly enjoyable.

30. A fine long letter from Tom Darker full of such interesting news; he is doing well in all ways, hedging, thinning, draining, selling cattle, managing admirably. The Frasers are the best possible tenants; the boys' schoolroom is fitted up, Mr. Moore and the Doctor gone to Dublin to choose a master; the draining on *my* two experimental farms has answered beyond hope, my dear Colonel with your Malvolio smiles; everything prospering except such little things as we cannot expect will get on without us. The papers tell us of railroads *begun*, capital flowing in, all since agitation has been quelled.

31. A very bright Sunday. Church beginning to look a little empty, so many people have gone away already, and more will go as soon as the weather and their health permits, these quarrels making society here very disagreeable. War still rages between the partizans of Drs. Taylor and Hazelwood; no compromise, the cry. The Rev. Mr. Kerr wrote a letter upon the subject to Dr. Taylor in the worst possible spirit, so it has been represented to us by those who have seen this Christian pastor's performance so arrogant, so abusive, so uncharitable in every sense that it has completed the disgust which his pharisaical manners and doctrine have caused more than half the society here to feel towards him. The smaller remains are however very influential, very keen, and very much interested in supporting his religious views, admiring even his denunciations from the pulpit; he insists on preaching in the evenings when he fulminates away dealing death and destruction on all hands. A great schism is therefore sprung up. So many never go to Church in the mornings; so many only go at that time and propose opposition prayers in a private apartment in the afternoons. The main chance a'n't forgotten either by the puritan. Mr. Hedges, the chaplain, of course sent his book round for his Easter dues, and Mr. Kerr, the self-elected assistant is to send round his; but the churchwardens refuse to sanction such a tax. Mr. Hedges sent him a handsome sum for his services while doing duty for *him* during his illness, and because he refused it equally handsomely there is no need of the English publick making up the difference.

All these strivings and jealousies and heartburnings make it anything but pleasant to go much among our countrymen. It is well for us that we live so retired.

THURSDAY, APRIL 4. The newspapers keep us busy for the world is all in a hubbub. M. Guizot and his clever master have weathered their storm but in England there is great perplexity. Amiable, though foolish and obstinate, Lord Ashley has placed his friends in the most awkward position out of which some people hardly suppose they will manage to get. A sort of 'maudlin philanthropy' some one calls this benevolent mania which has prompted him and many more to interfere in what should not be meddled with. Like the Landlord and Tenant question or any other question of private morals it must be left to private feeling which is only to be reached through individual worth or individual deference to publick sentiments.

The Protestant Church in Ireland is making itself odious; bigotted beyond belief are most of the clergy of the establishment; the Presbyterians of the north half frantick about their Marriage Act. The Scotch kirk neither quiet nor settled. A general move in the *Church* everywhere – to be expected where the vulgar mind is enlightening so rapidly; by and bye when the ferment is over the effect will be found to have been good. Early shop shutting for the purpose of the mental improvement of the tradesmen is becoming universal; there is a letter in *Saunder's* from one of Harvie's young men stating that in their establishment and at Todd & Burns' in Dublin there are libraries containing above 1,000 volumes, and reading rooms with most of the newspapers, magazines, and other periodicals, supported by the young men assisted by their employers, and that most of them devote their evenings to different branches of instruction. This, and the changes in our publick schools, and railroads, etc. will cause a revolution indeed – one little suspected perhaps to its full extent at present, but the time will come and before very long either when either the nobles must let themselves down gracefully to meet the uprising of their then equalised surrounders, or they will be set aside, removed perhaps, as unnecessary memorials of feudal times, unsuited to the improved condition of the world. 'Sceptre and crown will tumble down',[1] there can be no doubt of it, for they will by and bye not be wanted.

5. At present we are all occupied about a romance that I never believed to be more than half fancy till last night and now can only think of to laugh at, but it will require both reflexion and action being no less than a real and true love affair of that dear little precocious monkey Janey Gardiner, with a much more substantial hero than M. Antoine Le Gras, and much more opportunity of fostering a young passion on both sides. There of nothing against this little comedy but the extreme youth of the principal actors one don't exactly know what to do, a considerable degree of intimacy having been established, the advances of the gentleman's Papa and Mama having been quite met by the lady's before a thought crossed any of our minds as to consequences. Lady Fanny Cole was quite right in saying that when her daughters began to ride she would take to riding too. Young women should not be let out of sight of their parents. A chaperone don't do. Mr. Gardiner however is nobody; he would see nothing were he there and his daughter can make him see and feel too just as she does. Her mother thought Janey so young she forgot her natural precocity to which her long management of herself and of most things else at home has given an independence of spirit and a self-possessed manner quite like that of a woman of two or three and twenty. How it will end it would be hard to say.

I shall detail the progress for future amusement. It was at Mrs. Campbell's ball that Janey made her conquest; five times that evening she danced with Mr. Eliot, but her impression was not equally deep for she could not make up her mind on that occasion whether to prefer him or old Captain Straton. The next event in this history was a series of family attentions on the part of Mrs. Eliot, the mother, who in her many kind calls both at this house and at the Basse Plante was always accompanied by the son. Captain Eliot, the father, then began calling upon one pretext or another, and stopping the Colonels to talk over

1. 'Sceptre and Crown/ Must tumble down/ And in the dust be equal made/ With the poor crooked scythe and spade.' James Shirley (1659).

various interesting particulars relating to the quarrels here and other Pau affairs; he also made enquiries respecting my father. The son meanwhile who has a pretty talent for drawing began to make caricatures; the first one was sent to Mrs. Taylor, all the rest to Mr. Gardiner and these were followed by visits of course to laugh over the fun of them. Poems and letters came next – all relating to Pau politicks certainly, the first good enough, the latter ones tiresome, but they answered the purpose of introducing the writer in every possible way to the notice of the family.

A ride, a walk, two concerts and a dance at Mrs. Fox's had made some of us begin to suspect the cause of all these attentions, and Mary, rather annoyed at the last great packet of nonsense declared it was a little too bad that they were all to be deluged with these silly effusions on account of the bright eyes of her daughter. Meanwhile twice a week rides have been arranged between this daughter and Mrs. Taylor, Mr. Eliot to be always of the party, his mother engaging to alter her husband the Captain's dinner hour so as to suit the day whether hot or shady. The son then proposes a walk with his mother to Janey who waited in all day to be disappointed for no mother came. A note at night from the lover full of apologies talking of nervous agitations, distress, regrets, etc. his mother had been obliged to pay visits, so we concluded that she had had no part in the walking arrangement. However yesterday I paid a long neglected visit to her; she was out and we came away.

About ten o'clock at night as we were all finishing our game at Loto, little Johnny Gardiner with us, up came Tommy out of breath to thrust an open note into my hand directed to his sister; three long pages from Mrs. Eliot, in despair at having missed me, whom she has not seen above half a dozen times, for she was in, and looking out of the window, and rang and called to bid the servants shew us up, and how to apologise (for what!), how to excuse her rudeness or recover from her disappointment! she knew not, trusted all to dear Miss Gardiner, whom in page the second she hopes will kindly walk with her whenever she feels inclined, and play and sing to her whenever her Mama is better. Page the third contains a very indiscreet sarcasm on the affectation of Mrs. Blair whose studied attitudes on rising from her cushion in church prevent Mrs. Eliot who sits beyond her on the same bench from getting out into the aisle time enough to talk to all the congregation. A P.S. announces the intention of learning the base of some difficult duett to play on the pianoforte with her dear young friend. This startling communication coupled with previous advances has set both Mary and me a thinking – a troublesome business.

6. All went to church yesterday but me. I spent the morning with Mary whom I found free from any alarming symptom yet not thoroughly easy mind or body – the calomel was deranging the one and the Eliots the other. We know nothing about them, who or what they are, who are their connexions, what brings them here, etc. They don't spell their name like the Border Elliotts, nor does he appear to be Scotch, though they have been a good deal in Scotland; he has been in the Navy from boyhood, is the particular friend of Sir Charles Napier by his own account and was Admiral of Don Pedro's fleet! He talks of several brothers, one of whom, another sailor, is a friend of Colonel Litchfield's naval brother. They are all musick mad, and everything also mad, I should say – play on quantities of instruments like professors. Captain Eliot's violincello is first rate; he is free of the Opera House, directs and assists and is in fact a principal in all musical associations. Very like a gentleman – clever, witty, odd, and agreeable, and six foot three or four. This is all we know of him. The wife is very little, very sickly looking, must have been very pretty and is said here to have had money. In air and voice and manner she is a thorough Englishwoman of *very* middling rank – not unlike my mother's old maid, Mrs. Lynch. Clever*ish*, very talking, a little *blarneyish*, and exceedingly odd.

The son appears to be a very fine young man – clever, intelligent, advanced for nineteen, well principled, active in habits, with cheerful simple manners; he is going into the Church from conscientious preference for this profession, and he is to inherit 30,000 from his mother, so he told his particular friend M. Puyoo.

Mary says if he were the most eligible of sons in law she would not hamper her Janey at fifteen with any engagement to which I added 'nor with any *preference*.' 'She is too young to have her mind thus occupied.' Mr. Gardiner says: 'Let it alone, nothing may come of it; and if anything does, why in four or five years there would be no objection.' I think this is wrong – unfair to such mere children, and having given the matter very serious consideration I shall urge Mary to let as much of the intimacy drop as can be managed quietly. She don't like to put a stop to the rides because of a new hat and feather à la Wouverman's[1] which it makes Janey so happy to wear; so she trusts to wet days and so on, and will discourage the walks, etc. It will be another M. Le Gras business, I suppose. The fault has been in having no steady companion for that young girl, in allowing her to select her own acquaintance, to go out visiting by herself, to be in fact her own mistress. Her time is thus completely idled, her thoughts employed on follies, and a very trifling turn encouraged at an age when a higher order of habits should be so carefully fostered. Poor little girl, it grieves me to see these errours without having the power to correct them.

8. We had very agreeable letters from home to-day. One from the doctor who has been at Cork with which place he is charmed and so are the Gladstanes; the climate is delightful, scenery beautiful, society pleasant and good, and so much yachting and other sea and land amusements going on that it is a very desirable place for delicate people to winter in. Mrs. Gladstanes has grown quite fat, all the party, including our old horses, looking well. He did not go round by New Ross but, as his attractions there are expected to settle in Kilkenny, he hopes to have frequent opportunities of visiting them more conveniently. The other letter was from Mr. Frazer, a very nice and merry one; he has arranged with Mr. West to remain at dear Baltiboys till the end of May when he goes as usual to the Clyde; he is charmed with the house which he has found admirable in all respects; much pleased with the labourers and servants particularly those he has had most to do with and to whom he has been very kind, having had old Peggy and Paddy Dodson and the gardener and John Fitzpatrick to dinner on Sundays. Mr. Moore is to write to me in a few days

---

1. Philip Wouverman (1617–1664) was a Dutch artist amongst whose specialities were equestrian scenes.

about the boys' school. How much I wish we could spend the summer in the north of France, try Cork in the winter, home in May, and should I still require a milder winter residence arrange for Cork again. Or put off all this for one more year perhaps as we are here to get French perfected, it is of so much use. We must be patient not being our own masters.

9. Mary in great spirits, feeling pretty well, and the mercury beginning to act upon her. She has also had most satisfactory intelligence concerning the Eliots who are of the St. Germans family, the elder brother of Captain Eliot being heir presumptive to his cousin the present Earl, and Lord Eliot as yet either having no children or only daughters.[1] Captain Eliot's father was a distinguished General Officer; he married his cousin, a daughter of Lord Heathfield's, and had a very large family. Still Captain Eliot has some private fortune independent of his naval pay, and his wife of whom as yet we know nothing had this £30,000, the interest of which only she can draw at present, but as we understand the matter, upon this son coming of age the principal becomes his, though his mother is to enjoy the interest for her life. All this is very comfortable as it seems settled that there can be no cessation of intimacy.

10. This is not a romantick part of France – nothing very picturesque in the manners of the dull Béarnais; there is an apathy in their character very unlike the fiery Celts by whom they are surrounded; yet they are of the same race with a little Moorish blood added; the climate induces this torpor in a degree, its effect being to diminish the circulation, compose the nerves, etc., and therefore it suits but few constitutions, certainly not mine. The *natives* have all been in their holiday dresses this week past, and yet they look very ugly. On Thursday last everyone high and low was abroad, it being obligatory on all the *good* to visit every church and leave an offering on every altar. Good Friday there seemed to be less to do. Saturday

---

1. William Eliot, second Earl of St. Germans (1767–1845), certainly shared the same surname; his only son by the first of what turned out to be four marriages was Chief Secretary for Ireland at this exact time (1841–1845) and he was succeeded by two of his sons to the title.

immense baskets of flowers were bringing in all day from the
country to decorate the Churches on Easter Sunday; little
children had little chairs in the streets covered with aprons or
petticoats, stuck over with bits of looking glass, old prints and
flowers, and little girls stood beside them all day with china
saucers in their hands begging for sous. Sunday there was great
church-going; Monday dancing – musicians perched up on a
stage under the trees in the Place Royale and a great crowd
of peasants dancing round them. A man with the band called
out the figures and the Contredanses went on with spirit – the
figures of our quadrilles with hornpipe steps to hornpipe tunes
– generally but two couple performing – vis à vis – occasionally
four, and even six, the women modestly moving along with
their eyes on the ground, the men cutting every kind of caper,
heeling and toe-ing, shuffling and double-shuffling, cutting,
entrechatting, and swinging round with an air of audacity
altogether very like our highlanders. They were all neat and
clean with thick shoes; the women plenty of dark petticoats
and the eternal handkerchief headdress; the men mostly in the
Blouse of dark blue, and by the bye *they* pay the piper – a sou
for every dance. They have all very common countenances,
broad features, good-humoured expression and no grace in
form or action. They are a happy race – few wants and they
mostly well supplied, no ambition, no restless desire for other
enjoyments than they have been used to; plenty of comfort
in their own coarse way, quiet and industrious. It would be
almost cruel to raise them above the commonplace existence
which seems to afford them so much tranquil happiness.

20. Went upstairs last night to hear M. Barthe play, Mrs. Campbell
having very kindly begged us to join a very small party and to
bring the girls. The playing was quite wonderful and he has
expression and feeling as well as the most brilliant execution.
I prefer a different style of musick, this Holz and Thalberg
way of overloading a fine air with a collection of sounds
equally applicable to every melody, partaking too largely
of the wonderful to be the least agreeable, is such a mere
display of the agility of ten fingers that all character of musick
is lost. I can't think either a German or an Italian would feel
his heart satisfied with such a jargon. Were such dexterity
conjoined with good taste in the delightful art of producing

harmonised melody it would be almost too much to listen to frequently. I should like to possess the power of using my fingers as adroitly, as correctly, as certainly, as clearly and as powerfully as this wonderful artist, but I would never execute variations *à la Française* upon the beautiful airs in Bellini's Norma; there is a young brother, about twelve or so, who will play as astonishingly by and bye; they are both sons of the organist at Bayonne and the elder has been in the Academy at Paris – the premier élève. After the concert we had dancing. Janey and Annie were much admired. I was complimented at all hands, both on their dress and their dancing, and I was quite pleased to feel they deserved admiration. Janey stoops which very much spoils her; otherwise she would look remarkably well, really handsome. Annie is a graceful little girl – not pretty at present.

22. Janey quite well, and quite inclined to be still unwell, requiring nursing and coaxing and flattering and far too much taken up about her little fat self to think much about her mother. She don't go near her till desired a dozen times, does nothing for her and leaves her soon. Can talk for an hour to Mrs. Eliot though who has been twice to see her, bringing the son to wait in the anteroom and they *both* write to her, and the son presented rather a heavy silver-mounted whip in lieu of the broken one which lay on the sickbed for ever after. I am sure I hope all will end prosperously for the evil is done. Mrs. Eliot is an indiscreet woman, idle, nervous, and a great chatterbox; of course her neighbours afford subjects of discourse; altogether I should call her an injudicious acquaintance – far from a good companion for a girl like Janey, idle herself, forward in many ways, backward in many things, overindulged, and, if I may use the expression, over stimulated.

23. One of the Vigors – Stanhope I think – has been killed riding the Garrison Steeple Chase; he was leading, when his horse baulked at a ditch or wall or something, threw him, fell on him, etc.; he never spoke again. Duelling beginning to be out of fashion it would be well to raise mankind above steeple chasing whatever may become of racing – low in the scale of amusement as is this last method of squandering time and debasing feelings it is so far comparatively harmless that it don't peril human life while demoralising the principles, but

steeple chasing is just as much murder as is duelling and 'tis high time to have done with both.

And now for poor Mary – very weak and ill was she all yesterday; a bad night, great deal of coughing, voice still broken and very feeble, hardly heard indeed, eating nothing, looking quite worn out. She may revive; she has done so, so often, but it don't look likely. Her little daughter was taking her breakfast in bed at nine o'clock laughing, talking of all her visitors, all her beaux, her voice, her new galoppes. Far from having been to see her poor mother she did not even know what kind of night she had had. I never knew anything so strange – her father may have concealed from her that her mother is dying, but she must see that she is very very ill. It makes no sort of impression upon her – occupied most completely about herself she has not a thought for anyone else. She does what she is bid cheerfully enough, but of herself nothing. She is of no use in any way, and in my opinion possesses no feeling. Want of thought some call it – where there is feeling there can be no want of thought. Defective education may have encreased this selfishness of character but there must have been natural apathy to begin with. I am hurt by her unfeeling conduct more than I can express, and unfortunately her suffering mother is hurt by it as I know by her endeavours to excuse it. What will become of the little girl when left with her ill-judging father whom now she can turn round her finger. All is for the best; perhaps it is happy for poor Mary that she is called away from cares that would but disappoint. She is spared at this moment many pangs for *she* too thinks too highly of herself and all belonging to her and she could ill bear the mortifications she would hourly meet with on finding her estimation so much above the world's.

26. Mr. Pearsall gave Janey Gardiner her last lesson yesterday morning when to oblige poor Mary he sang [Handel's] 'I know that my redeemer liveth.' It was almost too much for her, for I never heard anything so fine. I accompanied him *through my tears*. Voice, skill, expression were all perfect; we none of us recovered the effect for long afterwards.

WEDNESDAY, MAY 8. Great racket in the streets now. All the flocks and herds which have been pasturing on the Landes during the winter are travelling slowly towards the mountains; it is rather pretty meeting them and their drivers on the roads in the evenings. Have been reading three little tales by Madame de Souza,[1] all ridiculous, but *Adèle de Senanges* pretty. I remember hearing that when her son Count Flahault brought over his wealthy bride, Miss Mercer Elphinstone, to Paris, Madame de Souza received them in *novel* style – hung all her house, and dressed herself, in tartan – like George the 4th fancying all *Scotch* must be Highland.

11. Our little queen is economising at a great rate – making reductions in her establishment to the amount of nearly £30,000 a year, for the purpose, it is said, of assisting her husband to pay off the very heavy personal debts of his late father.[2] It don't appear to be exactly honest to take English money, the produce of taxes on the industry of English people, for any purpose however praiseworthy in itself, which will take that money out of the country to be spent abroad among persons who had nothing whatever to do with the making of it. The large allowances made to these very nearly useless royal personages are intended to be restored through the medium of their expenditure to the country from which they derive them, though it has unluckily been the custom of the House of Hanover to support half the paltry German Courts connected with it, out of these state provisions. We British squander our wealth so absurdly, we are so ostentatious and so arrogant that at this time of day foreigners have got to look upon us as fair prey, and the aim of all is to get as much out of us as possible. We are fleeced on all hands, and all that is left to hope is that we may be driven home again in disgust to spend among those who more deserve our help.

13. They are gone – went between nine and ten this morning [for Avranches]. Mary looked wonderfully well, was in good

---

1. Botelho Souza was her name by her second marriage; Adèle, Comtesse de Flahault (1761–1836), was the mother of E.G.'s Edinburgh acquaintance who featured in the Memoirs.
2. Ernest, Duke of Saxe-Coburg-Gotha, died (E.G. reported on 18 February 1844) of 'spasmodick cramp in the stomach'.

spirits, and was roused to the whole exertion so as to appear to make it with ease. She was dressed most comfortably, yet with the greatest care. Planté the valet carried her down as he would a child and laid her emaciated form on the couch prepared for her. All the cordials, etc. requisite were at hand; Janey next her; Johnny and Mr. Gardiner in front; Sarah and Planté outside; plenty of luggage and three good horses to drag them. Colonel Smith says it is the best thing that could have been done – that it has been done in the best way, and whatever be the issue there was no help for it. A few minutes after they were gone we found the Turkish cushion the Duchess of Gordon had given Mary; borrowed M. Puyoo's horse and sent it after them, for she always requires it at her back; half an hour after we found their keys. We have hired a postillon to gallop on with them, by relay, if necessary, and bid him bring us word how Mary bears the motion.

19. The politicks of the week are very satisfactory. Sir Robert Peel has carried the factory question by a large majority. All seems to be quiet everywhere. The Irish state trials still dragging their slow length along, almost unheeded, for the whole world is weary of them. The repealers meet weekly but get little money, make no sensation and seem to be dull in every way. The fairs are brisk, weather beautiful, Louis Philippe has it all his own way in France, the tumults are over in Portugal, faction still busy in Spain. A bloody revolution broke out in Hayti; Scotch kirk matters queer enough, many seceders returning, many more desirous to return, the Episcopalians encreasing quite wonderfully.

We have been much occupied Tommy and I writing musick – the girls drawing a little, Miss Hart reading 'Widow Barnaby' to us to beguile the time. Clever woman, Mrs. Trollope; some of her hits are admirable, scenes quite comick, story interesting, but it is a regular caricature of human nature, and she is herself so vulgar, so coarsely minded in her own way of feeling and acting that the persons she intends representing as ladies and gentleman have not the very slightest resemblance in any one point to people of the most moderate refinement. In her later works after her celebrity had introduced her to a higher grade of society her quickness of observation enabled her much to improve the general manner of her polite life.

Delicacy a'n't to be taught late in life. There are certain feelings as well as certain features and a certain air that must descend through several generations to grow into the fulness which belongs to a gentle race.

22. The Colonel has just come in with a dish of Pau politicks. Far from the question of the doctors having been settled by the late decision of the French Government backed by the opinion of the British Ambassador, persevering Dr. Taylor applied to Lord Aberdeen and to the Universities of Edinburgh and Aberdeen, which two learned bodies have taken up the business of the transferred diploma very properly I daresay since it was laid before them and poor wretched little Mr. Hazelwood is going to leave Pau without delay in dread of the consequences. Ill as he is, and clever as he is, it must be allowed that his crime deserves punishment; his principles cannot be honest, and when these sort of swindling transactions are discovered they must of necessity bring both disgrace and ruin on the unhappy impostor; had his imposture done harm, had he been pursued on publick grounds we might applaud the moral courage which detected a great mischief. As it is I think an almost equal degree of contempt must be felt for the jealousy which has kept this little place in a ferment for the last four years and which is likely to meet with its fit reward even in the moment of success. Mr. Hazelwood goes, and Dr. Smythe gets all his patients and almost all Dr. Taylor's too. Ten were counted over to me by name leaving him but *eight* by his own reckoning to Mr. Gardiner; so that he who began the season with very nearly all the practice of Pau, by grasping at the whole, loses 'even that he had' and is left nearly *alone* to exult over the ruin of his rival.

I can't think him a clever doctor; he has had neither sufficient education nor sufficient experience and I do not feel that he has watched Mary sufficiently; perhaps that was not his business; she tried to conceal from him, too, her disobedience, her imprudence, and that excessive indulgence in eating and *drinking* which is killing her as surely as her disorders; but I think he ought to have impressed on Mr. Gardiner the necessity for a properly regulated sick-room; he was always so occupied with his own quarrels and his own fame that he thought little of his medical duties in comparison; kind he always was; skilful in an emergency; but too careless to have the charge of a chronick disease; the certainty of its inevitably fatal termination not lessening in the very least the duty of employing every means to prolong her life. Dr. Smythe managed her worse, clever as he is, he did not know her well enough to take the strong measures necessary, nor was he aware that the depression which so frightened him was but the depression which always succeeds over stimulus. Alas! I can grieve, but I can do nothing more.

24. All these musical people agreed that by far the best musick master here is Pol, a Spaniard, the organist of one of the churches. I find the Spaniards generally to be quite as musical a nation as the Italians; they have a natural love of harmony, cultivate the science to a high degree and have native musick of the utmost beauty particularly some of the wild melodies of the mountain provinces. A second year in Pau I could turn to much more profit than this first; here are good masters whom we have lost, and a very superiour society to be selected; and a number of additions to our stock of knowledge and accomplishment and happiness within our power – with a much cheaper plan of life than poor Mary put us upon. I shall be wiser at Avranches, but I much doubt that little place possessing the advantages I have too late discovered in this. We should never judge in a hurry; nor trust too much to the opinions of others.

26. No letters; it is possible that they may come by a later post; if so we may yet hear before night. They ought to have reached Nantes on Thursday and we surely ought to have heard to-day at latest; the post comes in two days from Paris much further off. I doubt all having gone well; false excitement supported poor Mary at setting out. We can't start for the mountains in this uncertainty – otherwise the two little girls, the two Colonels, and I were to have set out for the Eaux Bonnes to-morrow on a cheap plan concocted between Jacques and me. We hire our carriage of one man, our horses of another, Jacques drives, and acts courier as well, taking all trouble and all responsibility and assuring me he will do it for much less than we should otherwise, making his little profit too. The Colonels not speaking French it is much better for the servant to take all the bargaining with the set of sharks we live amongst

hereabouts. It is a disagreeable office for a woman. Besides they will use Jacques better for fear he should bring them no more prey; and of course he understands also the ways of the country. The Colonel has gone to Church in hopes of hearing Mr. Trench. I am waiting for the French service to hear M. Buscarlet, which I wonder at myself for not having done before, he is considered so remarkably eloquent.

The newspapers are full of Mr. d'Israeli's new novel, 'Coningsby' which I should much like to get. It seems to touch upon the true evils of our social position and will perhaps astonish the pride of old England, open the eyes of the *great* to coming events, for there is an influential class rising from the trade of England which must some day grow to be what feudal Barons were. War being over all it fostered fades. As we civilize we shall learn truer notions of greatness, polish of manner soon follows polish of mind and strong good sense the produce of application lasts many generations before becoming enfeebled. Now that the economy of morals is beginning to be understood there is no foreseeing a limit to human improvement.

30. We set out [for the Eaux Bonnes] Tuesday between twelve and one. Colonel Smith, Janey, Annie and I inside a comfortable very low carriage. Colonel Litchfield on the box with Jacques. Tom [Gardiner] looked a little dull at being left to pursue his studies with Mr. Scott. Miss Hart bore remaining very well and it will do her good to let her understand that she is with us to be useful and not to be amused. But my poor Johnny was near breaking his heart; but it will do him good too, for he is too much made of. Our children are so completely part of ourselves that they are unaccustomed to be left out on any occasion; having but three, and living so quietly, they are our constant companions; and dear, sweet Johnny having been with his Papa and me ever since we came to Pau, fancied he would miss us. Besides he can't bear Miss Hart though she is really very kind to him. It spoilt the pleasure of the pretty drive to Louvie, recollecting the sorrowful face of my Johnny.

It began to rain before we got to Louvie where we rested the horses and it rained unceasingly till we reached the Eaux Bonnes and was piercingly cold, but we forgot all discomfort, for the scenery became so very beautiful as we advanced winding amongst mountains whose heads were lost in clouds, by the side of a rapid rocky stream, through a gorge sometimes no wider than the road and the river, sometimes opening into meadows, sometimes even into plains; a great deal of wood, gay looking villages, and here and there a glen diverging on either hand as if there were no end to intricacies. On reaching a wide plain full of villages, two or three streams running through it and the marble quarries appearing among the forest which clothes the surrounding mountains, a road turned off over a pretty bridge and up a steep hill, three kilomètres in length ending in a ravine along one side of which on a narrow ledge runs a row of high white houses built for the visitors to the Eaux Bonnes. We put up at the Hotel de la Poste the master of which had cast his nets round us at Louvie where he was resting his horse at the time we were resting ours. We had intended going to the Hotel de France but we find ourselves very comfortable here, only the cold this first night was very nearly intolerable.

Wednesday morning neither Colonel Smith nor Annie were equal to sight-seeing. Hal had had asthma the whole night never having been in bed all night. Annie's stomach was deranged and she had to lay up regularly for the day; they would not hear of the rest remaining to nurse them as they felt quite equal to the care of each other for Hal was perfectly well after breakfast. Colonel Litchfield therefore took charge of Janey and me, and we set out about eleven for the Eaux Chaudes and Gabas. We had to travel back to the great plain and then turn to ascend about the steepest hill I ever went up in a carriage – very long too; just at the top the rock appeared to have been cut through to admit of passage and here stands a tiny chapel to the Virgin who is supposed to protect travellers during the dangers of this singular journey, paying her for the same. Up and down we continued to go through a ravine so narrow that the road was cut out of the rock at various heights above the foaming river. Mountain rose over mountain – rock towered above rock – in every fantastick shape their many peaks could form. The black pine mingled with birch, oak, and a few other hard wood trees clothed the whole range to a great height; the underwood was generally box; the patches of verdure were of the richest green literally enamelled with the greatest variety of the loveliest wild flowers, all to be spoken of in the superlative degree for none other would do them justice. Sheep covered the lower hills, cattle grazed near the river, a few mares and foals among them; sometimes a goat upon some pinnacle; eagles soared above; cascades innumerable fell on every side; here was the retreat of the wolf and the wild cat; there the path by which the hunters tracked the bear.

All through the forest were lying the pines lately felled by the woodmen reminding me of Rothiemurchus, only here the manufacture of the timber is carried on in the most primitive manner by manual labour alone without any assistance almost from machinery, a very small handsaw with which two men cut up the log into planks being all we saw with them; the branches are made into charcoal on the spot by the most hideous old women in dark dresses who also seem to gather the bark. When the men find any very large tree it is sent off to Bayonne for the shipping; the general run of the timber is used for building and firing. Where all these woodmen live we could not make out as no houses were visible after leaving a few cabins scattered along the narrow valley within a couple of miles of the Eaux Chaudes till we got to Gabas, the dirtiest place that ever was seen in this world – dirty, nasty, miserable, to a degree we have no notion of even in Ireland. Three hours from Gabas we should have entered Spain through scenery equally beautiful with that we had been travelling among, but we had arranged to go no further, so after refreshing the horses and saying farewell to a solitary gentleman rather shabbily dressed whose business in that wretched spot we could not at all make out, though he had a fine pointer attending him, we returned to the Eaux Chaudes, which we had passed through after descending the hill from Our Lady's chapel.

About a dozen small houses, low and wretched looking afford the only accommodation as yet to the few invalids who resort to these hot wells; the Bath house is very miserable in appearance, but on going over it we found it very comfortably arranged, and a cookshop, confectioner, grocer, wineshop, all in a row in the long corridor connecting the two wings of the building. A new Bath House, quite a palace, is in progress which has a very imposing effect at a little distance; the old row of shabby houses being hardly perceptible when this new edifice first strikes the eye, it has the look of a fine castle well placed on a promontory shrouded in rocks and washed by the river; it has been five years in building and will not be ready for three more, showing the dilatory movements of French artizans. There are to be baths, pump room, library, shops, etc. below, and good apartments for the sick above. It was six o'clock when we reached the Eaux Bonnes when we found the Colonel and Annie quite recovered.

31. Colonel Litchfield and the two little girls set out before seven in the morning, on poneys, with Jacques and a guide, to wander over the mountains. Colonel Smith and I took the nearer beauties more leisurely on our feet; the narrow ledge on which the fifteen handsome hotels are built just contains these houses, the road, and a strip of shrubbery bordered by a rivulet at the foot of the rock; the street after ascending some way pretty steeply turns into the hill with a crook, just long enough to hold five or six houses let out in apartments, the pump house, and a chapel. The place is generally quite filled during the summer months; the company in the hotels have private sleeping rooms, dine together in large salons, and sit together in the evenings in a large handsome drawing-room, well lighted, containing a pianoforte, etc., so that they have plenty of musick and dancing. The houses are prettily furnished, beautifully clean, in some the cooking is good, and I hear the place is not dear for a residence of some weeks if a bargain be made. We were in a very clean house with good attendance but most wretched eating and the charge quite extravagant – two francs a night each bed – three francs a head dinner – two francs breakfast – children little less, and so many extras: fire, candles, black coffee, etc. *that* our bill for two days amounted to sixty-eight francs.

There is no end to the walks and rides in this splendid neighbourhood; some mere paths; some made with care; over the hills; along the valley; by the side of the river which tumbles along deep deep below the houses among rocks of every size fretting away in noisy leaps except where a larger obstruction than usual forms a regular cascade several of which are well worth the trouble of walking to; the air, the pure water, the cleanliness and the extreme beauty of this singular place made us drive away from it with real regret about two o'clock. We retraced our steps as far as Louvie and then striking to one side crossed the fertile plain skirting the foot of the mountains to Oleron, a large ugly town built about two fine rivers with a few trees and some fine fields as foreground to the distant mountains. Part of the scenery we came through was very park-like, very English, and in many places pretty – the villages all look pretty at a distance, but they are very disappointing on coming to them – so very dirty, some houses so very mean, the best so very untidy; no gardens, no courts, no thresholds, to some houses no glass windows, stables in front of parlours, mud floors, muddy streets, and the inhabitants all dirty-looking too: no linen to be seen on any of them, dingy clothing, dull worsted garments, the women dark aprons, dark shawls, dark handkerchiefs upon their heads; the men with dark blouses over dark trousers; the children are however very redeeming; the roads too are perfection – all under government controul, men constantly employed on them in gangs *numbered* – the glazed hat and the pole for marking distances and the bag for refreshment all bearing the number of the owner. Women sometimes work at breaking the stones, and in the fields they do more work than the men and hard work too. In this part of France we have seen the wife digging while the husband walked up and down with the baby. In the shops the wives keep the books. In the ménage *Madame* is everything – her will, her orders, her arrangements, are final. Monsieur is of no account – no one appears to think of him.

We drove to such a wretched hotel at Oleron which we reached at six o'clock, that with my Eaux Bonnes' experience of Jacques's friends in that line, I rebelled, and set off with Colonel Smith to find a better – one where we are very comfortable – airy rooms, excellent eating, civil people and not very extravagant charges. We have driven to-day a considerable distance up the Valley d'Aspe, another way of reaching Spain – very beautiful of the peaceful pastoral style – very different from, not near so sublime as Gabas but well worth seeing; more like Welsh scenery; a rapid river with wooded banks, and fertile meadows, numerous villages, hills of fantastick form cultivated nearly to the top, divided by hedges into strangely shaped fields and dotted over with small thickets. As we proceeded, far in the distance rose the blue peaked mountains and beyond Bedous, where we turned, we were told the scenery became more rugged as the road got into the higher part of the Pyrénnées. We saw very little snow to-day. While the horses were resting we walked across the river and along a rugged mountain road to a curious little ugly village containing about 80 very miserable houses, all amid dirt and half ruined, the residence of three hundred Protestants who thus isolated from their brethren of the reformed creed have maintained the true faith these three hundred years nearly, from the time of the Albigenses. I suppose from their most wretched appearance they have been intermarrying too. They are in a fair way of improvement now having a very intelligent young man as schoolmaster, but a most stupid pastor to keep down the progress. Too sleepy to write more.

SATURDAY, JUNE I. Oleron. We dined at the Table d'hôte yesterday – an excellent dinner – one other guest only – a young man from Bordeaux travelling for the wine trade with a nice little boy about eight years old. We found him an intelligent person capable of conversing very agreeably. It is very stupid of my Colonels not to apply themselves a little to the study of the French language just to learn enough to make themselves one of the company. My own Colonel is so quick he would speak it well enough in a couple of months if he had not an interpreter beside him and my other Colonel understands it so much already that very little application would set him quite afloat. It is an unpardonable omission in the education of young Englishmen that of the modern languages, certainly the most necessary of all the means of advancement in life. Mr. Canning [P.M. 1827] owed his rise entirely to his knowledge of these useful tools. No member of government nor any member's secretary of that day could write a French letter. A Spanish one could not be read except by him. Madame de Navarez told me nothing surprised her more when she went to England than to find no *man* who could speak to her. The women all of them spoke several languages more or less well – French in general admirably – not a man could make himself understood. While she and her friend the Duchess of Leinster talked by the hour in

a language foreign to them both the Duke stood by *en Dumby*.
Yet in the face of this there is Mr. Gardiner cramming his
boys with Latin and Greek. French, Italian, and Spanish and
German all round them, unthought of – history, geography,
every science, and all modern literature, sealed treasures.

I found the school at the miserable little village of Osse
conducted upon the same plan as our national schools.
Tablets on the walls, the large black board, and excellent
progressive books prepared by the Evangelical Society of
Paris which supplies all the reformed congregations liberally
and pays a moderate salary to every teacher all of whom are
brought up in the Normal Schools there. The pastors are paid
by government, according to the extent of their flock – a small
stipend apparently for it was a very poor dwelling the minister
lived in at Osse – humble, very, but clean and an air of thrift in
the bright lined kitchen shelves, the wheels, the clews of yarn,
and smoked hams hanging against the walls. The Duchess of
Gordon had presented the lamp which hangs in the simple
church. A large subscription too has been raised among the
English at Pau for enlarging the schoolrooms.

Two or three miles beyond Bedous a little off the road is
a fine water fall which we thought it would too much fatigue
our little ponies to carry us on to see; there is a column erected
on the birth-place of a famous poet who wrote beautifully in
the Béarnais language and lives or did live in a fine castle a
few miles further on in Spain, for the next post, Urdos, is the
last French town in the pretty valley d'Aspe. On returning we
remembered to observe an inscription on the first rock after
crossing the river at the entrance of the valley – it is Roman –
announcing the advance of a cohort at least 1,000 years ago.
At Sarrance we stopt to see a very pretty church in that very
pretty and very clean village, where a fat priest disgusted us
by quitting the confessional soon after our entrance, pushing
aside ever so many kneeling penitents and insisting on taking
us up a stair behind the altar to shew us an image of the Virgin
dropped from heaven in a miraculous manner seven hundred
years ago and found upon the banks of the Gave. Our Lady
of Sarrance who cures all sorts of diseases and is resorted to
all through the summer by crowds of sick pilgrims, is a black
doll of a foot and a half long – stone – her features much

defaced by her travels, dressed in white silk embroidered in gold, a crown of white roses, a necklace and sparkling cross, and is shut up in a decorated box set up endways and on hinges so that she can look out from the top of her altar on the faithful below, or turn as to us in her private chamber. It is thought to be an image of the Goddess Minerva brought by the Romans and lost in crossing the river. Superstition is much the same in all ages, and with all creeds. What are our own *elect* but idolaters after their mystifying fashion. There is as little true religion in their narrow view of piety, as there is in saint or image worship, or in the Jewish austerities they imitate, and which Christ preached to abolish. The fine air of Sarrance is a great assistance to the little ugly black doll's knowledge of medicine.

2. A rainy day of course. It always rains at Pau. We left Oleron at ten yesterday in the finest possible weather such as we have been fortunate to enjoy all through our excursion after getting beyond the influence of Pau till we returned to its steamy atmosphere again. About half an hour before reaching Gan it began – a storm in earnest. Such rain is seldom poured down out of the tropicks. Luckily all of the road that was new to us the sun shone on and very, very, beautiful was the scenery – rich, with fertile fields and fine trees and thousands of cottages, and some country houses, an undulating country, all heights and hollows, very like Tunbridge Wells and that part of Kent but here we have the grand range of the Pyrénées as a background. And then opens out the valley of the Gave with the pretty town of Pau, its *parc*, its bridge, its castle. We found all well. Jack crimson with delight; he had been very good.

4. This morning finished all last month's accounts, and settled with Jacques who knows very well how to manage for himself; his economical method turned out to be but precisely the same expense as a voiturier would have been, only we had the benefit of his services in the inns. The five days were expensive enough – 241 francs, £9 odd. As he leaves us to-day he introduced me to the French style of dismissing servants by announcing that his trunks were ready for my inspection. It seems these are always looked through by the masters previous to a servant quitting the house, locked, corded, and despatched at once

– a farce – for a dishonest servant has a thousand better ways
of disposing of his master's property without a chance of
discovery. We have been reading Peter Simple again, and are
now busy with the Widow married – most absurdly amusing.
A fine day for a wonder. Everybody is leaving Pau.

5. All this morning the two Colonels and I have been running
about the town in the heat bargaining about conveyances
to the mountains. We had able assistance, Captain Straton
having come down yesterday to buy supplies. He sat an hour
or more with us in the evening arranging our proceedings of
to-day, and certainly I have learned more and seen more in
his company than nine months' experience of Pau without
him had taught me. We were in the kitchens, bedrooms,
stables of ever so many *voituriers* and diligence offices and
very well amused we were. At last we found a sharp looking
little man, a Jacques, with premises within the walls of the fine
old ruined church in the Place Royale which was destroyed
in the revolution. He has agreed to travel with us for six days
for one hundred francs and a present of ten, if he gives us
satisfaction; his voiture holds six; he will have three horses,
and take up saddles for such expeditions as a carriage can't go
on. Then at the inn at St. Sauveur Captain Straton has made
a bargain for us at five francs a head per day, *tout compris*,
children and servants half price. We are all in great spirits of
course – the little girls half wild. Tom goes up this evening
with Captain Straton; Colonel Litchfield has a cab for himself
at five francs a day, but then he has to feed his horse – two
francs more. If the weather only prove propitious how happy
we shall be. Now Jacques Fort, our late man servant, could
manage nothing cheaply of late for us – his economical trip
last week turned out not to be so saving a plan as he pretended
– principally from a long string of after thoughts he added to it
on returning home, charging me too much too for feeding the
horses; the love of money-making is so strong in these people
and they are so little scrupulous about the ways and means of
acquiring it that it is a considerable drawback to the comfort
of living here.

6. We set off at half after seven this morning: Colonel Smith and
Colonel Litchfield in the gig, the rest in a roomy vinaigrette
but with only *two* horses; there is no dealing with these people

– cheat us they will one way or the other. We were therefore the whole day performing the journey, including two pretty long rests. The first was at Betterham which is a curious old place – a mere village with a fine old church attached to a monastery, and a bridge nearly covered with ivy hanging down in festoons nearly to the water. We had followed the Gave all the way from Pau, *up* the stream, through a country extremely rich, beautiful from fine trees, verdure, and ripening fields, but not otherwise very interesting, the *coteaux* being little varied, the mountains very distant. One house on a hill we much admired, lately purchased by an American, quite capable of being made into a really fine country place. The old chateau of Corrazes where Henri IV was principally educated stands well upon the river with a handsome *parc* stretching along the banks. It was the Fête Dieu; the church crowded at Betterham from whence to Lourdes the same sort of country continues only in narrower compass and of course more picturesque.

Lourdes is quite a town, containing many excellent houses, several hotels, a good *place* with a handsome fountain and a small detachment of troops. The situation is curious from the stony nature of the hills around; the old castle is the garrison, once the residence of a baron of great power in the feudal times. The road quite doubles back along the other side of the ravine at the end of which stands the town, there being no way of crossing this narrow defile sooner without a bridge of too expensive a construction to be undertaken. We merely stopt a few minutes here, when turning up in earnest to the mountains we proceeded to Argeles which we reached at two o'clock every step of our journey to it encreasing in beauty. Still it was not the sort of scene we looked for among the Pyrénées, more like North Wales a great deal, hardly indeed so wild, and the different nature of the wooding from any our northern ideas had conceived of mountain forest made the scenes appear less grand to us. Chestnut, walnut, acacia, with an underwood of box is so unlike what we have been used to among rocks. Along the valley of Gabas the birch and the forest of black pine suited my taste so much more that that still appears to me the finest part I have yet seen of the Pyrénées.

Argeles is, however, beautiful and the drive up the valley

or gorge rather, to Luz is very fine indeed; the road is cut out of the rock but it is wide with a parapet and not generally very high above the river, a torrent, for which there is just room, the rocks nearly touch in many places or at least appear to do so, throwing the water on from the narrow opening in a wild jet that is very striking. The whole ravine is well wooded, the rocks finely varied in form. Luz is a small, pretty, scattered village with neat houses and neat gardens about the centre of a small plain at the foot of a picturesque hill crowned by a ruined castle; so hemmed in by mountains rising all round higher and higher as peak after peak appears in the distance, that after entering the plain there is no finding out any possible way of getting out again. Still each of the three streams which rush across this green meadow leads to a higher region, and following the Gave de Pau for about a quarter of a mile we came to a fine bridge, climbed up a steep ascent and drove along a ridge like the Eaux Bonnes on which is built the village of St. Sauveur. The first house in it Captain Straton is living in; he had met us before we reached Luz and ran along by the side of the carriage till we all got out at the foot of the hill. Tom met us at the top and we were very soon at our late supper at the comfortable Hotel de la France.

7.   Daylight discovered to us the full beauty of our situation; nothing can well exceed it; the terrace runs along a considerable way, wide enough at one part to have a double row of houses. A street, with plenty of shops on the ground floor of the many hotels publick and private it consists of. Where the Stratons are, and where we are nothing is before us but the green hill on the opposite side of the ravine; below the ground falls steeply to the river; behind rises rocky hill again from which every here and there foams down a cataract; the roar of one at my elbow here kept me awake the first part of the night; high up all round are the blue mountains – plenty of wooding; the loveliest wild flowers, green banks and terraced fields, torrents, cataracts, rocks, and a foaming river, with fine houses full of luxuries in the midst of this most beautiful wildness. We are extremely comfortable in our hotel, nice apartments, excellent eating, and the most obliging of hostesses.

Our little ponies being a good deal tired with their forty-two miles yesterday we only took them to Barèges to-day – an ascent and a good sharp one the whole way of not more than five miles though it took us a couple of hours and a third horse. It was very beautiful; a smaller stream than our Gave pouring down over rocks which kept it in perpetual foam; a narrow margin of meadow on one side through which is carried an excellent road; several cottages among the thick wood here and there; the bank rises directly from the opposite side, sometimes rocky, sometimes green, always wooded. Before us the whole way was a blue peak but not in appearance high for as we were rising towards the snow the effect of the distant mountains was diminished by the ascent and by the intervening ground. At the foot of a steep hill one mile in length we left all that was lovely and gradually losing trees and shrubs and verdure climbed up into a narrow street almost touching the bed of the stream enclosed by grey rocks bending back towards the mountains.

The sulphur baths here are famous for the cure of every cutaneous external, superficial disorder and for old gunshot wounds; the place is full of disgusting looking invalids and there is a hospital for maimed soldiers who are sent here or anywhere else that will do them good by a government which seems to have an eye to everything. A good many visitors come for a course of the waters which are said to effect the most wonderful cures; the smell is intolerable; the bath house would be a publick nuisance anywhere else, particularly one dreadful steaming den where twelve objects bathe together, and another range of pools separated for the itch patients who are sent up in hundreds to be cured in three or four days. Altogether, the dismal scenery in which there is not much variety, added to these other annoyances, Barèges would never be endured for a week, nay a day, by any who were not precluded from a chance of life anywhere else.

To a traveller it is interesting enough for an hour, for the snow is within an easy walk. Tom, Miss Hart and Colonel Litchfield reached it and kept us soberer members of the party in a fright during their wise expedition lest any of them should get under the glaciers or fall from the precipices. It is also curious to see a smart French town in such a wilderness;

green shutters, gay draperies, marble tables, gilded balconies
in just such a place as Glen Ennich without the lake. The drive
back was infinitely more beautiful; all the desolation was left
behind. Every step brought into view additional fertility for
high up upon the mountains every level spot is cultivated: rye
and hay and lint waved with the stirring air on every of the
thousand little patches of soil around us, and the mountains
beyond Luz standing high above the plain towards which we
were rapidly descending formed the grandest background to
the moving picture.

8. This day we have spent in our saddles – that is we have all been
on poney back nine hours, for we set out at half after seven, got
back a few minutes before six, having rested in the little inn
at Gavernie not quite two hours. The object was to reach the
cirque [corrie], a circular field of snow which fills a hollow at
the foot of the wall of mountain which terminates the valley
of the Gave de Pau presenting an almost impassable barrier,
in the direction between France and Spain. The distance
from hence is about 12 English miles. By the side of the
river the whole way a torrent, of course, from the rapidity
of the descent and a foaming torrent from the number and
size of the rocks over which it has to force its way. It flows
from beneath the glacier we were going to see, the Cirque,
and as it tumbles down along its narrow way, it receives on
either hand innumerable smaller streams, some rushing like
itself from some diminutive pass diverging here and there,
some dashing down from rock to rock in full cascade and
still more startling cataracts, roaring increasingly throughout
the gorge. There is to a degree a sameness in all mountain
scenery, beautiful though it be – these must be the hills,
the rocks, the narrow pass, the occasional plain, the narrow
meadow, the cataracts, the torrents, the rapids. In the valley of
the Gavernie, we had them all with the addition in one place
of a mountain of blocks of rock, as if some enormous creation
of granite had been thrown from heaven by power, infinite,
and had broken into gigantick fragments where it fell. The
enormous masses rested upon one another in uneven angles,
here and there shewing the river far below them through the
irregular loop holes left between their points of coherence: it
was the grandest part of our journey: the beginning or entrance

into the gorge was the most beautiful from the richness of the scenery: the termination was the most sublime. We walked from the village of Gavernie to the top of a bank just above the road and there suddenly looked up upon a theatre of mountains. Walls of rock rose in steps one above another, the terraces on their tops covered with snow, till on reaching the clouds this enormous barrier shot up into every form of peak or point standing darkly out from the clear sky.

The Brèche [Gap] de Roland is concealed here by a sugar loaf peak which stands immediately in front of it – the false brèche is in full view; both can be seen at the same time from the village of Gêtre a few miles further back in the valley. They disappointed me for the cuts are not deep enough; just like what a person's jaw would be were a couple of teeth taken out of it leaving a couple between the gaps. The cirque lies at the foot of this rocky mountain. As the snow melts a cataract is formed which by and bye expands into a small lake out of which the Gave again issues; but we were too early in the season for these additions to the scene; it was grand enough without them; and if I had ever seen it and anyone had ever told me I should have been of a party to explore it, I should have thought such person mad. They magnify the terrour of the enterprise greatly both in books and on the spot; danger I fancy there is none, for the guides are steady, the ponies sure-footed, very gentle and well accustomed to the work, the noise of many waters not affecting them, abrupt turns, stony descents, wooden bridges, and sudden rises, never disturbing them. The road is cut out of the rock, but where highest above the stream and most precipitous below, it is wide and level; where it becomes narrower and more unequal it is nearer to the water. Still it is not an agreeable ride at all. I have not head enough to feel my feet dangling straight over a rocky river 400 or 500 hundred feet below them, without my heart beating much quicker than is heroical. Neither Miss Hart nor Fanny Straton had a guide, nor any of the gentlemen, Tommy included, and we met several women of the country riding home from the market at Luz to some of the villages we had passed all alone, late in the evening. One young woman was leading a second horse, an unbroken colt too. An urchin the size of Johnny was sitting on a stone beside a waterfall herding three or four cows pasturing in a place fit only for goats or roebuck. The noise confuses me always, more a good deal than the height. However this pass up the Valley of Gavernie has given a shake to firmer nerves than mine – danger though none there be. Colonel Smith said I behaved wonderfully.

9. Sunday at St. Sauveur.[1] The same lovely weather, as hot as it ever is up here for the sirocco is blowing. Yet to me sitting here quietly in my room it is delightful. We all dropt off to bed last night soon after our really good dinner tired out completely by the journey of the day. Most of us had tea in bed, and we slept till seven this morning in spite of aching bones which we felt stiff enough on beginning to move. The girls with Miss Hart, Tom and the restless Colonel are all off up some mountain. Jack and my Colonel accompanied them to a certain height when they very prudently turned back and found me sitting cool and quiet with Captain and Mrs. Straton who had walked up to pay a visit.

We are to drink tea there again in the evening. They have been most extremely kind to us in every way: sent us up their newspapers by which I see that Mr. O'Connell and suite are safely lodged in the Penitentiary without the slightest appearance of riot. The sentence is very light: nothing the least proportioned to the offence as a *punishment*; but that was not wanted; it was only necessary to disarm him for ever by shewing that the Law could reach him – the ordinary Law – reach him, check him and so put an end to him, for his rabble followers being no longer deluded by the belief of his immaculate power have already ceased to make any particular fuss about him. For party purposes even it is no longer possible for the licentious press to make out a ferment from the very few shouts in Court given by the young liberals; out of doors there was none; the carriages of the prisoners drove to the jail without a guard, rendering Mr. O'Connell's proclamation requiring peace perfectly unnecessary – no one seems disposed to break it. The whole thing has been admirably managed; it has been so left to take its course, so little looked on as a grand event, and the Traversers have been treated with such

1. For Mrs. Ellis this was 'the little Cheltenham of the Pyrenees.'

courtesy throughout. And their prison with its airy rooms and fine garden, is so little of a dungeon that there is nothing for them to complain of, to a publick warily allowed to get sick tired of the whole proceedings. Sir Robert is swimming along famously.

The Emperour of Russia has really arrived; more to visit our various scientifick works than our little Queen who is however receiving him with great splendour. The King of Saxony is in England too. Times are changed with the sovereigns of the earth, and much for the better; it is a new habit for them this visiting of each other so unostentatiously. They are flying about in all directions now, without ceasing. Our Queen Dowager and the Duchess of Kent are both on the Continent, at present, and the Prince of Denmark in Scotland.

10. This day we passed very happily, yet it has been very fatiguing. We set out by seven in the carriage and cab for Cauterêts, thirteen miles. Our ponies with the guides, Captain Straton and Tom went the same way as we did down the beautiful ravine between Luz and Pierre Lafitte; there the ponies struck into a bye path over a shoulder of the mountain we had to skirt the foot of, which shortened the distance to them. We in the carriages had to ascend by the new admirably engineered road which strikes off from the road to Argeles, quite suddenly up another ravine almost equal in beauty to the one we had left. Cauterêts is a large town full of handsome houses, plenty of fine hotels, shops, etc. but although backed by a very striking conical mountain, and built along the bank of a rapid stream, it is not by very many degrees so beautiful as St. Sauveur.

We drove through the stables, not the stable yard, but the stables of the Hotel de France and alighted in the midst of our ponies who were feeding in a long row before a manger. We mounted them without delay and soon leaving the gay streets began again to ascend the stony banks of a torrent. The different paths are scattered at intervals upon the sides of the stream which falls here and there in pretty cascades, positively smelling of sulphur – strongly. Steeper and steeper grew the road as we advanced into the pine forest; it was quite magnificent; high fantastick rocks, the dark firs creeping to their summits, bare blue mountains, green hills; a few hard wood trees at first, then nothing but the evergreen forest; the path, stony, steep, winding like the wild torrent it skirted. I was often reminded of Rothiemurchus: the fir trees, the odour of turpentine, the hoary looking roots spreading far and wide for nourishment, the blaeberry, the bog myrtle, the granite, the rude log bridges covered with sod crossing the many rivulets which rushed over our path; the granite blocks below, and the grey craggs above, all reminded me of my own dear highlands; but the height and the picturesque outline of the mountains and the height and the magnificence of the cascades far exceed any scenery it has ever been my fate to wander in. I have never in my varied life beheld, nor is it likely I ever can behold again anything surpassing the grandeur of this day's journey. The two Colonels, Captain Straton and I have all been travellers in many lands, and there was but one voice among us.

At the end of the defile two rude paths lead on either hand up the almost precipitous mountain. One goes on to the Baths of Pantacousa in Spain; the other to the Lac de Gaube, the waters of which, augmented at this season by the ever melting snow, fell just in front of us over the rock down to the ravine below, in one wide, stormy, dashing, deafening cataract, worthy of ranking among the wonders of the world; the gloom of the forest, the traces of desolating tempests, all around, the solitude, all impose upon the senses and heighten the effect of the wild grandeur around. We stood upon the Pont d'Espagne, a bridge of logs thrown over a pause in the downward course of the mighty torrent, and looked up at the foaming water and down on more foaming water, till I felt frightened out of any sense the noise had left me. The path up the rocky mountain by the side of the cataract to the Lac de Gaube is very difficult to climb. How the ponies managed it is quite astonishing; for it is extremely rugged as well as very steep, though winding in a regular zigzig with sharp enough corners too, and with big stones in succession in many places; the ponies had often to stop to rest for it was a tedious ascent. And after reaching the plain at the top we had a good bit to go before arriving at the lake and snow to cross besides. A narrow slip too much in a hollow for the sun yet to act on, over which we went on foot, in the marks trodden for us by the guides, who drove the horses over afterwards, and one pony stepping aside sunk to the girths owing to his indiscretion. Snow was above, below and all round us, in fields rather than in patches; the little dismal lake in front, deep in the basin formed by a wall of rocks as rugged as at Gavernie.

On a large block of stones jutting out into the water is a square iron railed enclosure containing a head stone of white marble erected to the memory of a young husband and wife – English – on their bridal tour, who perished in this lake a very few years ago from incautiously venturing by themselves into a little coble used in fishing along the shore for trout by a man who lives during the summer in a sort of *bothie* on a green slope near this rock. Here during the season a party of any size may get a good luncheon or even dinner with wine, spirits, coffee, confectionery, and the delicious trout from the lake and fine dried fruits smuggled over the frontier from Spain served under an awning with considerable comfort for two francs a head. We were too early for anything beyond a savoury omelet of ham and eggs, bread, spirits and plates, etc., but having a basket with us of our own provisions we made a very merry meal at this elevation of eight or nine thousand feet from the sea. Monsieur and Madame de Gaube, as we christened them, do not live in this high sphere during the winter – they only come up for the season; the priviledge has been hereditary in Madame's family for many generations. She is rather a good-looking woman, a little weather-beaten and very obliging.

We walked down again to the Pont d'Espagne none of us choosing to try such a descent on pony back. The mounting was quite a pretty scene, as each filed off, onwards through the forest, a guide at each lady's side, except Miss Hart's who disdains everything feminine and galloped off by herself as soon as the nature of the road permitted, to explore the village of Cauterêts. One of the guides was the sister of the handsome Michel Canton who conducted Annie, and the wife of the sturdy little Larrose who had charge of me; she is a handsome woman, well dressed in solid clothing probably all of her own making, for the distaff is in every woman's hand in this country. She wore blue knitted stockings, very neat shoes, black jacket, black apron, blue petticoat and a pink handkerchief upon her head; the men, bonnet and all, might have stept out of any hut on Druie side [on the estate at Rothiemurchus]. We met a great many Spaniards both going and coming, in large groups, the men very fine-looking figures with the open jacket, the sash, the open knees, cross gartered sabots, and smart cap and tassel worn on one side; the women wore the jacket and petticoat so common to the peasantry everywhere, but no big apron with pockets, nor neat shawl to conceal the high made dirty shift; their hair hung in a big plait down their backs, and they generally wore a skull cap without a border tied under their chin. They were all very dirty in appearance; going, they carried large packages upon their heads – goods to dispose of at Cauterêts probably; returning they were loaded with bedsteads, chairs, tables, and other furniture which we suppose they were carrying to the Baths of Pantacosa, and they bore them like the Coolies in India, on their backs, supported by a band across the forehead.

11. The girls with Miss Hart and Colonel Litchfield rode up to the peak of Bergeon, a three hours' business with a great deal of walking and were hardly rewarded for the extreme fatigue of the expedition by getting a view of mountain-tops and valleys no wider than ribbons with streams in them like silk threads. I never think the scene from a mountain-top the least interesting so Hal and I staid quietly at home. They were equally long coming down and found the descent extremely disagreeable. Captain Straton sat two hours with us at least, maundering on as usual.

We also went up to a fine spring in the hill above recommended for asthma but found the door of the cave in which it rises locked. We also looked at several apartments in case of ever coming here again, enquired the traiteurs' terms too, and made out that the year round we should live at half what it cost us at Pau and in better rooms fully as well furnished, linen, knives, etc., provided into the bargain. Even during the short season of two months properly managing matters it would be far from a dear place; the air is delightful; the scenery beautiful beyond idea; the whole country interesting. It all belonged once to our Norman Kings; the Castle of Lourdes and the Castle of Luz were the two last strongholds which surrendered to the French after the death of our Black Prince. A botanist could never weary here; a mineralogist would find plenty of occupation also. In the valley of Gavernie several ores abound. Very fine iron mines were worked with success by an English company about a hundred years ago till the forest failed them when for want of fuel the mines had to be given up. Marble abounds near Bagnères de Bigorre which place although little out of the way we shall not have time to visit. It is in the plains much like Pau but prettier and at this season full of dressed up company, Parisian gamblers and so on. Capberne is not worth visiting. Bagnères de Luchon reckoned the most magnificient part of the Pyrenees is between forty and fifty miles from here, and out of the question. The woollen manufacture at Luz seems to be a large establishment employing many hands for all the fine soft mousselines and toiles de laine and Barèges gauzes are spun by the hand; therefore unapproachable in beauty by our cheaper framework imitations. I regret not being rich enough to lay in a stock of a few dresses, shawls, scarves, etc. for they are very dear out of their own country but not cheap enough in it to authorize extravagance.

We are too poor to do all we wish; our rather costly tour through those splendid regions must be luxury enough for one while; this last happy week will cost about £16. £9 before makes £25, of which Colonel Litchfield will not be allowed much to relieve us; so that adding our journey after poor Mary, and rent till September for the apartment in Pau we shall leave now, we must be prudent in other things at present. Never was money better spent; it has been uninterrupted pleasure of the purest kind the whole time – pleasure to look back upon for years to come; which must have a good effect in every way upon the little girls at an age when impressions are not easily effaced. Kind Captain and Mrs. Straton came up to carry us down to tea, and we parted with mutual regret, there being much to like even in him and she is very agreeable. We return to Pau tomorrow. Much as we were tempted to remain, we determined upon well considering the matter to follow our duty to Avranches. So adieu to the beautiful Pyrénées.

12. Bade adieu this beautiful Wednesday morning to the loveliest ravine in the most magnificent mountains that ever it has been my lot to look upon – the happiness of *living* in such scenery no one but a mountaineer born and bred can properly feel to the

full extent, though all who have any love for the sublime and beautiful must thoroughly enjoy a highland dwelling-place. All our party delighted in it; all left St. Sauveur with regret. There was nothing new to remark as we descended except the ever varying forms of the same fine scenery; and a curious old monastery near Argelès which I had missed on coming up the valley. It was built in the time of Charlemagne and there it is still in good repair surrounded by a pretty village standing on rising ground well wooded at the entrance of a glen running up from the plain among the mountains; this and the school for priests at Betterham, once a monastery also, were all the traces of the superstitious institutions of that unhappy form of religion still too prevalent, which this part of the country showed us. Neither monks nor nuns are heard of, very few priests are seen, no wayside images, no religious processions. In most of its religious habits Béarn remains true to its protestant days. We heard of a ceremony on the fête Dieu.

On this day all the girls of the district have their dolls christened; they go up to a little chapel somewhere on a hill where a boy in borrowed canonicals performs the ceremony. Excellent training for the young.

There are ruins at Luz of a Castle once belonging to the Templars and in the wilds of Gavernie some bits of old wall are said to have been once an out chapel of the order; twelve skulls altogether in a deal box are shown still, as having been the last of these once splendid knights who had their heads cut off on the suppression of the order in the year heaven knows when [1312]. The heat became very oppressive as we got down towards the plains. We reached d'Estelle a little after ten for we set out very early, at five, and there we remained till four – hours of actual misery – the heat was fully Indian without any Indian contrivances to lessen the distress produced by it; the Inn disgustingly dirty; the luncheon extremely nasty – greasy dishes, dirty forks, horrid wine. We were very glad to get away.

How hot and airless we found Pau which we reached soon after six; the cabriolet[1] was near an hour behind us, the poor

1. A light, two-wheeled chaise drawn by one horse.

worn out old mare they had sent in it having fairly knocked up from the heat, and though we paid her every attention she was very nearly exhausted. Hal and I and Jack refreshed ourselves with ices; the girls took a bath. Two letters were waiting for us – one from Avranches. Mary had had an inflammatory attack of the stomach which taking for wind she had treated with her usual brandified remedies; they just called in the English Doctor time enough to save her; she had been leeched twice and was better, but very ill, and it is plain from what Mr. Gardiner says and the low spirits he writes in that this Dr. Pollard thinks just as despondingly of her case as the doctors here. Janey writes to Tom also – pleased with Avranches, but not in raptures; the place is pretty, on the sea, and they have found a house they think will suit them and another they think will suit us. The other letter was from Jane who had been raised into a kind of extasy by poor Mr. Gardiner's sanguine letters during the journey. She sends me all she has yet made out about Captain Eliot. Little enough. A Sir Charles Shawe knew him slightly and thinks he is Irish. Sir Charles Napier hardly knows him; he said he was coming out to take the command of Don Miguel's fleet, when luckily the enemy took it before the new Admiral arrived; he added to William Craig that he believed he was a fellow that was fond of fiddling. Uncle Frere does not think he is a man of any property but he is too much engaged just now with some business of importance to think any more about him. So our enquiries have not produced much as yet. It is plain that there is nothing but the worth of the young man to attract us, or rather *them*, for I don't approve of the matter at all. And the bad health of the trio, with the moderate fortune of the lover and a certain oddity among them makes me as well pleased that there is a separation for a while which will give Janey time to understand herself. I like them all three, but wild and uncontrouled and vivacious as is the Captain, I like him best.

13. The heat of Pau is so dreadfully exhausting after the pure air we have been breathing that we are all nearly dead – it is really most oppressive.

15. We have had great consultations about our plans. The Eliots with us every day trying to wile us from the path of duty.

It is so hot, so exhausting here, so pure and cool in the mountains; such a pleasant little society will be gathered at and near St. Sauveur, and Colonel Litchfield so much wished us all to settle there till autumn that we were very strongly tempted. Indeed it was so arranged and Miss Hart and I had been as busy as we dared to be in such heat preparing for a three months' residence among so many agreeable people. I did not approve but I really could not disapprove. Colonel Smith has done so much, put up with so much to gratify my wish of being near Mary; and her movements are so uncertain there is no knowing how long it may suit her restlessness to remain anywhere. Mr. Gardiner is only going to take a house at Avranches till September in case she should tire there as elsewhere; so that there was a reason of some weight for waiting till we knew more of this new place she has gone to. On the other hand is poor Mr. Gardiner's anxious condition, alone with so much to perplex him; the expectation of our following them quickly and the possible fretting it might cause her were we not to fulfil the implied promise. So Hal having been kept awake all Friday night by his own champaign and Mr. Valpy's ices and the heat, turned over all these arguments in his mind and announced yesterday morning that he was going to take the seats for Bordeaux.

17. Dear Jane's birthday; there is another pleasure in prospect for the summer – Jane will come over to see Mary and we shall be all together once more. Last night, exhausting as was the heat, we went to hear M. Buscarlet and not the worse of being exceedingly handsome. I never can fancy the French language suited to the sublime therefore I never feel affected by their religious discourses and the Scriptures read in that language are truly disagreeable. The singing is perfectly beautiful – in parts, the singers properly instructed, and arranged in order on the three first benches in the Church. Mrs. Buscarlet's voice is as fine as her husband's, and her style admirable.

Very busy this morning, packing, paying, ordering, settling, so many *last* things remain to do. We have just entered our own room after our busy day and we have been refreshed by an hour of kind M. Puyoo's enlivening conversation and by a fine thunder storm accompanied by very heavy rain; it will prepare the roads nicely for travelling and cool the air;

otherwise I really do believe we should all have been laid up with brain fevers. I am sorry after all to leave Pau. A second year could have been passed much more profitably in every way, and having some idea now of the ways of the place I could have avoided many mistakes in future. I must only be wise enough to act for myself at Avranches; probably we shall find it suit us equally well.

There was a letter this morning from Tom Darker full of agreeable news. Frazers left the house in high order. Wests seem anxious to keep it so. Country quiet, all the disaffected being much cast down since Messrs O'Connell & Co. were sent to jail; harvest not promising owing to the long drought. All the rain came to Pau. New schoolmaster, clever and attentive; 22 boys already; Miss Gardiner's school increasing also. Old pensioners all comfortable; orphans ditto; except our young tailor who seems to be doing little good. James Ryan is building his house, and four of our respectable tenants did not pay one farthing of rent – the two Quins, poor Kearns, and Bryan Dempsey; Commons only ten guineas: such a set. All our neighbours well, and kindly enquiring for us. I wish I were home again but that can't be yet.

18. Poor old Massa [the Pole] came to see us off, and M. Puyoo with a present of oranges, and kind Mr. Valpy. We were up early and all ready a good hour before the time thanks to our military habits – the best after all. It rained nearly the whole day – an unspeakable comfort – the air was quite cooled, the sun concealed, and as there is nothing very striking in the scenery upon a second review, it little mattered. Here and there an elevation of some little extent cultivated, wooded, and inhabited, breaks the wide sameness of the Landes; and Aire is a pretty old town with its steep banks and its handsome river, its archiepiscopal palace and its fine old church. Mont de Marsin is pretty, where at five o'clock we dined. At nine at Roquefort Jacques who had arrived shortly before us with his malle poste [post box] came up to bid us in earnest good-bye. I think he would gladly have kept one of our party back to aid him in his road to riches, and truly I believe the lady's red eyes confessed that her good sense had carried the day against inclination – for Jacques, 'brave homme' as he may be, is quite a Frenchman, quite a Gascon, quite a Béarnais,

more likely to be an agreeable lover than what *we* should call
a good husband.

19. We went on all night, sometimes sleeping, sometimes waking,
with rain and without rain, till we stopt at six for very good
café au lait to be served to those who wished it. We drove
into the really fine old town of Bordeaux about eight, and
were settled in the Hotel de Nantes, in fine rooms, all looking
very right, in an hour; the Hotel de France was nearly full;
we did not like the appearance of the only rooms they could
give us. Our old friend the Hotel de la Charrente we did not
remember with particular pleasure; so we have tried this at
Mr. Valpy's recommendation, and I hope we shall continue
to like it for we can't get off to-morrow – diligence full –
to-day was gone; Friday therefore we must wait for. I am
glad of a rest of one day but should have been better pleased
to have been spared another. Our dinner at five at the table
d'hôte was very neatly served, everything clean, everything
good including attendance; but there was very little to eat:
four French gentlemen besides our party of eight: one sole,
two pigeons, one chicken with four slices of lamb and one 1b.
of bouilli – after soup of course; then four vegetables with tough
roast beef, and one small rice pudding and one vanille cream;
dessert in little saucers – six bunches of currants in one, three
macaroons in another, and so on; there was plenty because
some went away; each dish was taken off in succession, cut
up, and handed round – about two mouthfulls to each person,
so that all those who ate of everything got enough I daresay
but besides that eternal variety being disagreeable to me the
length of time thus consumed at dinner is most particularly
tiresome.

It was a nice cool evening and we walked out for two hours;
up and down the noble quay more than three and a half
miles long and very handsomely wide. Large old-fashioned
houses, really handsome many of them, look over this fine
causeway to the river full of shipping wider than the Thames
at London Bridge; the Bridge lately built here is therefore
from its length very striking – seventeen arches – 1400 French
feet; the pavement asphalte, beautiful to look at, so smooth
and clean and delightful to walk on from its firm yet soft
feeling. Really the curious old gables and arched doorways

and ancient gates and queer towers, etc. with the numerous handsome streets and the constant succession of handsome shops make this a very remarkable town though the situation is nothing particular – quite flat, no banks to the river nor variety in the neighbouring country: only the two spires of the grand old cathedral and the equally fine old tower of St. Martin's rising above the roofs of the long long lines of houses. The better class of inhabitants seem to be all in the country just now for we met very few in any of the *places* or promenades, and but little bustle is in the streets.

20. We have just had a very comfortable breakfast in the publick salon at a sociable round table which just held our party. Most of us are off to the flower garden, picture gallery, etc., but I prefer quiet to sight seeing, not feeling quite well either. We were disturbed during the night by more company in our very smart bed than we wished for. I in particular was made such a victim of that I had to get up and settle myself on the sofa. Colonel Smith lighted a candle and went a-hunting – caught one gigantick enemy and destroyed him; the rest of the phalanx disspirited by the loss of their gallant leader retired from the field leaving merely a few light troops to skirmish occasionally. Nasty, dirty people, the French, with all their shew. Disgusted with the table d'hôte: such a low description of people, eating such quantities, so few to wait on them, so little to give them, and such a long business we were quite sick of it. A military band attracted us to the *place* where we found an immense crowd in full dress – both the scum and the dregs of Bordeaux, I suppose, for such a collection of detestable looking creatures male and female could hardly belong to any class the least respectable. It was an airless evening and we shortened our walk to prepare for our early start to-morrow, leaving this unhealthy town without the least regret.

21. By six the porters had called for our luggage; by seven we had breakfasted, reached the boat and started. I can hardly call the scenery pretty; in one or two places a neat country house with its appurtenances, a road behind and garden in front seemed cheerful for the moment, but after leaving the town there was nothing to compensate for the loss of the noble quay and its fine row of houses; flat banks, scantily wooded, unrelieved by an interesting feature. The river widens considerably just

about the junction of the Dordogne and villages of some size appear on every hand most of which we touched at to set down passengers which greatly lengthened our voyage. We did not land at Mortagne till one o'clock. The deck of the pretty boat was very much crowded at the beginning not however by any persons above the class of tradespeople – civilly inclined however. One very chattering maidservant very much amused us by her perseverance in talking down every human being, beginning with an old widow who was knitting and taking everybody in turn to the Captain and the sailors. A handsome active girl with the handkerchief of the country a little coquettishly arranged over her fine dark eyes. A party of three we found were to be our fellow passengers in the diligence – an intelligent middle-aged man the doctor of a regiment shifting its quarters from Perpignan on the Mediterranean to L'Orient close to Brest! His wife a nice-looking young woman with pleasing manners and prettily dressed, who had dirty nails, and managed her baby herself, nursing it and otherwise attending to its wants before us all without a blush. An officer's wife, their friend, was travelling under their care to Nantes to join her husband. We got rather friendly by means of the baby, and found them pleasant companions.

The landing at Mortagne at low water is disagreeable; a very long wooden pier having to be traversed under the burning sun; then we had to wait in a perfect oven of a wooden box at the end of it while the luggage was landed and packed on the roof of the diligence which had been standing till nearly burned through so that it beat down hot on our heads, when we entered, from the burning top. We had to pay ever so many sous to pass through a gate kept by two old frights in the pillow case caps peculiar to this part of the country. The road was hilly, the country frightful, the heat intense all the way to Charente. I never suffered more in India from the sun; the people were ugly too and the dress of the women with those extraordinary varieties of hideous cap, each appearing higher, wider, stiffer than the last, completed the disgusts of the journey. Had we not got as many ripe guignes [Scots: wild cherries] for four sous as all of us could get through our ill humour would have made us ill. Charente is very pretty –

a clean little town on rising banks well wooded, the stream a good width crossed by a beautiful suspension bridge worth suffering much to see. We walked over it paying a sou apiece, all the iron supports shaking as the heavy diligence moved on at a foot's pace. At Rochefort which is also pretty in the same style there was dinner, but it being so late – eight o'clock – we chose tea or rather coffee which we all enjoyed. It was near midnight when we passed La Rochelle which I regretted as the fortifications are in good order and a few fine streets and a place full of trees looked rather well in the lamplight.

Daylight shewed us a most frightful country – the termination of the Landes – all this part of France has been reclaimed from the sea; it is monotonous to a degree, very unhealthy, and though generally well cultivated, rich in cornfields at least, and some fine cattle, it is quite ugly to eyes fresh from the Pyrenees. A new kind of cap began here to present itself, quite as big as the drums and the pillow cases but carried out behind like the flags of the lancers or the old prints in Froissart's chronicles[1]. The men instead of the bonnet or the neat glazed hat, all appeared in night caps with a great long end hanging down their backs. We noticed that the horses were much finer looking as we approached the north, the people more alert looking, the women much less quietly industrious, not half the spinning and knitting we had been accustomed to.

22. We entered La Vendée early this morning passing among innumerable little fields hedged and hedge rowed, the farms separated by those rugged bye-roads which were such a resource to the poor Vendeans and such a puzzle to their enemies. We breakfasted at Bourbon Vendée, a rather considerable town half way between Rochelle and Nantes. This was luckily a cloudy day, the heat not therefore oppressive so we journeyed on in comparative comfort through the same flat scenery, reaching Nantes before two o'clock. A large straggling town, the parts we passed through offering nothing of particular interest – neither turrets nor spires nor any fine buildings, multitudes of narrow streets with good

1. These mid-fourteenth century accounts, principally of the Hundred Years' War, occupied a special place in her father's library at the Doune in Rothiemurchus.

houses and remarkably handsome shops and the Loire with
fifty branches or tributaries flowing through many of the
streets crossed by multitudes of bridges, some handsome,
others only of wood. Being warned against the Hotel de
France we have settled ourselves in the Hotel des Colonies;
very good apartments but dear – fourteen francs a day – eating
at the table d'hôte 3. frs. 50, breakfast 1 fr. 50., children as
usual half price; the eating is not particularly good, wine is
bad, attendance very bad; the house is new, only in progress
of furnishing the people having but just taken possession of
it, therefore a little confusion as yet of course.

23. Sunday. I never was more done up than yesterday; it was
so hot in the office when paying up our seats, counting our
luggage, and arranging for our onward journey, the hunting
out an hotel and battling about the bargain; good-natured
Miss Hart went down to the kitchen and made us all some
tea, the greatest of all refreshments. At the table d'hôte were
only two gentlemen, rather agreeable men. I talked quietly to
mine who seemed quite content with his companion. Miss
Hart made such a noise with hers that upon this as upon
many other occasions she made me quite ashamed of her.
After dinner she stationed herself at the window of my room to
make her very audible observations on all affairs in the streets.
Seeing Tom at a print shop below she called to him to ask if
he would go to see the Cathedral – to wait for her then as she
would go with him; and off she went without a thought of her
pupils or a word to me, and returned after eight – long – when
Janey was in bed quite tired and Annie and Jack were sitting
by me who had been obliged to decline a little stroll in the
cool air with Colonel Smith because the children could not
be left. A more unfit person for a governess could not be met.
An obliging clever young woman, but so taken up with herself,
so idle, so restless, so free and easy, so coarse in manner, and
so indelicate in feelings that she must not remain with us on
any account. I have tried in every way to improve her, but
her unfortunate idea that she needs no improvement puts an
end to all hope of doing her any radical good. I must therefore
endeavour to get quit of her as speedily as possible with as little
disturbance as possible. She has no sort of notion of the duties
of her station, no idea of its responsibilities, no pleasure in its

employments. To amuse herself at Colonel Smith's expense is her whole aim. So mine shall henceforth be to be done with her. Our Avranches life will be so little to her taste I don't anticipate much difficulty. Colonel Litchfield too will stand fire I think. Even though M. Puyoo has been sacrificed to him!! In this part of France the table d'hôte is not on the plan it is in the north, or was twenty years ago. Then and there, the family of the host really partook of the meals with the travellers, and the dinners were certainly infinitely better; here are none but the guests who fare all the worse for the separation.

24. The sultry air of this close town was cooled by a great thunderstorm during the night accompanied by a great deal of rain. Our walk through the narrow streets of this curious old city was quite fatiguing from the want of air and the quantity of dust; crowds of people smartly dressed were flocking towards the Place Louis XVI, where the statue of the poor King still stands upon its handsome pillar though the inscription at the base has been defaced; the Place itself is long, narrow, all gravel, with a few rows of stunted trees, and handsome flights of steps at either end, down to lower streets. Many fine houses surround this walk; the Prefecture is a handsome building; there is a fine hospital; one or two other handsome publick offices; the old Castle down in a hole; the old Cathedral hemmed in by shabby houses. The tower end is very beautiful – the inside light and lofty and imposing: the tomb of the last Duke of Brittany very handsome indeed, well worth many visits; hours might be spent in this old cathedral – writing about it is another thing. One or two of the very old streets with their wooden houses and overhanging stories are very curious looking, but as a Town I cannot admire Nantes; nothing interesting in the situation, nor striking in the buildings. The shops are numerous and very handsome and there is a new arcade handsome in itself and full of handsome shops into which some of the windows of our hotel look. Everything is said to be dear here: judging of the rest by the hotel I should say excessively dear. We had neither bread nor milk enough at breakfast to-day, very scanty dinners, no attendance. I am glad we are off at four o'clock for we are hardly comfortable here.

25. Daylight showed us a pretty country highly cultivated, well

wooded filled with country houses, small villages and small towns; yesterday evening we saw little to admire beyond extreme richness, and the mirth of the peasantry which has been encreasing upon us as we travelled northward. Every party of haymakers returning home from their day's labour sang and danced along the road, and at the cottage doors they were assembled in groups gaily jigging away in couples young and old as I have read of but had seen nothing of in the dull south. The caps of the women though invariably immense changed several times in form during our progress; near to Rennes they became rather comely to the matrons being something like the old highland mutch.[1] The blouse is little seen among the men now, who generally are smartly dressed in round jackets and loose trowsers and glazed hats very like our sailors. Rennes is a particularly fine old town, really beautiful, full of fine old buildings, good streets, handsome shops and large houses. Early as it was it was all astir, the market full, many shops opened, and by five the active housekeepers were all trotting about with their little baskets. It seems to be a busy thriving town, diligences passing through to almost every part of the kingdom. It was a long journey to Avranches. The road was very hilly, very dusty, and we went but slow; it was fully two o'clock when we arrived at the summit of the tedious ascent which leads to the very unpretending collection of narrow streets formed of very ordinary sized houses which composes the little unattractive town of Avranches.

26. Busy house-hunting: how we toiled up one street, looking at so many and finding none to suit. Most of them so very small; all so very disagreeably situated, and unfurnished for the most part, the plan being to hire the bare house and then hire or buy the furniture. Of course a house is cheaper here than at Pau; it had need be for they are so very inferiour – just little boxes, dirty, ill-finished, and scantily furnished at the best. I see nothing engaging in the place at all. Country quite uninteresting, town extremely, shabby, sea at a great distance, houses very inferiour; the air delightful. We all feel revived by it wonderfully.

1. A close-fitting day cap of white linen or muslin worn by married women.

27. More house-hunting. Such a tiresome business. The Gardiners have got very comfortably settled in a very small house which it took them near a fortnight to get ready. Besides ordinary cleaning, there were several repairs, papering and painting quite necessary; then the furnishing – every article to be selected and watched on its progress from Mme. Hallais' shop; then crockery to purchase. But there they are really very neatly established in a small way – clean and tidy as hands can make them. We are so much less compressible a party it will be very difficult to find us a suitable habitation. Mr. Gardiner has a small garden in front of his house, a good large one behind; on the ground floor a drawing-room long and narrow yet small; a dining-room very small; a kitchen, pantry, and servants' sitting-room. On the first floor Mary's bedroom with her sitting-room opening out of it; his dressing-room – a mere closet; Janey's bedroom and Sarah's. The garrets are rather good – the boys have one, Planté another, the two French maids the third; for the remaining two are mere lumber garrets quite low and unfinished. It would be a second-rate lodging of the small class at an English watering-place. The situation is airy – at the corner of the Boulevards looking over the country. We have dined there these two days. Everything so neat – no attempt at cooking, their cook knowing almost nothing; they say there are no cooks here. Mr. Gardiner had good wines, good ale of course, delicious bread, butter, cream, fruits, vegetables and meat very fair; the brown bread and butter would do for me to live on, so that in the eating way I shall thrive here on excellent plain food instead of the greasy sodden stews I hate. I don't expect much from the dinner in our hotel to-day, judging from the breakfasts and the very dirty floors. Margaret scrubbed all our rooms out yesterday – the floors were like those of a barn before; the beds clean and comfortable and some pretty furniture in really cheerful rooms. The Bretons are so near, some of their dirt sticks. It is unaccountable how people can be so fine and so very nasty.

28. So miserable a dinner in our hotel yesterday we gladly accepted one to-day from Mr. Gardiner having no means of preparing one in the apartments we have taken in the Maison Colibeau – a wretched, dirty, dilapidated house in the best street in this

desolate looking town. The rooms being a good size and well arranged and the house being furnished after a fashion, we decided on taking it till Michaelmas, the usual term here, by which time we shall have had an opportunity of seeing one which may suit us better for a permanence. We are to pay 400 francs for this and supply ourselves with glass, crockery, etc. The old broker woman gives us very little furniture of the shabbiest kind but we must make the best of it.

29. Not half done cleaning though our new kitchen-maid is assisted by a charwoman and Margaret is worth half a dozen. The little girls and Miss Hart were busy too, washing the paint. The beds are comfortable enough, the rooms airy, and there is a large garden, but it is a sad dilapidated place; do what we will it cannot look nice. We have had great occupation seeing servants, replying to trades-people, hunting out our furniture, making our few purchases; the people are very tiresome, awkward and dilatory, spending half their time in talking; they are very obliging in their manner however; exceedingly ugly; very far from tidily dressed, that great steeple of a cap being almost the only clean bit of white about the women. They seem a half century behind even Pau.

30. Our breakfast yesterday and to-day in our own house was exceedingly comfortable; the bread, butter, eggs and cream all so good; the dinner last night showed well both for Margaret and the market, and though the little maid from the country don't wait exactly like a thorough-bred footman, she did pretty well and promises to do better by and bye, being really anxious to please. I have no time to-night to write up all my impressions so must leave them for greater leisure. I was all this Sunday morning with poor Mary who had taken elaterium and suffered accordingly. I can't say I see the great improvement in her. Her complexion is clearer and her cough is gone; otherwise she is unchanged – pain in her side instead of head – indigestion – weakness – increase of water – emaciation; however she is in good spirits which is a great matter, and good Mr. Gardiner is looking forward to her recovery I do believe. He is greatly improved in health himself, and Janey looks better.

MONDAY, JULY 1. A long morning with Margaret, paying bills, balancing her accounts, arranging household matters with her, so as to get into a regular method which will save both trouble and expense. The principal market day is Saturday when it is best to lay in everything that will keep a week. Beef can be got no other day, nor poultry; mutton, butter and eggs may be had on Tuesday; fish, fruit and vegetables every day; the poultry is bought alive very lean and has to be fed in coops; it is dear too; the other things are not. Avranches is getting dearer yearly as every other place is where English congregate; still it is cheaper than Pau, but not so comfortable. The best house in the town, furnished, would not be above 2,000 fr; then it is small, and not furnished well, though a good garden makes up for much. Men servants few people have. We therefore save that expense. Under Margaret we have only a middle-aged kitchen maid at 15 francs a month, and a nice little housemaid who waits at table and dresses the young ladies for 12. The washing we shall try to put out as it is troublesome where there is no convenience for it. The charge for washing is high, soap and charcoal both being dear. Charcoal is double what it was at Pau. Wood appears to be rather cheaper; many persons burn coal from economy and have had grates put up on purpose. After all these family matters were disposed of I went to see Mary. She was not suffering much though she had not passed a good night, pain in her side and shoulder preventing her remaining in bed. She is still very large in spite of the great quantity of water she got quit of yesterday. She fills so quickly I don't see how it will be possible for her to bear up long against the severe medicine she is forced to take so constantly. She was much exhausted by this elaterium yesterday. She had taken it five days before – four times within the last fortnight. I cannot see the great improvement in her. On the contrary she appears to me to be nearly as ill as anyone could well be and be alive.

2. Monsieur Godin, the Juge de Paix [Conciliation Magistrate] is the agent for Monsieur François Frault, the owner of Mr. Plunkett's house; he has been here this morning to arrange the letting of it; high enough – 1400 frs. unfurnished, without the kitchen garden and the tenant to pay the window tax. Yesterday Mr. Hickey, the clergyman, called, and Mr. Robert Poe, an invalid who lives out in the country, rather pleasant though a proser, gentlemanly, long

in India, advocate or Solicitor General in Calcutta, Irish, and his elder brother who lives immediately opposite to us was at school with Colonel Smith.[1] The queer little Dr. Pollard completes our Avranches acquaintance. This last oddity is formed after the model of Mr. Quilp.[2] if that deformed dwarf can be fancied with a benevolent countenance; he is said by some persons here not to have a regular diploma nor to have ever practised medicine in England, nor to have been always successful here, and we were warned not to let Mr. Gardiner trust him entirely. However, upon consideration we mean to say nothing; he appears to manage Mrs. Gardiner better than anyone who has yet tried it. She has confidence in him and he has power over her and his attention to her is unremitting. In fact he is more a nurse than a physician which really is what she wants; and he gives her as little medicine as he can well manage with, applying himself to diet which he endeavours to regulate most judiciously having forbid stimulants and rich dishes, and to regimen, enforcing early hours, exercise, air, all by degrees as she can bear them. He had the charge of a lunatick asylum near London and was making a fortune by the excellent management of his patients when he was completely overwhelmed by his wife running away and the law expenses necessary to get rid of her. He has two daughters married, and a third who lives with one of her sisters, and here he is by himself with nothing but two francs a visit from a few patients. He is a busy little body, plays the organ in church, sings glees, pops in at every open door, and seems to know everybody and everything and to have a very considerable opinion of himself.

6. We had a visit from the clergyman here, Mr. Hickey, which mentioning to Mary, she told me he was the famous Martin

1. This would have been either the King's School, Macclesfield or Haileybury and I.C.S.
2. This is the evil, deformed dwarf from *The Old Curiosity Shop* (1841) which she had been reading recently (see 21 January 1844); rather unkindly, this was the model that also came to her mind once when describing her Wicklow neighbour, the Earl of Milltown.

Doyle.[1] What has brought him here we know not. I remember
hearing in Ireland that his agricultural experiments had much
impoverished him and he has a large family. There are so many
English families here and the seats, though lower rented than
at Pau, are still sufficiently high to give him a comfortable
addition to his income.

8. The Colonels talk of an expedition to Jersey for the end of the
week, a visit to Dr. Eckford [an old Indian friend]. We made a
round of calls upon those obliging persons who have visited us.
Mr. Hickey is quite unlike my idea of Martin Doyle – absent,
fidgetty, uncertain in manner, unconnected in conversation,
with a little bit of a garden in disorder![2] The writers like the
preachers a'n't bound to practise. This poor man appears to be
in straightened circumstances from the style of house we found
him in. I remember hearing his agricultural experiments had
been very costly to him and he has a large family. We saw two
grown up sons and two grown up daughters and he talked of
five more, two sons in Australia, a barrister in Dublin, an elder
son married, and a sick daughter at Havre with her mother.

11. How oddly we stumble upon people all over the world. Who
should be living here but Sandy Grant the agent[3] of my father's
ruin, the mismanager of all his electioneering matters, who

1. 'Martin Doyle' (c.1785–1879): one of his more
   recently published pamphlets would surely have
   interested her ('Hints addressed to the small-holders
   and peasantry of Ireland on . . . health, temperance,
   morals etc.' of 1835) and one to be published two
   years later in 1846 ('Hints for the small farmers
   . . . of many parts of Ireland . . . to which is added
   observations as to the expediency of growing tobacco,
   with the details of its culture') would certainly have
   intrigued her.

2. It is therefore somewhat ironical that one of his last
   homilies was entitled 'An address to the landlords of
   Ireland on subjects connected with the melioration
   of the lower classes cottage farming . . . or how to
   cultivate from two to twenty acres.' (1870).

3. He acted as political agent for E.G.'s father in the
   ruinously expensive election campaigns he fought to
   become M.P. for Great Grimsby (1812–1818) and
   Tavistock (1819–1826).

lined his own pockets well, and lived and throve for a while on deceit and falsehoods. His first wife, a handsome woman who brought him some fortune, having died, he represented himself as my father's elder brother, and with my father's money, and a service of plate he had charge of for him, he managed to get for a second wife a Miss Thorold of a good Lincolnshire family. They lived in this neighbourhood at first in great style, a fine chateau, carriages, servants, and the plate, for years no one could get on here without an introduction to Mr. Grant.

But gradually all this glitter vanished and by degrees he has sunk into a small but good house on the Boulevards, the rent of which is paid by his brother-in-law Mr. Thorold; he is still in the best French society, but nearly avoided by the English on account of several ungentlemanly actions, of which his poor humble relations on the banks of the Spey would be ashamed to hear. I met him the other evening and knew him instantly – a little florid old man with a stoop and hair perfectly grey – the hook nose however not to be mistaken nor the downcast twinkling sharp grey eye. How often have I carried him down his tea to the study in Lincoln's Inn Fields where he and my father spent their evenings concocting expensive bye ways to distinction when the open road of duty lay so plain before them, leading through a life of happy usefulness to that true honour which commands distinction. Publick life begins in private. The Senate is an end not a means – it should be deserved before it be attained and then the fruits of experience accompany the honoured patriot into this enlarged sphere of action which he should enter not for the purpose of shining in debate but because he feels himself possessed of the ability there to forward the interests of his country. Sandy Grant has four children, two sons in Australia, a daughter adopted by her mother's relations, and another now in Paris with a French lady of rank.

12. The Colonels really go to-day to Granville on their way to Jersey, and how curiously one does hit on people. The Consul at Granville happened to be here and they took advantage of this to get introduced to him by the little Doctor and to give him their passeports to have visé'd and ready for them to-morrow morning. Who should this quiet grave thin elderly

gentlemanly Mr. Turnbull be who is thus obscurely existing on £300 a year, but the young dashing Lieutenant of Sir Wm. Wiseman's frigate who about twenty years ago, more sinned against, I do believe, then sinning, brought misery into a large family circle by forgetting every principle of duty. Bitterly have both suffered for their crime. After Sir William's discovery of his wife's dishonour, unable to leave his station himself, he shipped her off to her poor father's care, but she gave them all the slip after landing in England and joined her lover who of course had been dismissed his ship, somewhere in France. Sir James promised to receive his daughter provided she left Mr. Turnbull; her reply was to publish her own death in the newspapers; however want of funds, or repentance or something induced her afterwards to accept her father's offer, and she was established at Richmond with her sister Mrs. Rich who devoted herself to her care. Sir William divorced her. I remember hearing my father say that out of respect to poor Sir James Mackintosh the case was heard in the Lords with closed doors, as few as possible were present and *his* name scarcely mentioned in the reports.

After the divorce Mr. Turnbull married her and he has been very much pushed on in his humble career; he had to leave the Navy but he was made Consul in the West Indies somewhere with a high salary; there they lost two children so were glad to exchange at a loss to this more healthy climate; a third child has died here, and a fourth is dying of water on the brain inherited from their mother. She is known here as the daughter of Sir James Mackintosh; the rest of her painful history seems unsuspected; she is admired for her talents, and on account of her powers of pleasing forgiven for her extreme ugliness. I hope we may not meet, and that if we do I may be able to appear as if she were a stranger. It would be too humiliating for her to feel herself in the presence of Eliza Grant, though we would never breathe to mortal her sad tale. Colonel Litchfield too she might know for years ago in her youth about the time of her marriage he was daily in her company at Russara, and his name, as well as his appearance, is too uncommon to be forgotten. Mr. Gardiner also knew her well in India. I hope the gossipping Doctor may mention to Mr. Turnbull that Mary and I are Sir John Grant's daughters and that Mrs. Turnbull may thus avoid us – it would be too painful a meeting to all. Giddy, foolish thing! When we first knew her in Edinburgh, whither she had been sent by her father with her two little boys to be out of the way of some foolish flirtation in the South, she went on so flightily with Basil Hall[1] that my mother thought it right to check the intimacy between my sister Jane and her. Her elder boy was like her husband – dull and good-looking; Jamie was a Mackintosh, clever and ugly. He shot himself in the delirium of fever brought on by the fatigues of this Afghan war. I remember him so well in his little nankin dress dining with us in Picardy Place; my mother asking him what wine he chose, his mother replying while she pushed the water bottle towards him that Adam's wine was what he drank, and the monkey looking archly up and saying: 'I don't like Adam and Eve and Cain and Abel's wine'. She should never have been married to that worthy stupid husband; he could not comprehend her, and she had been too little educated to have patience with him. It was called such a good marriage too! I hate the name of good marriages.

By the bye Henry Eliot has been nearly killed by falling from his horse going up to the Lac de Gaube up the precipice from the Pont d'Espagne; he was picked up insensible, but is recovering under a *French* surgeon; his ladye love appeared very little moved by the intelligence. She is by no means so Eliotised as she was. It quite surprises me after the violent intimacy with the mother and all the encouragement given to the son, and the folly of the presents accepted on all hands.

13. The gentlemen went off to Jersey about half after two yesterday. Colonel Litchfield is so reserved there is no knowing from his manner what his feelings are, but Hal gets so cross when annoyed that I saw very plainly he had twenty times rather have staid at home. It is always the way with him: he accepts every proposal for moving with avidity & then longs to be off; generally affects this & all the people set it down as Mrs. Smith who obliges her husband to send excuses. 'She won't let the poor Colonel dine out even,' Richard Hornidge said!

All night long there seemed to be a sort of hubbub in this

1. This is all more fully documented in the Memoirs. See chapters 19 and 21.

usually quiet street. They told us this forenoon that a man in a fit of jealousy had stabbed another, been arrested, and brought into the jail here to be tried for murder. The servants say he will be guillotined in a fortnight in the market place; but their laws will be very unlike ours if so miserable a scene take place, for he had discovered his wife with her lover and struck him on the moment. The last execution in these parts was at Grandville eight years ago. Soon these barbarous spectacles will only be shuddered at as matters of history.

14. My Southern eye is now beginning to get accustomed to the tameness of Northern scenery. Still uninteresting it appears in detached parts pretty; the Town has lengthened and widened though shabby as ever. And as we can procure all we want in it, and the air is quite delightful, and the people obliging, we can get on very well here by keeping ourselves to ourselves. We have made the rooms we occupy in this barrack of a house really very comfortable. Colonel Litchfield and the maids have two good rooms on the second floor. We and the children fill the whole of the first floor. Miss Hart has a large room looking to the garden with closets attached opening into one of equal size with equal conveniences looking to the street which the little girls have. Next them and over the lobby is the Colonel's dressing-room and then my excellent bedroom with closets of course communicating with the equally large one into which we have put Jack and Margaret with their windows to the garden again. Downstairs we have the drawing-room and dining-room both well sized, a kitchen and servants' sitting-room and admirable cellars for fuel, meat, wine, poultry, running under the whole of this large house. We have put as much furniture as we could get Mme. Hallias to give us into these apartments, and scrubbed and scoured and tidied, and having filled our windows with beautiful greenhouse plants, we look altogether far from uncomfortable.

The other family who lodge here are quiet people – a French gentleman, his wife, two children and two maids occupying but three rooms on the second floor. The servants here are bad, – idle, gossipping and dirty, but exceedingly civil though very free and easy. The peasantry in general are very far from being handsome – they are little, without air, sallow, untidy.

Their appearance betokens anything out a healthy climate; they are ill-dressed, poorly fed, and have not the industrious habits so remarkable in the South. The whole well wooded, undulating plain out of which rises the rocky hill upon which still stands the ancient fortress round which the little town has grown, is fertile to a degree, and apparently illimitable on every side by one where spreads the Ocean; but in all this extent no landmark arrests the eye save one low rock upon the ugly strand formed between the arm of the sea and the little river. On this low rock is built the strong tower of St. Michel still used as a State prison.

A good many of the old nobility live in the neighbourhood on the poor remains of their often subdivided property, some few in the town keeping themselves quite apart from the *authorities*. The new order of things is hateful to them in all ways; towards the English they are very polite – never making any advances themselves, but meeting with alacrity any advances made to them. Thus the new comers call on all the *French* as at Pau, while the *English* residents call on the newcomers. Of these last there is a superabundance, odd-looking people for the most part; exceedingly quarrelsome they have been we hear but a large division having carried their ill manners elsewhere the remnant as yet appears to be better conducted. A great deal of visiting goes on among them and they seem to be quite annoyingly punctilious about their calls, etc.

16. Half the day with Mary, cooking, etc., but she relishes nothing; the other half family matters which we shall get put quite to rights during the absence of the Colonels and so have all comfortable for Hal and my time at his disposal. The wardrobes can be gone on with at odd moments; they are in disorder of course and will take time to arrange, but it is pleasant employment. I feel up to everything in this air and shall soon have all as orderly as in my 'busy bee' days. Poor Belleville![1] I am so sorry the stone fell out of the seal

1. This was the son of James 'Ossian' Macpherson (1736–1796), who spent his last years on an acquired estate whose name was changed to Belleville; nearer Kingussie, it was still close enough to Rothiemurchus for the families to be very close.

ring he gave me with the Bee he had engraved on it out of fun, which we had plenty of even in those anxious days. I have been reading 'Le Voyage autour de ma Chambre' with interest though it don't at all come up to my idea of what might have been made of the subject. Also 'La Picciola' with which I find the same fault though it is very pretty.[1]

17. Mary so seriously swelled in spite of Kyinsa[2] that it is necessary to give her elaterium. A disappointment about a cook has done more towards producing this access than weather. Slave to these luxurious habits of every kind so long indulged she cannot exist without a degree of personal enjoyment that would be utterly reprehensible were she in better health – poor spoiled thing – her dear little daughter is denied the necessary instruction, kept idle, moped, dispirited on account of the expense – ten francs a month not to be afforded to the drawing-master – fifteen quite beyond their power for musick – a governess, a companion totally out of the question, but two hundred francs to bring a cook from Scotland, and have her improved in pastry; so many more for nicknacks connected with confectionery or the toilette are never thought of for a moment as extravagance.

18. Mary wretchedly ill all yesterday – so ill that no one could be cross at her perverseness though she perils her life by her absurdities. I am tired inventing dishes for her – nothing is good except it belong to herself; she won't taste even; turns up her nose at what is certainly clean, good, palateable – at any rate better to take than medicine and said by her doctor to be as necessary. She is sliding back to her wine and ale, so I went down for the Doctor, who interdicted more stimulant till some nourishment had been swallowed. By coaxing, reasoning, petting, we got at different times a cup of good soup down by spoonfulls, with jelly stock in it, and she was greatly supported by it. It is very hard to

1. Two of the best-known works by contemporary writers, Comte Xavier de Maistre (1763–1864) and Xavier Saintine (1798–1865).
2. E.G. described this on 6 July 1844 as 'a French medicine lately adopted, which we hope will supercede the elaterium'.

manage her. The dose is to be repeated to-day so we have
brought the boys here to keep the house quiet for her. It is
their holiday which they would spend too noisily at home.
Mary under the influence of opium has slept through the day
and was comfortable this evening, ready for more elaterium
tomorrow.

24. To-day I have no hope; the struggle may be long but
I fear the end cannot be doubtful. No rest last night,
pain, breathlessness, swelling, how can her failing strength
support her under such continued suffering. She has had
on fourteen leeches again this morning. I have been much
interested in a French novel of the new school – 'Monsieur
de Goldon' – beautifully written, clever, witty, polished; the
first volume really good, the second perfectly ridiculous and
highly immoral. No one personage throughout the tale does
right. If such be French principles no wonder the nation
does not thrive. Nothing can thrive where manners are so
lax. A miserable sophistry usurping the place of Christian
principles; formal ceremonies instead of sober piety, impas-
sioned addresses to the deity full of worldly feeling instead of
true religious control over them; and the fear of God and our
neighbour in the place of the love of both. A set of little tales –
'La Plus Heureuse Femme du Monde,' etc. I found on poor
Mary's table, in the same seducing and immoral style the more
convince me that till religion and morality are understood and
practised in France they never can rise to greatness as a nation
or to happiness as individuals. Melancholy in reality is their
apparently gay existence; the unreflecting never enjoy; the
reflecting must, as all their lively pictures of their condition
prove, be very nearly wretched.

25. Our circle of acquaintance is enlarging. A Mr. and Mrs. Crane
from Liverpool whose cook can dress a dinner for two and
twenty people without other assistance than a girl to wash
up her dishes. Colonel and Mrs. Piper late of the 38th, and
Captain and Mrs. Stanhope Jones, whose card put me in mind
of the Smith Bouveries. I don't know why Bouveries should
sound so fine and Smith so humble. The armourer though
an artisan was at least better worth descending from than the
keeper of a cowhouse. Mr. and Mrs. Cowhouse would sound
anything but aristocratick, and so for all I know Jones may

analise better than Stanhope which the note of some future antiquary may deduce from the coachmakers with the usual accuracy of those learned in research.[1]

29. I hear a bad account of poor Mary – a bad night. I saw her yesterday in the afternoon, and hope to get to her this morning for I am better. It is a satisfaction to see her though I can do no good. She is hardly able to speak. The wine ordered by the Colonel has come from Jersey; the duty amounts very nearly to the price so I hardly think anything will turn out cheap, but the Marsala. Mrs. Lyon has written to me for information about this place which I have given very honestly. I do not wish her to come here for her inconsiderate way of speaking makes so much mischief. It is a great pity for she is a kind-hearted person and extremely agreeable. There really is no greater pest than a gossip particularly when quick-tempered enough to take offence easily and uncontrouled enough to burst out upon the first comer with all the fretfulness engendered by irritation. I keep all mine between myself and my journal; so far fortunate; it ought not to be set down at all, and I have a great mind to resolve upon giving up the system of feelings and setting down nothing but sense!

30. Mary speechless since yesterday morning, nearly unconscious, a state of coma, increasing, from which there seems to be but little probability of her rallying; and should we wish it? No. Her sufferings are too great for any who love her to wish to see them continued. Dr. Smythe predicted step by step the certain progress of her maladies; he told us that if she lingered, which he thought she would, a fusion on the brain must ensue and would be fatal and that it would be an easy death. Easy enough for she is totally unconscious now; her face is placid; it is plain there is no suffering; she is insensible to pain or pleasure and may it be God's will in his mercy to spare her worn frame further torture and to receive her sufferings, her patience, her resignation, as adjuncts to her faith, in atonement for human infirmity. He knows her weakness, her trials and her hopes.

31. It is all over – she is gone. Between two and three o'clock this

1. A stanhope (O.E.D.) is a light, open, one-seated vehicle originally two-wheeled; it was first made for the Hon. and Rev. Fitzroy Stanhope (1787–1864).

afternoon her sufferings terminated. I had left her to write to Jane intending to return to watch the effect of two large blisters one on the chest, the other on the shoulders. Colonel Smith said he would go up in the meanwhile and he was thus present at her death. She never recovered consciousness; suffered no pain; but her breathing became difficult and her features altered a good deal. Janey and Tommy were in the room; I forget the rest. I am thankful we are here to receive the children, to help Mr. Gardiner, to comfort and be comforted. My kind Hal has taken all painful preparations upon himself. I am well enough to manage all other arrangements, and everybody is very kind, particularly the little Doctor who is really unwearied in every endeavour to be of use. I have seen her body – stretched on a narrow mattress laid upon the floor in her nightdress with a muslin handkerchief over her face and poor Sarah sitting beside it. Mr. Gardiner also keeps watch there. To-morrow the expression will be more agreeable: it don't look like *her* now; it is not her; the poor worn remains of her once beautiful body, the case no longer wanted for the freed soul which dree'd its weird[1] indeed here and has left few equals behind.

The youngest of the three fair daughters of Rochiemurchus – the pet of the family – the beauty of the North. I always think of her as in our highland days, with her pretty manner and her pretty smile tripping down our barrack stairs something like what one could fancy Flora. I am an old woman now and these fairy visions of my youth should long ere this have faded before the more everyday scenes of this working day world. But there they are – deep in my heart of hearts – something like nothing else. The air and the hills and the lakes and the forest and the heather and the people and their clannish attachment, their poetry, their pibrochs, – all come back upon me in moments of sadness as if we were all young and gay and together again. And my poor father is in India occupied about anything but the scenes I so well remember; William has forgot his sisters; John has become selfish, indolent, eccentrick. My mother who has most heart

---

1. To submit to one's destiny, to suffer the
   consequences of any act (S.N.D).

of all is dying herself away from all but poor Jane whose warm feelings I do value and cling to tho' she is altered from what I have known her. It was Mary who understood me and whom I understood – Mary, full of faults, for she was human – pure and innocent and lovely compared with me who judged her. The first to go amongst us. May God preserve me to look after her children. Hal brought them home with him. They are nearly as dear to me as my own. I have them all to care for – mine and hers, and a sober kind of happiness before me. With the best of husbands and every comfort I have no right to repine at my lot, nor do I – far far from it – but I would fain have had Mary spared to me – God forgive me for the murmur.

SUNDAY, AUGUST 4. This day week I was very unwell, unable to go early to my dear Mary, and when I did go she was suffering under the dreadful effects of the last dose of elaterium she was ever to take. In the evening, furnished with Jane's letter, I went again and she smiled very feebly on hearing she was coming here; yet it gave her pleasure too. She was feeble from exhaustion and out of spirits at being so little decreased in size after all she had lost and all she had gone through; the water had been drawn from the upper parts but the lower portion of the stomach was as much filled, as hard as before. She revived a little before I left her, chose a pair of trowsers for Tom, bade me leave Jane's letter for Mr. Gardiner to read and was pleased at hearing the clothes for the man-servant had come home. She made Mr. Gardiner read to her as usual; the chapters she asked for were the 14th, 16th and 17th of St. John. She passed a bad night. Dr. Pollard had to be sent for; pain in the lower part of the stomach, difficulty of breathing, difficulty in speaking. Monday when I went to see her she was, they said, sleeping; it was no sleep: it was very nearly insensibility; she had spoken in the night, bade the Doctor good-bye several times in a sort of whisper, and this morning had said 'don't' to Mr. Gardiner when we were putting on the leeches. We tried in vain to rouse her. Once when I said: 'Don't you know your Janey?' she fixed her fading eyes upon her daughter for a moment – it was the last effort she ever made; the rest of the day she lay insensible – neither moving as she had done so restlessly for the two last days nor giving other sign of life but breathing heavily. Tuesday it was the same. Wednesday she died.

And after she was gone, and after I had seen her lifeless body stretched on the narrow mattress laid upon the floor in the little sitting-room she had furnished so prettily and which amid all her sufferings seemed always cheerful while she was there, and when I had looked for the last time on the face already changing, I went down to Mr. Gardiner and begged of him to have her opened; then accompanied Colonel Smith to buy the cloth to cover her coffin; gave his orders to the man who came to measure her remains; and bought in shop after shop the mourning most necessary for the two families; between whiles comforted the children, not by words, for they fail, but by occupying them. The girls we set to prepare their gay wardrobes for being packed away. Tom folded and sealed the many letters I had to write; the two little boys watered flowers. Colonel Smith had many persons to see for Mr. Gardiner, the French making as great a business of a death as they habitually do of every incident. It must be notified to the Mayor. A certificate of the fact must be procured from a physician, leave requested for the interment. The ground has to be purchased and conveyed in regular legal form to the purchaser; this is the perquisite of the hospital who furnish at a very low rate all that is required for carrying the body to the Cemetery and depositing it in the grave.

Thursday he and Mr. Gardiner had official business still to finish. I had the children and more letters and mourning preparations and arrangements for a collation on the funeral day. Mr. Loire[1] took his sketch very early for the features were fast disappearing – the moddler could not work from them which has been a cruel distress to us all. We had hoped for a *head* from which we could all have had a cast. The surgeons came at noon and were occupied some hours – luckily Mr. Gardiner was out. I had taken the children to

1. A Pau painter who went on to produce portraits
    of E.G. and her Colonel; according to 'Künstler
    Lexikon', there was an artist Léon Henri Antoine
    Loire, who lived from 1821 to 1898.

see him the evening she died and we staid and drank tea
with him. Miss Hart took them up this evening and they
were permitted to see her in her coffin and to touch her hand.
Friday I went up after cutting out all the hatbands with Miss
Hart and getting all other requisites necessary, in order; and
I found Mr. Gardiner watching by the coffin in a pitiable
state of distress. Seeing me did him good for it brought him
tears. We wept together till the pain of the grief was abated
and then we talked ourselves calm; for more than an hour we
talked of her; of all she had suffered; of all that she had been
spared; of her goodness; of her hopes; of what remained for
us to do for her sake. I left him when Colonel Smith came;
he was composed and remained so.

Miss Hart was in Janey's room to put the bands on all the
hats; the gentlemen were all ushered into the drawing-room
where a neat collation was spread – wine, coffee, fruit, cake
and sandwiches. As they entered they fitted themselves with
gloves a pile of which were placed on a small table covered
with a cloth in the lobby. And Sarah, whose mourning was
ready, received the hats and carried them upstairs to Miss
Hart; Mr. Hickey called here for Colonel Litchfield and the
poor boys and I took care to be home before as I dreaded
this moment for dear Janey. On their arrival at the other
house the coffin was carried down and placed in the hearse.
Mr. Gardiner who had never left it took his place immediately
behind it holding Tom by the hand. Colonel Smith with
Johnny followed. Colonel Litchfield and Dr. Pollard next;
the rest of the kind persons who were so polite as to pay
this attention to a stranger followed. In front of the hearse
went Mr. Hickey and the French commissary of police; thus
they passed, all walking, round the boulevard, through several
tortuous streets to the top of the hill near the old tower and then
down the steep road into the Cemetery. Mr. Hickey read the
service remarkably well. Mr. Gardiner bore up wonderfully;
so did our poor boys. When the ceremony was finished their
father took them home leaving Colonel Smith to see the grave
filled up. I had employed this melancholy time in reading with
the three girls the funeral service. Wonderfully it soothed us
all – those beautiful words full of love and hope and comfort
of every kind calmed us quite and we fancied we had timed

our reading so that we were all praying for her we so loved together.

Saturday Dr. Pollard came to read me the report of the French surgeons. It is so far satisfactory that it proves she has in the main been skilfully treated – that Dr. Taylor had had a pretty nearly correct idea of her case – that art had kept her alive longer than anyone could have supposed to be possible from the condition her body was reduced to – and that no skill could have much prolonged her life. It also proves, poor dear Mary, that her own habits much injured her and much increased her sufferings. The heart and the liver were both organically diseased; the stomach and every passage leading to or from it was in a high state of chronick inflammation; the dropsy had reached the peritoneum membrane lining the abdomen and the chest and the brain had been suffused during the latter days; the brain was healthy, the lungs perfectly sound. The Paris doctors all thought the lungs affected; so did Dr. Taylor and therefore he kept her in the south. Dr. Smythe fancied her brain diseased. Dr. Pollard imagined the dropsy was in the womb; they were all wrong in these points; all right about stomach, heart and liver; but there was no malformation anywhere. She was a finely developed woman. I wrote more letters; went to see Mr. Gardiner and the children and found Janey calm after having visited her mother's grave. Mr. Gardiner and the boys have gone to church, so have the Colonels. Miss Hart is with Janey Gardiner. Just one little week since I sat and talked by Mary for the last time. She knew me for a moment on Monday morning – that was all.

6.   I met this in the *Scotsman* – an extract from Mr. Josephus Lilley's *Agricultural Tour in Ireland*: he says: 'The landlord must first begin to build cottages for the labourers to make them a shelter from the winter. Next, farm buildings for his tenants to protect their cattle and to store their produce. His rents would then soon be paid up in full . . . his life would then be safe were he to reside among his people . . . whom by assistance and example he would improve to the third and fourth generation . . . and he would force the neighbouring proprietors to emulate his conduct.' I like to think of my dear Hal's wise beginning. John Fitzpatrick and Michael Byrne in their comfortable cabins; old Peggy; our poor old and young

pensioners; and his helping hand to the deserving tenants. Of course much progress won't be made during our absence but it is to be hoped that between Mr. Robinson and Tom Darker they will not much fall back. Interrupted here by Mr. Gardiner who walked up into my room and sat down as he would have done in Mary's. Poor man, he is cut up much and he is anxious about his Janey as we are about ours.

7. A letter to-day from Tom Darker. Poor Mary, she used to like his letters so much. She thought them so intelligent, so much to the purpose. All is going on well; the corn crops good; potatoes and hay but middling. Mr. and Mrs. West very agreeable tenants; they want the grate and the mantel-piece put up in the large drawing-room if convenient. The new schoolmaster is doing very well – sixty children in the schools. Dempsey has begun to drain. Young William Darker gives satisfaction to Mr. Richard Hornidge and likes his place, and Tom himself is quite well.

I wrote a long letter to my poor mother yesterday, full of all the particulars that I thought would interest her. These details, though melancholy enough, will take her mind off the one absorbing fact, the death of her much loved daughter. Her mind will wake to all the circumstances attending the last days of her we shall ever mourn when perhaps she would not allow it to be diverted by any other subject; at least in this hope I have written to her fully as if I had been sitting beside her telling her all the sad occupation of the last fortnight. Yesterday, in our evening walk, we passed the Cemetery; we looked down on it from the road to Paris – a pretty oblong shrubbery with a corner at the end hedged in – all that is allotted to the foreigners – this is an advance when hereticks are admitted within the same enclosure.[1] I did not go in nor wish it. My first visit to dear Mary's grave must be alone with my husband.

8. All day almost with Mr. Loire the painter, sitting with poor Mary's clothes on helping him out with her picture. It is perfectly like, without expression – as we never saw her therefore. He has coloured the skin from mine and

---

1. This graveyard is still impeccably maintained although the nineteenth century gravestones are very worn; there is still a protestant corner.

endeavoured to correct a little of the stiffness but it don't make an agreeable portrait. That it is not disagreeable is the wonder.

9. I was amused yesterday with the little painter; he belongs to *la jeune France*, of course, there will be no old France left soon if they continue subdividing according to their present practice, and his jealousy of England and dislike of Louis Philippe for his *concessions* to our nation is something altogether quite childish. I mystified him nicely. One thing is certain and comforting – the French are advancing like their neighbours. He showed me their *Musée de Famille* on the plan of our *Penny Magazine*, quite as well and as cheaply done; their press is beginning to abound with works of practical utility for the mass of the people so that like ours uprise in time they will and if there be not room in the hive for bees and drones too the drones must go, that is all; they have had their day, done their work, and when no longer wanted must change their nature or go. Like all this part of France the painter is a legitimist. I told him he would be disappointed – Henry V[1] announcing no talent and having had a defective education; he assured me I was wrong; adversity had educated him. No Bourbon wanted for talent and that he so far understood his *métier de roi* as to have highly cultivated his memory – recollecting persons, incidents concerning them, subjects interesting to them in a wonderful manner. *Au reste* it was to be supposed he would choose his ministers well, for that there is to be a commotion at the present King's death no one here seems to have a doubt of; the Duc de Nemours is so unpopular – yet too clever for them all I believe. The Duc d'Orleans was much beloved by this vain people; he was of the Napoleon school, fond of military parade, disliking the English, and extremely affable. We are never to be forgiven for shutting up Buonaparte in St. Helena. 'Blame his father-in-law,' said I; 'it was to satisfy the Emperours of Russia and Austria and the Bourbons that that troublesome *ambitieux* was chained.' How he opened his eyes. And when I described the beauty of St. Helena which

1. The Comte de Chambord (1820–1883) was the heir upon whom Bourbon legitimist hopes rested after the death of the deposed Charles X in 1836.

I had seen, the comforts provided for the prisoner who had refused them, the gentlemanly manner of Sir Hudson Lowe whom I had known, he looked as if I were telling fairy tales.

He is a singular man this painter; he superintended the building of his good house in the Chasse, is painting it himself, doing the stucco work himself, cultivates his pretty garden himself and has it in high order with only the stout maid-servant to assist him in digging it; he keeps the courtyard as neat as it would be kept in England; he has a cage for his poultry, the wire netting woven by himself; a carpenter's shop in which he works, making garden chairs, poles, palings, etc. And as we were looking out of the window at all these neat details he pointed out to me an arbour which he had planted to shield his wife's visits to a particular spot and bid me admire his choice of *fragrant* creepers which he had selected of the strongest perfumes in order to overpower less agreeable scent!!

10. Rain again – rain for ever – it seems to follow us wherever we go and to be fine wherever we are not, for in Ireland they have had nothing but sunshine. A letter from Miss Gardiner which we received last night gives a glowing account of the state of everything – many new, many old ones back; a good general attendance and an unusual number on the books. She gave over fifteen boys to the male school which is flourishing also. Mr. Moore chose the master out of the national training school and he appears to be a very competent person. As to the lending library Miss Merrey has twenty-nine subscribers and Mr. John Robinson is just about adding to the stock of books.

Oh how I wish I were among them, but it can't be yet. We must stay here till we have paid up the expense of moving – the journey to Pau was a serious slice out of a small income even with the help of kind Aunt Bourne.[1] It fulfilled its purpose,

1. Twice widowed (her first husband, James Griffith, had been Master of University College, Oxford and her second, Richard Bourne, who died in 1829, had been Professor of Physics and then Clinical Medicine, also at Oxford), she was very generous to her family. The bulk of her fortune went to E.G. on her death in 1865.

and has besides done much for the little girls. As to my health I doubt its ever becoming much better. While in the mild South the cough was quiet but I was otherwise far from well; here I am stronger, more active, free from headaches, and coughing away busily. My dear Hal suffers here from asthma; no bad fit, but the nightly dread of one, in consequence of which feeling he has to sit up hours in an easy chair – a poor substitute for the comfort of bed. He is otherwise well; far too hungry.

13. Went yesterday to Mr. Gardiner and announced to him our intention of parting with Miss Hart; he seemed much hurt, for her sake, more occupied with the effect of this measure upon her than with our reasons for taking it; which convinces me that one of the grounds of our resolution is just. She is a very dangerous woman in any family where she has acquired so much influence. After a few minutes I explained to him that she cost us at least sixty guineas a year and saved us nothing; and this was too large a slice out of £600 for a cheerful inmate, which is all that I could call her. I added that I could hardly better employ my time while here where I have little else to do than in sitting in the room beside the girls and their masters, and in walking out with them regularly. We mostly do this now. The fag of the musick is mine, the care of the wardrobes, the looking after Jack. Little remains that would not be a pleasure to a mother interested in her children he agreed. Then I went on quietly to state that I thought her an unsafe companion for girls near womanhood: setting the opinion of the world at defiance, judging from prejudice, not from reason: idle and luxurious in her habits; restless, unsteady and flirting even with Tommy whom she allowed to take liberties with her very unseemly to my mind.

He allowed the justice of all these observations. Still I see she has great hold over him. She is a dexterous flatterer where it is her interest to make herself agreeable. He asked whether we meant to send her off at once. I said: by no means – my feelings were much too kind towards her. I intended on her closing her year with us, on settling accounts with her to tell her our circumstances no longer permitted our retaining so expensive a luxury as a governess – that here where there are good and cheap masters to teach what she was unable to teach and what the girls required to learn, we must depend on them and on my watchfulness; and that she must endeavour to procure another situation without unnecessary delay; he seemed quite satisfied but repeated that it would be a great shock to her and that he wished she had gone to Mrs. Andrewes as he had advised her. I do too, I am sure; though she would not have staid there a month. I hope she may get a comfortable place and have the good sense to keep it but I much doubt any family enduring her: her acquirements are few: she is not sufficiently educated for older girls nor sufficiently careful of younger ones; and her manners are insupportable.

I had also to speak to Mr. Gardiner about his Johnny; that boy is really an anxious charge; he has taught Jack language only used, I hear, in the lowest pot-houses among the depraved frequenters of vulgar debaucheries; and he has instructed him in particulars of such coarse indecency that I quite shook when Margaret related the conversations between these little creatures. He gave the Bible as his text book of wickedness, and the finding all sorts of horrours there justified the use of his evil chosen expressions and precocious knowledge. We cannot make out how or where he learned these early lessons in vice. Perhaps at Pau in his infancy, when utterly neglected by Miss Hart he spent his day with a perfect rabble of blackguard companions, brought home sometimes by somebody's servant, sometimes by the police; and after he was sent to an English school by his father at eight years of age to keep him out of vice came pouring in a whole host of little debts, sous borrowed of the pig woman, and spent with the cake woman, etc; his governess all this time receiving company in the drawing-room, occupied flirting with Charles Bell, ogling M. Puyoo. Alas, the ill-consequences of early want of care can be regretted but once; they influence life; poor little Jack! to think of what that little innocent mind has been exposed to; he will forget it I trust by occupying his fancy with other things. I shall keep him with myself and devote myself to his amusement – separate him entirely from his cousin. I won't give up the cousin, poor Mary's child. All I can do for him shall be done; it won't be easy, and it will require prudence; but a word in season often avails much. I fear the boy is a little hypocrite already. God help them all! Without a guide, poor things.

I had a letter from [brother-in-law] James Craig last night. My mother is bearing her sorrow almost better than Jane; they have been so long prepared for it the shock was much lightened. Colonel Smith had a note from Richard Hornidge between whom and the doctor we have got quantities of Irish news. Mr. Brown is going to let Stormount on lease to Mr. West who will build an addition to the house and Mr. Fraser will take Baltiboys off his hands. The Milltowns have lost their lawsuit with the Cootes [the fourth Earl's wife had been the widow of the third Baron Castle Coote] and have to pay £8,000, raised by insurance on her life. Mr. Butler's action for false imprisonment has gone against him and he has some hundreds to pay as damages. We shall have a thick neighbourhood on our return.

14. Letters in the evening – a very incoherent expression of deep sorrow from poor Jane, who really was overcome for the moment far more than ever I thought she would be. My mother is bearing it better; probably age may have much blunted her feelings; she may also feel that at her years with her infirmities her own time among the rest of us will not be very long, and that may in part reconcile her to the loss of those who have gone before her. I think of my dear Mary as still living, though absent; I see her constantly in her pretty dresses with her graceful manner and her sweet smile as she was at Pau in those few weeks of ease; at Malshanger when we first landed from India; in the highlands when we were all young and gay together. Dreams all – as is all past life save in the principles events have developed in us. I will steadily occupy myself about my children, bring out their talents, confirm their good inclinations and try to save them some of the many griefs we had no help to shun. The little Doctor came to tea last night and played whist – a right good game as we say in Ireland with only a little too much emphasis on some card he occasionally hazarded uncertain of his partner's accurate apprehension of its value.

18. I told Miss Hart we were to part. She received the news very well, cried more than I expected, but was perfectly reasonable. She spent the remainder of the day at Mr. Gardiner's with whom she wished to consult about her plans and she has

decided upon proceeding at once to England to visit some friends by whose assistance she expects to be soon in a good situation. Our conversation was very friendly. I really have a regard for her; I admire her talents, and I think that where she is interested her feelings are warm; her want of controul over them renders her an improper companion in my eyes, for the age at which our Janeys have arrived. She was much spoiled by the Gardiners, and situated as we were she would not unspoil with us. With strangers she will do better; her duty was to this house, her heart was in the other, too difficult a position for an ill-regulated mind. I feel for her, poor thing, beginning the world again; it is a sad life though she and all her class earn its sorrows by so misconducting themselves. No set of people are more in need of proper education than those we employ to give it. They are positively dangerous to youth in their present unreformed condition.

24. A year yesterday since we sailed from Southampton in the *Calpe*; how time flies; nearly a year, within a very few days, since I met my dear Mary after a separation of more than six years; so changed she was that I never should have known her: so worn and exhausted and faded that I never thought she would have been spared to us for eleven months more. How often during these months of anxious suffering on all parts have I thought at night I should not find her alive in the morning – in the morning that she could not struggle through till night. I shall always miss her. When we were apart we used to write so constantly that I always knew what she was doing, almost what she thought, and the blank is very dreary. Dear Jane and I never suited so well; though truly attached to each other our dispositions are so different we never were so intimate as Mary and I were. Then Jane married before all the distress in the Highlands came on – Mary and I went through it together. Her Janey will never be very interesting to me: a good sensible nice little person, but in most things taking after her father's family – little in person, neither gay nor graceful, boisterous when she is happy, moody when she is dull; without imagination, self-satisfied; not even pretty, though very nice-looking; a neat little figure; chirping away with a Cockney voice nineteen words to the dozen. Oh, how unlike her Mother – height, complexion, dignity, grace, ease,

gentleness; with a play of features and a flexibility of voice, and a mind of natural power highly accomplished, she was such as one reads of but seldom sees.

We had a letter last night from Mr. Cockburn with the balance of the quarter's pay; he tells us Tom Browne is dead. He began life the head of a respectable family, inheriting a decent fortune, the little property of Glenmore just opposite to Baltiboys, next to Russborough, with connexions able to assist his progress in any line of life he might choose to follow. But the idle Irishman fancied his small income sufficient not only to hunt and shoot and drink with but to marry on; his wife was well connected with a little money and clever but not accommodating; they lived unhappily together for several years when having squandered all his own property and all he could lay hands on belonging to her and his mother and sisters, he left her with four children to manage as she best could. The boys have all perished miserably: one was shot, another was drowned, the third has never been heard of for years and years; the daughter alone has turned out creditably, earning her bread cheerfully as a governess – she the well descended gentlewoman. The wretched man himself after various difficulties went out to Bombay in the Company's service as a common soldier. There his cousin Hal, a younger son, who never had one penny but what he made for himself after getting his Cadetship for the small fortune his father left him was never paid him, he befriended this ill-conducted spendthrift and got him on to some situation he might have done well in; but he lost it from his dissipated habits. With difficulty they got him invalided instead of being dismissed, so that he received a small pension on which with some trifling addition from your father, dear children, he has been existing for years in or near London; he married again, some low woman, who has brought him two children; he died in an hospital and Hal has paid for his funeral. A common tale of the last age; I firmly believe few such belong to this better era. What a circle of sorrow the one bad drop expands into.

29. A very miserable night and equally wretched day. Hal's neglected asthmatick symptoms have ended in a more violent paroxysm than he has suffered under for a great length of time; he became so exhausted, looked so pallid

that we had to send for the doctor who promises as is usual with him quite to restore him to health, which indeed could perfectly well be done without him had my dear husband the necessary command over himself, as we know perfectly how to treat him, ill or well, also know what produces the fit, what alleviates it and how so to live as generally to avoid the recurrence of it. The air here I do not believe to suit him, it is too keen; but he could live in it perhaps were he careful; he was quite well here when we first came while his stock of travelling health lasted and that the novelty of this scenery engaged him to take exercise in it. Then he got idle; next anxious and uneasy about poor Mary; then her death and all the melancholy consequences much affected his spirits and thus increased his indolence; as is usual he tried to recruit himself by stimulants his stomach was no longer fit to bear, and this extremity of suffering is the result. The fit will yield in time and while the dread of its return lasts he will be prudent; the doctor is of no use except to amuse him, all medical remedies being of little service; diet and regimen are all we have to trust to. It is a distressing complaint.

WEDNESDAY, SEPTEMBER 4. There is a large high unfinished house near the North Boulevard in a lane leading to the Mill which an elderly woman in black at the head of a long line of merry healthy little girls issuing from it told us was an orphan hospital. This evening we went all over the establishment to please this same elderly lady whom we took to be the matron. So she is, and the founder too, for instead of being a publick institution it is all the work of a very humble female, the daughter of a small farmer and publick house keeper close by on the Paris road. She began by instructing some nurse children of her mother's; a few neighbours persuaded her to teach a few more till by degrees she got a little school. She found all these poor children deplorably ignorant, idle, fretful and stupid. A little observation brought her to feel that the peasantry hereabouts are in the lowest state of intellect, dull, inactive, mind and body, unfit to bring up their families, not improveable themselves. She therefore felt as if she had been almost led into a position by which much good was in her power. It would be a work pleasing to God were she to consecrate herself to the education of the children of the poor and the care of as many orphans as she could manage to support.

Her father gave her her small portion on which she began – bought ground – began her building – gathered her children. She begged of the charitable and met with great success; the tradespeople trusted her and she is nearly out of debt; her fields and her garden and her court are still unenclosed; the centre of her house is still incomplete and the intended wings are only marked by the irregular stones left in the walls by the masons; the second floor and the atticks of the main building are not yet habitable; on the first floor are two large rooms, one on either side of the spacious staircase; they are lofty, airy, well-lighted, and each contains 15 small beds very neatly fitted up; 14 orphans and a young girl in charge of them sleep in each room. A small closet over the entrance no way superiour in its furniture is the founder's own room. On the ground floor are the school-room and the chapel, underground the kitchen where the children also eat and the cellar in which was a good stock of wood for fuel and two large hogsheads of cider.

The children were at supper. A large slice of bread each and plenty of juicy pears; they have soup twice a day, for breakfast and dinner, not always made of meat, 'c'est selon,' bread, and cider after dinner, bread and fruit for supper. She dresses them all alike, in a plain coarse clothing, in good order. They are taught reading, writing, ciphering and needlework, and they assist in all the work of the house and garden, her intention being to make them good servants for the rich and good wives for the poor. The day scholars of whom she has many for she says she can refuse none who want her aid only get their dinner from her. Those who can't pay her are welcome; those whose parents are better off give her help according to their means. She takes in plain work which the children do beautifully; a box for charitable contributions stands in the school-room, and she keeps fowl to supply the market with fresh eggs – these are her funds.

But she says God has helped her. She is furnished cheaply by the tradespeople. Some send her presents, such as fuel, cider, fruit, etc. And the Minister of Publick Instruction at Paris, informed by the préfet here of her undertaking, has twice sent her handsome sums of money – first 2,000 francs, last year 1600. So her building debt is nearly paid. She is not of a first order of minds – the better fitted for the low state of intellect she has to deal with – humble, patient, zealous in her good work she will greatly advance a generation and prepare a second for higher improvement. It will take many to make much difference in the dull natures here. They are below even the English. I shall never complain of the volatile, excitable Irish again. Their cleverness, and their intelligence, and their alacrity render it quite a pastime to try to direct their talents into useful channels. The apathy of the stupid race of these parts is almost hopeless. In the South they were so industrious, so cheerful, that although little educated they were quite interesting. There is nothing here to redeem want of principle, bad faith, falsehood, etc.

8. Dr. George has put off his visit to our great disappointment. Some *interesting* ladies cannot part with him before February. Mr. West wants leave to sublet our house as he has taken a lease of Mr. Brown's and enters into possession in November. The Doctor calls himself very dull and very unhappy for want of the friends he loves best, and we, were we to consult only our own inclinations, we would fly home directly. I would give up much to be there. Hal does not get on well here at all; he is very far from well and I fear the air don't suit him; he is going to battle on a little longer however in hopes to become accustomed to it as the children are doing so well here, Jancy nearly herself again, Annie thriving, Jack well, and they are all improving in other respects beyond belief, their minds expanding, their accomplishments encreasing daily. Masters are good and cheap and living moderate, and our journies have been so expensive that we require to live reasonably for a while. £600 a year goes but a small way with a family to educate and to move about with two invalids at the head of it – one of them seldom able for exertion, the other who would like to be spared much that must be taken. It is therefore of some consequence to us to remain where we are though I doubt our being able to stay.

Judgment is reserved in O'Connell's case and out of prison he must come – a sad calamity in every way – most unfortunate indeed; he and the radicals will crow, the ministers be discomfited, and agitation may recommence;

very very unlucky; three Lords for him, two against, the English judges against him.

11. There are to be very grand demonstrations of respect to the Liberator all over Ireland on occasion of his triumphal release. Most unfortunate, just as the country was forgetting him, the people all turning their minds to their business, the whole country thriving, here comes out the mischief maker to put everything into confusion again. However if the man's sentence were illegally pronounced it is all right that it should be reversed – it is only very unfortunate.

12. Bought all our wood by the help of kind old Mr. Poo – 30 *cordes* at 24 fr the *corde*[1] brought to the yard; then it has to be cut up – 2.50 a *corde* besides, making the year's firing at least £30 – dearer than Pau a little; this is however cheaper in other respects, not in the marketing much, but in style much – no men servants, inferiour ways altogether though we make ourselves very comfortable in this our lower estate; groceries are dear in France – fruit and vegetables cheap, milk and butter cheap, meat dear, here – poultry dear and bad – wine of the country cheap – furniture cheap, – crockery very dear – the shops in general all dear except the milliner's. Still for a few years' residence with children to educate this place would be cheap.

13. Tired out with perpetual annoyance about Nanon the cook-maid we first had who left us without warning a few days before her month was up. I resolved by Colonel Smith's advice to lay all my griefs before the *juge de paix* who is probably an honest man for none of the litigants are satisfied with him.

15. Politicks very quiet. Mr. O'Connell's release happening on the nativity of the virgin is ascribed to her prayers; crowds attend him to and from Mass where he goes without delay, and the Archbishops make grand discourses; he is quite in fashion again, shouts and cheers and bonfires blazing, but all quite peaceable – beautiful weather in Ireland, fine prospect of harvest, no war between France and England.

---

1. According to the O.E.D. this measure of cut wood might consist of a pile eight feet long, four feet broad and four feet high.

And for private news Peggy Allan has been discovered to have been an incorrigible drunkard for years. Robert could conceal it and put up with it no longer. So he has sent her to the highlands to her parents with her baby, entrusted his other children to the care of his nephew and his wife, and borrowed of his master the money necessary to redeem his furniture almost all pawned by wretched Peggy. Robert drinks himself more than is good for him.[1] They were all taught the vice during the negligent management of my father and mother when almost every servant we had went tipsy to bed nightly. An immense responsibility rests on the heads of a family. Young as I was when the charge of my father's devolved on me, I remember I thoroughly felt this, and laboured earnestly to do my duty in the household. I did hold the reins tight – gross cheating, open debauchery, I put a stop to, but new brooms when daughters hold them cannot always sweep their parents' chambers clean; besides want of money to pay up and discharge the ill-conducted prevented a thorough reform. What anxious days to me were those.

My work all the week has been mending, mending, the thumping style of washing keeping a needle busy. My reading has been another little book of M. Balzac's – the 'Médecin de Campagne'; so very pretty and so really *good* that I thought at first of translating it for Mr. Chambers' *People's Library*, but it is too French to suit the British taste without considerable alteration. I read very little. Colonel Smith can't bear to see me with a book. I have been playing whist instead and winning all night and every night. As my husband won't play with me he has lost all I've won so these hours of hard work have gone for nothing!

16. Poor Miss Hart went at two o'clock by the diligence to Havre – to Caen at least – from thence by water to Havre and then to Southampton, London and Norwich. What a curious creature she is. When I gave her the check for the money due to her and she perceived I had paid her up to the day she made a fuss

1. In the Memoirs E.G. explains some of the pressures that might during the family's final impoverished years at the Doune have contributed to this state of affairs: 'Our establishment consisted of poor Robert Allan who was butler and footman and gamekeeper.'

about taking it because she had not earned it; true enough.
'Oh, you must not pay me for these last few weeks, I am sure
I have hardly thought of you.' 'Not much, Miss Hart, but I
can make allowances for you and you must take your money.'
'I'll take it as a present then – a kind present which I didn't
deserve.' She had indeed spent her whole time at the Gardiners
coming here but to sleep. The Colonel was so extremely ill as
to occupy me completely day and night. Margaret, my right
hand, has been laid up with a sore finger and a bilious fit;
the kitchen-maid had left us without warning so that we had
a servant less. A little attention from Miss Hart to the children
would have been an assistance under these circumstances. I
did not expect it, knowing how little she thinks of her duty
in comparison with her pleasure, but her conduct confirmed
the wisdom of parting with so ill-regulated a character.

20. Such a change, so very very unhappy to me yet so necessary.
Hal had a miserable night, just in bed one hour from eleven
to twelve and all the long cold weary time from thence till
morning he sat in dread of a severe attack; he is thin, so thin,
and he looked so ill. I came down to breakfast quite uneasy.
Colonel Litchfield went up to see him and he determined to
carry him away and they are gone – the one to Jersey to try
the air of Dr. Eckford's house, which suited him before, the
other to go on to London. What the result will be I know not.
A letter from Dr. Eckford says he expects Dr. Robinson to
join him and accompany him over to Avranches. I hope he
may have prevailed on George to move as he will then see Hal
and prescribe for him; no one else ever does it so successfully.
Oh how I wish I were at home in our own nice house beside
our best and kindest friends. I never felt so desolate as this
evening; it was so hard not to be able to go with him, to
see him in the rain mount to the top of that nasty diligence
without the slightest protection from the weather with his
liability to cold and I cannot hear from him for days with
these roundabout posts. I did not wish him to stay to suffer
but his going looked very wretched.

24. Tom has been reading to us from the Irish paper where it
is very well given the Queen's landing at Dundee and her
progress to Blair Athole. It puts me in mind of my visit
to Edinburgh two years ago only this is very much better

managed by the authorities and much more comfortable to the Queen, being altogether without parade – a private visit of her and her husband to their Highland shooting quarters. The weather was beautiful, so that the crowds on shore and the thousands who ventured to cover the beautiful Tay with gaily decorated boats, had no drawback to their loyal pleasures. A fine procession of burghers, trades and officials met her landing. The 60th Rifles commanded by Mrs. Eliot's brother Major Crowdie received her. The Prince had her on one arm, the little Princess Royal in the other hand; they walked up the steps and along the quay some way to their carriage amid acclamations which actually rent the air so charming was the family air of the party to people who had never seen their sovereign since the Stewart days. The Scots Greys escorted her to Dunkeld where she lunched and showed her daughter to a mob in extasy, and on to the gates of Blair where she was made over to 200 Highlanders accoutred in their own style half of them with Lochaber axes, the other half with broad sword and target. They will be half wild with delight – glorious days for the hills and the glens and the beautiful North – never to be forgotten by the enthusiastick inhabitants. The morning after her arrival she was out walking in the grounds I don't know how early.

We have had a rainy afternoon again, have not seen Mont St. Michel since noon. I should like the look of that curious place better could I get the convicts confined there out of my head. The silent system does not work so well with the French as they say it does with the Americans; the prisoners here frequently go deranged; none leave the penitentiary as strong in mind as they entered it; and few are reclaimed by the discipline to lives of virtue afterwards; the mark is set upon them and they cannot recover cast. Originally this rock was a religious stronghold. Part of a very fine old Cathedral crowns the very top where mass is still celebrated for the few inhabitants and the convicts. A sort of castle wing, once the Abbot's house, is occupied by the superintendent of the jail and the State prisoners, now only twelve in number, confined for various terms according to their degrees of offence, some alone, some in pairs; they are well lodged, are permitted any luxuries they can pay for and are allowed for an hour every day to walk in what was once the Cloisters, from which however, there is no view as they are covered. Some pots of flowers carefully tended in this melancholy place reminded me of 'La Picciola.'

What was the monastery is the penitentiary. Large, airy, comfortable dormitories above, workshops below. An aisle of the old Cathedral is the eating-hall opening on to a platform where the convicts walk for half an hour after each meal. A nunnery lower down was burned and not re-built. A narrow street only wide enough for foot-passengers, consisting of near 80 mean houses winds round the foot of the rock. A barrack stands on a ledge above the gateway, and the Commandant has a good-looking house near the site of the ruined nunnery within the walls of which he has a garden. Many little patches of garden are lighted on here and there, and this little fortress not bigger than the Bass in the Firth of Forth contains with its guard of soldiery above 1,000 souls. The formalities required before getting in, the many steps to mount, the guard, the great gates, locking and unlocking with enormous keys for every visitor, all impose on the senses and add a gloom to a place miserable enough from the guilt there expiating. Petty theft is the general crime, but there are hardened sinners there. One or two rather in favour let out to carry loads, working as masons, carpenters, tailors, were merry-looking enough; others as we glanced at them through the windows of the workroom very forbidding. They weave a great deal of good cloth and on leaving the prison get a share of their earnings. It is better to begin with the children – save all this expensive machinery of punishment and cover the land with infant schools. Two or three generations hence human nature would be altered.

25. I like my quiet hour at night after the busy day for though we do not seem to do much, the children and I, yet being always together the hours appear fully occupied. We take our time all of us in the mornings for these are our holidays. Breakfast at half past eight, read two chapters in the Bible afterwards; then the girls write. I am forming their hands as Mr. Scott formed mine, and they will both write well; then they cipher; then they do translation of French or Italian as may be parsing a sentence accurately; then they run out in

the garden after a light luncheon of fruit and bread. If it rain they work and read. We have neither musick nor drawing with us. Johnny reads a paragraph from the *Rudiments of Knowledge* over several times till he has any new words perfect and the sense quite in his head; spells a line, does a sum and writes a little. In the afternoon he reads a page of something amusing and we have a little talk about geography or metals or animals or something; the girls read a little French or Italian. We dine at three; walk out till dark; crack our walnuts round the fire, drink tea at half after six, read and work till bed-time; this is our life. We have the Notte Romani – Silvio Pellico – Madame de Sévigné – L'Esprit des Lois – Shakespeare – the *Edinburgh Review* – and the Club periodicals. To-night they read each a tale out of Bentley's Miscellany and very well. I finished two Acts of Twelfth Night which was greatly admired.

I had a letter this morning from Dr. Robinson. Mr. Frazer comes again to Baltiboys. Dempsey is draining. James Ryan has built himself a nice slated house. There is no agitation; the people are quiet enough though poor enough, patiently waiting in hopes something may turn up for them. *He* sends a prescription to complete Janey's recovery and seems to think little of the Colonel's asthma – he did not see him suffer. Not a word from Hal. Was there ever such a post? Just six hours distance and it takes four or five days to hear from Jersey. I like the Hermitage so much I wish that we could stay in it. The pretty walks all round, the nice gardens which we are to begin immediately to put in order, and the small warm cheerful house. With better servants we could be very comfortable here.

That little wretch has been wearing all the children's stockings. A suspicious circumstance determined me to have her room in town searched: eleven pairs of stockings, two pairs of sheets, a brush of Colonel Litchfield's, a glass, a bottle once having contained wine, etc., etc., greeted the astonished eyes of Margaret. This agreeable discovery having completed a long list of errours, I feel no compunction at having dismissed the useless idle monkey. Maybe we shan't replace her with better but we must try. The servants are said to be bad here and we have had three wretched specimens. Victoire told us one day she was going the next, and she went. She had got herself a place she liked better in a nursery and suddenly found our work too heavy for her. And I thought her slow and idle beyond bearing.

26. A letter at last from my attentive husband. He got quite wet unprotected from the weather on Friday evening as it poured rain during the whole journey; but he had no asthma till he was getting up in the morning to go on board the steamboat – a slight attack only then which he drove away with black coffee; he has had none since to speak of though he has been eating and drinking whatever came in his way, but he has a bad cold in the head, no wonder. Dr. Eckford is ill too, and Colonel Litchfield gone to London. My affectionate husband waits till the *Tuesday* to write to me. I all the while half fevered with anxiety about him. I shall never again take the slightest interest either in his asthma or his travels, throwing away my feelings upon such an icicle – he had best remain where he is so comfortable – nobody wants such a piece of apathy here. I went in for this amiable letter having some calls to make and some debts to pay.

   There is also a letter from John Robinson. The harvest is good: nothing failed but the hay which is dear in consequence; people he thinks ready for any mischief and not unlikely to turn on O'Connell if *repeal* so long promised be delayed again. O'Connell supposed to regret being let out so inopportunely, not knowing how to amuse his mob, dreadfully frightened of the volcano he has lighted and a little uneasy at his own position. The rent comes slowly in – how will it all end? Pat Quin obdurate: he will neither pay his rent nor give up his land on the kind conditions proposed; so he must be put out; and with his vindictive disposition this will be a disagreeable business.

27. We called two evenings ago at our Landlord's Colonel d'Almar's to ask for an under gardener to come and put our garden to rights here. An old man in a white nightcap who told us he had served his master upwards of forty years took us all over the pretty well-kept grounds. The French keep their servants for ever, work them well, pay them little, scold them immensely, but they must use them kindly for much attachment subsists between them. The old gardener lives in a good house with a large garden attached, and he promised me the services of the porter who is accustomed

to the employment and lives with his wife at the gate in a smaller house with a suitable garden. Yesterday there came a little dried up old man to beg we would employ him to arrange our garden; he had dressed the vines for twenty years and more and he would not like anyone else to touch them. He ravelled on in the usual style about his capabilities, but knowing them all now, I trust none of them, and entrenched myself in the utmost deference to the advice of M. le Colonel, who there-upon came to visit me to-day. He is an agreeable old man, tall and large and stately rather; he complimented my daughters, asked many questions, gave us his own family history, and then walked round the gardens, pointed out and named the finer kinds of pears, told me when they would ripen, lamented the state things had fallen into from neglect, said the porter should come and trim the potager [kitchen garden] for twenty-five sous a day – he had asked thirty – that he should bring women to weed at eighteen sous – he had told me twenty – that the boaster should attend to the wall fruit and must have thirty sous and that two francs worth of gravel should renew all the walks.

30. No letter from *him* again – a week since he wrote – twelve days since he left us and he has written once, but I must not be unreasonable; he is quite well, Colonel Litchfield assures me of it – happy and busy and hates the trouble of writing; only he did not use to be so indifferent. As women grow old they should expect to lose power, prepare for a change in the sentiments of their husbands and submit to it as to their fate – a useful lesson perhaps though not a very pleasant one – proving that personal charms have much to do with the love of one sex for the other and that no other qualities will make up for their failure. We are not impressed with this sufficiently. Yet after all this philosophy if I find he has written and that his letters have miscarried I shall dress him up again in a superiority to all other husbands and restore him to favour with little questioning.

On looking over my journal for the month I find I was quite wrong about my father's birthday; it was the 21st not the 19th. Old age is beginning to play tricks with my faculties, memory in particular. I cannot for instance recollect any new name now, nor catch it up as formerly. I must have it repeated, perhaps spelt before I got it rightly; then maybe forget it after all. Also I feel deafness beginning and stiffness of the joints, and I walk heavily though not *leisurely*, for they accuse me of carrying the post. I sometimes think can this be me. All the atoms that were me must long ago have dispersed in different directions and been replaced two or three times over by some heavier sort clogging the soul and altering all. Youth is very lovely, very gay and very bright, and very cheerful and very happy; even its sorrows are light; old age can but be venerable; its enjoyments are very sober; while the intellect remains it still possesses a very high order of pleasure, but when that begins to fail, existence but drags along. I never regret that my life will not be a long one; I only wish to preserve it till the children require me less, till the girls have got over the first few years of their womanhood, and Jack either been enlisted under the care of premature good sense, or gained some kind protection through the dangerous season of opening passions. At ease about their happiness, I hardly care how soon I am required in my next existence. My part is nearly over in this, and I dread living to be a burden to my husband – to be what dear Mary was for so many years to poor Mr. Gardiner. But it is not my will, but *thine*, I have but to say Amen.

TUESDAY, OCTOBER I. We took a nice walk to-night through lanes and fields and woods with rocky pathways as far removed apparently from the hum of men as is the happy Queen in the wilds of the highlands. We came upon one of those fountains where the washerwomen in cold water so unmercifully beat our linen; they stoop round the squared pit thumping the wet clothes after soaping them against the wooden frame of the fountain assisted by a flat *butte* [mound], just as in the South they went on at the side of the river at Pau, or in India on the broad stones near the streams. After this there is a grand boiling in wood ashes, to burn the things white instead of bleaching them. And they don't do them up well here; they do nothing well hereabouts; very stupid backward people. Our Queen leaves Blair Athole to-day. One paper observes curiously enough that it wants but one year of the century since it was a sovereign of a different race that the Highlanders guarded so jealously. Who in that '45 could have predicted that in the next, the lads from 'the Tummell and the Garry' should be leading a Queen of the house of Hanover over the Athole hills in love and reverence and that there in the stronghold of the Stewarts she should come to receive from Athole's Duke the white rose he holds his lands by offering – or that the heir of those princely glens, and the Princess Royal of England should be playing there among the wild heather together. Strange times but improving ones.

4. A letter at last from Hal. There is only a post twice a week from Jersey. Poor Hal, he got my three letters all in one day – last Saturday; so he calls me unreasonable for not allowing for this chance and for not knowing how irregular the post is. I knew nothing, and judging by the time it would take for a person to go from here to Jersey, six hours, I did not suppose the post would take six days – they do things so well in France. However I restore him to favour, though he ought to have written by Grandville last Friday, whether he were well or no. I should have been less anxious to have heard of a little asthma than not to have heard at all. My good-humour is restored nevertheless and if he comes home tomorrow he shall be quite forgiven.

6. A grand agricultural meeting at Naas; to believe the report all the finest specimens of the animal kind have been *achieved* by the members; they praise each other's property up to the skies, dine all together, gentlemen and farmers, and part in high glee. A regular system of such meetings is a better check to Repeal than all the soldiery.

11. Hal returned – really much better – not looking so well as I could wish, but better than when he went away; he has got a prescription which acts like a charm; he never yet was ordered anything that proved so successful. It is stramonium[1] tobacco and poppy seeds in equal parts smoked through a common pipe; it relieves him immediately and entirely, and hitherto has not become weaker in its effects from use.

12. Hal passed a good night; his prudent way of living at present, black coffee, and this smoking mixture will certainly cure him and then this fine bracing air will strengthen him, I hope, recover him from the ill effects produced by the debilitations of the South. We must try in future to keep our hours of

1. A narcotic drug produced from the Thorn Apple.

study sacred. Our rule is to have our 'Chapters' read and our breakfast over by nine; then to twelve we are busy. Janey practises an hour while Annie writes her copy and her exercise and Jack reads, spells, writes and ciphers. The next hour Janey and Annie reverse their employments and Jack is off. The third hour is singing half an hour each, sums and reading aloud. Till four we had for exercise and dinner, and then the three hours of musick again, more than we mean to give to this charming accomplishment by and bye; but while we have the master we think it right to work for him. While one plays the other draws, while one sings the other reads to herself. We vary the readings and the exercises daily to take in French, Italian and English, and vary the subjects too, and on M. Moulin's days we now get an hour of work, needle work, for each at his house while the other is playing; and we have to give up the second *lesson* of singing though they often sing for their own amusement after tea. Jack also loses his second lesson of reading on these days. We can't overtake all, and walking in and out again takes up time for it an't enough *walk* alone. The dancing master has come who will still further derange us, but he is very necessary, and an Italian is come, an excellent one, it is said. How shall we manage to have him and M. Loire too. Without a room in the town I do not think we can do it. Too much to do is just as hurtful as too little,; too many different masters cannot be properly attended to. I had intended devoting this winter to musick and drawing because we can't promise ourselves these advantages at home, and six hours a day is quite enough work. Kalkbrenner's exercises are fatiguing.[1]

27. I get no time now for my poor journals. The kings and queens travel about unnoticed by me. Mr. O'Connell bites his nails and quits repeal without one comment. Willie Cumming at Inverary meets the young Marchioness of Lorne and all the grandeur that welcomed her bridal progress to the Highlands, nay he sat at the same table with the Duke of Cambridge and danced with the still lovely Duchess of Sutherland, without remark of mine. Now the weather has changed, and we thought

1. Christian Kalkbrenner's 'Traité d'harmonie' was published in 1803.

we were poisoned by some horrid acid in the shape of salt. Yet I had no time to dilate on these exciting subjects.

A look at the newspaper to see how the world goes is a treat now but occasional though I have contrived to skim over two rather amusing novels of Mr. James's, in which there are interesting stories, much good moral, many excellent passages, amid a deal of nonsense. The 'Ancien Régime' and 'The Gypsey.'[1] The Book Club is a great addition to us; besides the periodicals it has many volumes worth reading. We have the Dublin University Magazine to-night always good. I had a nice letter from Jane Cooper [a former governess] quite ready to return to us and full of news, and I have been writing to Ogle Moore about my boys' school which has failed under a Protestant teacher. Mr. Germaine[2] is opposed to all education, the people so difficult to satisfy with a good one, there are so many conflicting interests and such a variety of prejudices to encounter that I doubt much being done in our absence. Still we must try and keep it on. Every little helps and if they won't learn from a Protestant we must give them a Roman Catholick trained by the Board and of course in a degree enlightened. We can only work with the tools we can procure but a skilful hand can do much even with bad instruments. As to the *real* religion of either sect I look upon them both to be much on a par – the one as far out as the other, but the political bias is a different thing – priest worship more dangerous; then to cure these evils we must enlighten the people, raise them into having opinions of their own, into judging for themselves, into reflecting, comparing, etc. A boy five or six years in a national school though under a papist teacher will be several degrees nearer a rational being than his father was ay or his Protestant neighbour of the Orange cast. Storm if you please, my dear

1. George P.R. James (1799–1956) was a prolific, mostly historical, novelist (he published over one hundred); his achievement was recognised when William IV appointed him his Historiographer Royal.
2. Ogle Moore was the somewhat feeble Church of Ireland Rector in Kilbride and Arthur Germaine the Roman Catholic priest in the neighbouring parish of Blackditches; in their different ways, each had taken up a good deal of E.G.'s time.

husband, passion and prejudice are the children of ignorance, says an old fable I learned in my youth.

30. My poor journal! It is sadly neglected. The little girls occupy all my day and the evenings are short for we go to bed early and there is always some job of work to do, or musick, or whist, or backgammon or something. A bad end to October. Janey is far from well (either), so unwell indeed that I have had to put her under Dr. Pollard who is considered very successful in his treatment of young ladies at her time of life. I think myself she wants her Baltiboys life – her poney and the hillside, and the large airy house with its various conveniences; however, these being for the present unattainable we must submit to medicine with regimen.

TUESDAY. This is really the 12th November and during all these days I have never felt there was a moment for the journal. The weeks steal away with little to mark them but there is plenty to do in them. The children and I rise early and whether we go into the town or remain at home the day slips busily over. The masters are good and the pupils are coming on fairly. The book club is a great resource for those who have little to do and even we who are fully occupied find leisure now and then to peep into a good novel.

We had an anxious week with Jack. And Janey is very far from well – I have faith in no one but George Robinson and I heartily wish for her sake and her father's that we were back near him; for the Colonel is still asthmatick though this mixture that he smokes relieves his breathing effectually for a while, but it returns regularly all the same. Still he sleeps, eats and can take exercise all weathers, and he is in good spirits; the life here must be dreadfully dull for him: no wonder he is satisfied to smoke the greater part of it away. It is an odious place, this Avranches, at least as we see it, knowing none of the French and the British for the most part being little worth knowing. Mrs. Cumming dined at Major Larrell's the other day and would not go through such another evening she says if she were paid for it. No musick, no conversation, quantities of wine drank at dinner; the drawing-room full of card-tables, those who did not play betted on those who did, ladies as well as gentlemen going about jingling their purses and calling one another nicknames – Smike, Jerry – Poke, etc. I do hope we may get away from this out of the way place in May and go off home to our own nice place where there is everything to interest us and where if I mistake not we are much wanted. Not that I ought to complain of Normandy – the air appears to have quite set me up. I have not been so well for years. How happy we all are without Miss Hart; the children are as merry as crickets, a load seems to be taken off the house; latterly she taught them nothing and as she never had saved me trouble she was really a good riddance.

13. Janey too unwell to go in to the masters, Annie and I therefore went alone; the Italian is certainly deranged. The moment there is any allusion direct or indirect to the subject of his most unhappy country off he flies like a sky rocket or a lunatick; full of an extraordinary enthusiasm for some chimera these excitable creatures imagine to be patriotick liberty, without sufficient discretion in their conduct to ensure success. When the Italians deserve liberty they will achieve it; till they are sufficiently disciplined to be capable of managing themselves it is very fortunate anyone can be found to look a little after them, willing to trust his head among such distracted people. This unfortunate being Masoni and his friend Massa at Pau were as unfit to make part of any political movement as the most ragged half-cracky Irishman in Kerry; he seems to be quite capable of teaching his own language, if we can keep him from wandering to the carbonari.

18. I like those of the French I have seen much, and were we to remain here should certainly cultivate their acquaintance. It is my place as the stranger to make the first visit and Mrs. Cumming being quite willing to join me we really will get a list of the old noblesse and go and see them all. Many people of consequence whose fortunes have suffered during the convulsions of their country, unable to afford the expense of Paris, have settled here. They keep quite aloof from all government functionaries, hold all lately risen to greatness in contempt, dislike their king, dream of their fat prince of the proper branch of the Bourbons [Comte de Chambord], and pass their quiet lives in interchanging friendly visits.

30. Saturday night, November gone. Time flies rapidly indeed with the elderly, and there being little to mark it here we have no landmarks to look back upon, and our days being fully

occupied they slip unmarked away. A letter from Miss Hart to Janey Gardiner. She is engaged after Christmas at a salary of £70 in a clergyman's family, a widower, to take charge of his two younger daughters, girls of fourteen and sixteen who have four or five elder sisters. The Miss Gardiners at Twickenham procured the situation for her and luckily nobody referred to me. In so serious a business as placing a governess over pupils who are motherless I would have spoken the truth – possibly she may answer these people well. At any rate their salary should answer her and encourage her to endeavour to keep so lucrative a situation.

A letter from Tom Darker who had turned a little fortune out of the farm; he has paid all its expenses – all the school expenses, all the pensions, etc., never applied to Mr. Robinson nor touched the rent for the house, has bought stock to the value of £120 to feed upon the turnips, and has £70 in hand to meet the winter with. This is very encouraging and may bring us fairly up before the world, for our expenses here are now very moderate – £50 a month the outside and I think it possible they may be hereafter even less as we learn better how to manage, and Colonel Litchfield pays a share of this.

My picture was finished to-day. It is said to be remarkably like and is upon the whole a pretty little picture. It is not flattering certainly, therefore Colonel Smith is not satisfied. M. Loire has not the genius of Sir Thomas Lawrence to catch the best expression as it passes; he can only faithfully copy the features when at rest. At such times I am said to have a serious if not a sad air quite unlike the animated look speaking produces; this picture therefore is me as people seldom see me, as they don't quite know me, and I should say it is rather odd but very like. The dress is pretty – Aunt Bourne's silver grey tabbinet, my mother's point collar and cuffs, a small half dress cap and velvet scarf. The position easy, leaning back on a chair. It is for the little girls and cost but fifty francs. They are in hopes of prevailing on their Papa to indulge them with his. Mr. Robertson is sitting and his portrait will be admirably like. It is easier to paint gentlemen M. Loire says, added to which he gives me a bad character – perpetual motion!! and delicate regular features admitting of no poetical licences. My picture has a look of my dear Mary though her features were much more pronounced.

SUNDAY DEC. I. The last month of an eventful year. This time last year we were all in anxiety at Pau, daily, hourly; now, anxiety is over. Life is often very dull to me with every thing around me to make it cheerful. Time will bring all right. If I were more easy about my husband I should be happier here, but this asthma is sticking to him. Smoking parries the attack for the time but the disposition constantly returns, just to be driven off for a while again, and a drowsiness is growing upon him that I cannot judge to be healthful; it may be the effect of the opium, the air cannot suit him, the life he leads certainly must be hurtful: no exercise beyond the walk from here to the reading-room and a game or two at billiards; there is nothing to rouse him or amuse him or interest him here; his appetite is too good also. Billiards he is so fond of it would be hard in this stupid place to give them up and all doctors declare them to be of use to him, but I have never known them so; he was well here till he began to play, well at Pau till he began to play, and never for one day afterwards; the same at Cheltenham long ago, and he is always freer from oppressive breathing on Sunday nights. I have watched this patiently and proved it.

We had a curious sermon this evening, a set of documents read from the pulpit concerning the Bretons, our Celtick neighbours, a million of whom know no other language than the Erse. By the exertions of the British and Paris Evangelick Society the Bible translated into that tongue and innumerable tracts have been circulated among them and they are now anxious for churches and pastors of the reformed faith, a Welsh Mr. Jenkyns, not ordained, officiating at present. In many other parts of France the old Huguenots are reviving, and in Ireland *priests* are daily abjuring the errours of Rome. We of the Anglican church should purify it a little further and then bright results might follow. I had a curious conversation with M. Loire, the clever little painter on these subjects when he surprised me by his knowledge of the Scriptures and by his perfectly '*Channing*'[1] views of the doctrines of the New

1. William Ellery Channing (1780–1842) was an American Unitarian Minister and writer.

Testament. Frenchmen in general being perfect freethinkers I was unprepared for his opinions. The women hoever are wretched bigots still most of them, as in Ireland.

8   DEC. Sunday. The great occurrence of the week was a regular ball at our Landlord's. We were invited there last Monday to spend the evening and to bring the little girls, so never dreaming of more than a dozen people and anxious to see the ways of the country we all accepted. We heard during the morning that it was to be a *soirée dansante, beaucoup de monde*, etc. and I was a little startled though not in the least prepared for the whole house being lit up, four or five large rooms open and a hundred and fifty people at least in full dress most of them crowding into the largest where was the attempt at dancing. The house is very handsome. A large entrance hall where we were assisted by tidy maids to take off our wraps, a wide staircase up which a servant preceded us to the first landing where one of the handsome sons met us and giving me his arm conducted us through the crowd to his mother. The corridor was lined with sofas, the large richly fitted up drawing-room on one hand prepared for dancing, a smaller opening from it with folding door was for musick. To the left of the corridor was another drawing-room full of tables for Ecartez and beyond Madame's bed-room for the whistplayers; the beautiful bed remained and at the end of it was a door into the dressing room into which the ladies went in small parties perpetually.

All these arrangements were perfect, the lighting brilliant, the attention of host, hostess, and the two fine looking sons, to all the guests unremitting, the profusion of refreshments extraordinary. Large silver waiters were for ever performing the grand tour in pairs, the first loaded with every variety of cake and tartlet, the second full of the innocent drinks the French like so much, syrops made of different fruits, orgeat, and *eau sucrée*; by and bye came at intervals a gold waiter full of little china saucers, a gold spoon and some delicious preserved fruit in each; then a still smaller golden waiter made the round, lined with delicately cut white paper on which was laid a variety of dried fruits. And then the large salvers with the cakes and syrops came again. At last rum punch was handed all about really unceasingly and drunk by ladies and gentlemen in plenty. The whole company ate and drank enormously, seldom nodding away the service like good Mr. Balquhidder.

At twelve o'clock all the ladies were sent to *supper*; the gentlemen accompanied them to the door of a room beyond the musick room where we were all left as many as the space would contain to the care of the Messieurs des Mares, father and sons. It was Monsieur's bedroom, but the bed being in a recess was concealed by curtains; the supper table was set round the three sides of the room; the host and his sons officiating behind it assisted by several servants. All the dishes and all the candlesticks that were not silver, were gold, except for sweet things which were served off china. Soups, potted meats, pâtés, cold poultry, ham, etc. fruits and confectionery; hock, claret, champagne, beautifully arranged. After the ladies had refreshed themselves the gentlemen took their places. And before taking leave we were all carried to this same room again to drink thick rich *chocolate à vanille* out of cups of Sèvres china with gold spoons and a crisp biscuit.

The musick was admirable mostly by amateurs; the pianoforte was played by two ladies, a different pair for each set of dances all arranged beforehand, and written down on a bit of paper so that there could be no confusion, accompanied by M. de Caen on the violincello, M. Boulle on the violin, M. De Sautier on the cornet a piston, with two *artistes*, a flute and a violin to keep the *ball* going. The amateurs played admirably, all of them, and we are not in the habit of considering the French a musical people. In a small provincial Town at home I am pretty sure we could have got no *two* ladies to play as perfectly as the ten or twelve who succeeded each other so quietly, so simply, quite as matter of course, during this evening, nor almost anywhere could be displayed half such skill among our amateur *gentlemen*. It was a very agreeable evening, wanting but ice which is not made here, and less of a mob in the dancing room; a limited number of couples and no intrusion on their *chalked space* would have been a great improvement. The ladies were prettily dressed without much jewellery. A great many old women were there as gay and as gaily dressed as the young ones; ladies as plenty at the card-tables as gentlemen. Janey and Annie looked as nice as any there and danced better and danced all night; they were much remarked and Janey in particular much admired.

Mrs. Cumming put off her party on Thursday on account of the cold which really is intense; it enters every pore from all the many chinks in French carpentry with a piercing strength we Irish are quite unaccustomed to and which I hardly think was ever quite as intense to my feelings even in the highlands. The natives don't seem the least to mind it; they wrap up certainly when going out, the upper classes at least, but there sit the shopkeepers in their open shops without a bit of fire except in the *chaufpieds* [foot-muffs] and the servants run all over the town without either shawl or bonnet. Yesterday I was sitting huddled up like my grandmother and with a silk handkerchief tied over a warm cap like a Musselburgh fishwife.

Mr. Moore has written me a long letter about my school; the change of masters appears likely to succeed, at least Mr. Germaine has withdrawn his opposition. Miss Gardiner don't seem to be succeeding with her girls – in fact the thing won't do well till we are back among them all, which I am sure I wish we were. Hal's reasons for remaining abroad another year are undoubtedly good but they may be matched on t'other side. To save a few hundreds and bring forward the education of those dear girls is some moment. But the discomfort of this country and the want of us at home are deserving of consideration.

Two things much struck me at the Ball. I observed every now and then between the dance particularly half the gentlemen fussing about all over the rooms speaking to different ladies and then writing busily on small tablets they carried – they were engaging their partners for the evening. Any gentleman may ask any lady to dance, there are no introductions; it is not to be supposed that any individual would be invited whom all might not consider proper acquaintance; it was therefore sometimes necessary for the gentleman after engaging his partner to have to say with his pencil in his hand: 'Votre nom, Madamoiselle'. How odd we should think this in England. I am learning every day. I find morals strict beyond anything *in idea* – an attentive delicacy as to actions thought very innocent with us; appearances must be saved: as a whole family falls

from the imprudence of one member, disgrace clings to all
for ever from one *discovered* fault. Sin away in *secret* as hard
as they can 'tis no matter. While concealed there is no guilt.
Anything you like behind the curtain.

11. We had a dinner party here on Monday: Mr. McLeod,
Mr. Robertson, and the little ridiculous doctor who made
everybody half tipsy and himself quite so. While they were all
playing whist I was reading the *Bombay Times* and stumbled
upon a fine appointment given to my brother John almost
immediately upon his landing – Commissioner to Mysore[1]
a fine climate, great allowances and delicate employment. A
character of him by the Editor quite first-rate – the 'ablest
servant of the Company'.

There are great changes preparing in the Established
Church, the Puseyites beginning to disgust people, the
supineness of the clergy generally to irritate and the numbers
of dissenters to frighten. Reform must begin. A petition
bearing many great names has been sent to the Bishops,
but one doubts their ever doing anything unless forced to it.
The offertory about which there has been such a fuss paid
with such ill-will, extorted so peremptorily, it is discovered
has been all misapplied, instead of the poor receiving it, they
have used it for the dissemination of tracts and other sectarian
purposes which has made people furious.

15. Sunday. A pleasant change in the weather – a thaw. Still
very cold but not that piercing, stinging very painful degree
of excessive cold which paralised every faculty. Out of
doors with the exception of two days of north east wind
which rendered the air unmercifully sharp, we could keep
ourselves warm enough by exercise, for it was dry underfoot
and overhead, though gloomy. But within the house it was
wretched; not only are the walls thin, in some places there
are cracks or holes; the roof made of shingles is excessively
thin, no lathing or mortar even beneath it in some parts;
then not a window closes; every door has an open space near
an inch wide all round it. We have hung up clokes, stopped

1. As secretary to the Governor-General, he had been
   appointed Commissioner for the payment of the
   Maharaja of Mysore's debts.

cracks, etc. as well as we could for the moment and I shall take advantage of this milder weather to prepare for the next frost in earnest; the thin calico curtains, the want of carpets, the wide fireplaces altogether make a very comfortless winter residence of these pretty summer houses. It is wonderful to me how anyone accustomed to the luxury of a British home can voluntarily submit to the actual misery of a French one. I would rather myself live in the smallest of our own well built houses with but one *good* English servant to wait on me, than in these gaudy bandboxes with the ignorant, idle, dirty *bonnes* of this country and subject to the dishonesty of all around us. From the thriving merchant in the best street of the Town to the old market woman with her basket of pot herbs, cheating, extorting, lying, is their sole notion of trade, and when their extortionate demands are resisted many of them become actually insolent; like the carpenter the other day who made the most absurd demand for flooring Colonel Litchfield's room; he would give no account, so I would give no money, so there the matter rests in spite of his shower of impudence. We can't buy a nailbrush to pay for on the morrow that they don't add ten sous to the price immediately and aware they asked it from the first. Then in frosty or rainy weeks the washerwoman can't bring home our clothes; she has no fire at home to dry them with: none of them have; they put up with everything, so we must put up with everything. Charming country.

I have been wearing a warm shawl, a handkerchief over my cap and jail boots these ten days to protect myself from the draughts of icy air. The little girls even had to wear shawls, Colonel Litchfield his greatcoat, and we had the fear of want of firing before our eyes besides for the wood merchant who was bound to have thirty *cordes* delivered by the first of November has by dint of pressing messages given us five; and the woodcutter who was engaged to cut up the whole supply after working one day we saw no more of in spite of messages and Abel with the kitchen hatchet had to do his best to keep the evening fires up on Monday last; this properly represented to M. Bellais infinitely distressed him and he immediately favoured us with another day's work since when we have not seen him. Sometimes with all these and fifty

other annoyances of a like nature, the intolerable idleness of
Abel and Marie, the too often recurrence of poor Margaret's
over-powering headaches when for near two days she lays
utterly insensible, and for two more remains half stupified,
and my own sufferings from cold and discomfort, added to
the plague of rousing up the girls to exertion and of checking
Jack's almost equally tormenting activity, I sometimes feel
growing crazy, my head quite confused and temper souring.
And there that abominable husband of mine shaves away as
unconcerned, two or three hours at his careful toilette, two or
three more at his billiards, and then he eats with the appetite
of a school-boy when I can't break a bit of bread. Some of
these days I suppose I shall laugh at all these distresses: just at
present when the cold wind is whistling through every crevice
and all looks and feels cheerless, 'brighter days' seem to be a
long way off.

22. John Robinson writes again about Hal's contumacious tenant
Pat Quin who in May next will owe near £80, without the
means of ever paying one pound; he is however becoming
more tractable and will now consent if well bribed to give up
his almost ruined farm to another, even to the Colonel, and
luckily our economical living abroad has enabled us to buy
the poor ignorant ill-conducted *ruffian* out: John has £300
in hand – a new era in our affairs. Hal therefore seriously
inclines to remain here another year: it would give time
for these changes, put us fairly before the world and the
girls would continue to have the advantage of these good
and cheap masters; his health and the want of our moral
influence among our people and the uncertainty of a tenant
for the house at Baltiboys are what we have to set against
these advantages; I can't make up my own mind upon the
subject so shall leave it to chance or rather to Hal who will
decide for the best most likely without consulting me.

The newspapers . . . are principally filled with the folly of
the Bishops supporting the Puseyite absurdities of the clergy,
who think to improve the religious feeling of an enlightened
age by restoring vexatious ceremonies, useful only in times
when *forms* were requisite to keep alive the spirit of devotion,
when what was *material* only was comprehended. There must
be another reformation: we require it, a few more years will

see it: a quiet revolution, as much needed as the former tempest.

Still murders in Ireland, misery beyond idea in London; more, much more, however, done to relieve it than used to be.

Commerce is steadily reviving; the increase in the Customs is again most cheering, peace and quiet everywhere; so they who have nothing better to do may rail at our Sir Robert as they of another peaceful time railed at the great man it is said he studies from. May he vex them for *twenty-two* years![1] They hardly deserve it.

I have been vexed in my kingdom too – plagues everywhere. Our washer-woman begged we would recommend her to Mrs. Cumming since when she has been getting very careless with us. Mr. and Miss White having also employed her she has thrown us up not wanting us and the distance we live at made our business over fatiguing to her. What she wanted was a bribe instead of which I have given her a successor who may probably use us as cavalierly after a while though at present she promises well. Then Abel and Marie are so careless and so idle. We give them double what they would get in a French family yet they don't serve us one bit the better, on the contrary; Marie would get six or eight francs a month; we give her twelve, which is more than the best cooks get though very moderate ones ask us fifteen. And how wretchedly they live – soup made of coarse vegetables, bread and grease for breakfast, the same for supper, soup and bouilli for dinner, with two *maigre* [lean] days every week; with us, whatever is going: tea, coffee, ragout, etc. The French say we spoil them and they never get a place after leaving us. Seven thousand francs or £280 is the average of French incomes here. There are families which are richer, many poorer. We don't expect to do without spending almost double so little do we understand their economy, or rather so much higher is our idea of comfort.

1. William Pitt the Younger was Prime Minister for
   this length of time, most of the years 1783–1805;
   Sir Robert Peel's second ministry at this stage had
   only another eighteen months to go before it sank in
   the aftermath of the repeal of the Corn Laws.

We could not half starve our household, sell our cast clothes, underclothe the poor servants, go without fires. Our habits are quite different in almost every essential, our morals too. And I suppose we are happier as we can occupy ourselves without frivolous excitement and are most of us independent of the worry of their little attempts at gaiety.

24. Christmas Eve. How the years fly, so quick as we grow old. In my youth a year was an age; now, it seems but a small portion of the small space yet allotted to my days on earth. And how much seems to remain to be done in that little time to come; how little to have been done in all the time passed. And the time of the world itself almost appears to march in the same progression. All the ages past hardly developed the genius of humanity as have the few years of my individual recollections. Our world in my childhood and our world in my decline of life are a thousand years apart, from the improvements we are to measure existence by. Above all, far above the progress of science, we may hail the progress of virtue. A more benevolent as well as a more enquiring spirit is abroad – tenderer feelings to our kind – juster notions of our duties, a more rational estimate of our relative positions, is beginning to prevail in the different societies of our race. *Truth* has dawned; it will rise, encrease, and brighten into perfect day. Knowledge is but Truth and Truth is Power – infinite, eternal, that cannot fade away.

25. Christmas Day. The first that finds a break among us. I have lived forty-seven years and never till this year have I had to miss one of the band that played around my mother's knee. We grew up, we five, together. I was twenty-eight when Jane left us – married and left us. Still there she was for us to drink her health and happiness on Christmas Day. I was thirty when my father carried my mother and Mary and John and me to India leaving William behind to begin life amidst a thousand difficulties. John went to Bengal, Mary married and returned home. I married, and since then I have never spent one Christmas with any of them. We are never all to meet in the world again, and we must look to further breaks, prepare for them. I should be thankful, and I am thankful that so many are still left – that we were all spared so long, for it has been permitted us to remain to beyond middle life without having had to mourn for one departed. We were

widely scattered yet we were all there. Alas that is over –
the one most loved has gone the first, almost the youngest.
I must turn to the next generation, think of all the happy
young hearts rising round us and take care to keep sorrow
from them as long as possible.

29. Sunday. I have been at home nursing the remains of a cold
and reading in these idle days all sorts of unconnected works.
'Feats on the Fiord,' a Norwegian tale by Miss Martineau,
prettily written, interesting from the novelty of its pastoral
manners, describing scenes in every way so unlike any to
which we are accustomed. It is the eighth number of Knight's
Weekly Something, a well printed, convenient sized volume
offered for one shilling intended as well for the instruction
as the amusement of the lower ranks.

Another of these is really a curious production – 'Mind
among the Spindles,' a collection of essays written by the
Factory girls at the mills of Lowell[1] in America, very slightly
altered by the Editor and proving a height of intellect in
cultivation there quite astonishing; it is but a smattering of
knowledge they may have, with some absurdity and much
pretension; but tastes and habits and abilities are forming there
in the quiet evenings of study after the turmoil of the day's
hard work that must have an extraordinary influence upon
the following generation, the more particularly as these young
people seldom remain to waste their energies of mind and body
by a life of drudgery in the atmosphere of a cotton mill; they go
there only for a few years for the purpose of earning the money
necessary for some purpose dear at heart, and then improved
by the regularity required by their employment the industry
and the activity necessary to their advancement in it, and the
knowledge they gain in the Lecture Rooms, they return with
good health, light hearts, a bank book and minds elevated to
a higher range of feelings, to diffuse better means of happiness
around them. If there is no imagination in the tale, this will
really end in a moral revolution.

The rest of 'Martin Chuzzlewit' almost superiour to the
beginning. A number of Tait's Magazine in which an article

1. See her comments on Charles Dickens' reactions to
   these essays (21 March, 1845).

on the 'Politicks of the New Testament', a startling title, quite took possession of me and so I have read it twice. Not exactly correct in all his deductions, Truth is the writer's guide, the eloquence irresistible. October's *Edinburgh* has two good articles; the early ministries of George III in which is much that is fine, and a short notice of Young England, rather amusing. These and my *Feuilleton* [light novel] have made me quite idle. I have mended certainly but in these my holidays made nothing.

Yesterday I had a long walk with Mrs. Cumming and Mr. White; we called on Mrs. Wright, and we looked at a good many pretty prints in Des Jardin's shops. French *drawing* is as perfect as French *painting* is the contrary – nothing can be prettier than their lithographed sketches. We also took tickets for a concert which promised well from its programme, sanctioned of course by the Colonel who all smiles with his cue in his hand bowed assent with an air of good humour that Mrs. Cumming said proved success at billiards; yet as usual he meant nothing; he never meant, he said, to go, so I could not, nor the children, and I had to write to say so, a little loth, for I love musick, and I thought it unhandsome to leave my friend in the lurch with her box at the theatre empty though I sent her the price of our tickets honestly – ten francs for those delusive smiles. Everything always turns out for the best. It rained heavily after tea; we should have been very uncomfortable had we gone, perhaps have caught cold.

Mrs. Wright told us a tale of Mrs. Moggridge that brought all my poor mother's years of trial back to my mind. The same story though a different cause. Instead of electioneering expenses, swindling agents and neglect of business as in our case, in hers, horse racing, high play, and an extravagance almost reckless, has surrounded her and her eight children with misery. The estate is in the hands of Trustees who allow Mr. Moggridge a small annuity; he cannot therefore pursue his mad career in the same sphere as heretofore; but in this his humbler state he continues it in a lesser way, while debts are gathering anew, children are growing up, and difficulties of every description encreasing.

It forcibly brought back to me our two or three last years

in Edinburgh, our two or three last years in the Highlands, the many painful struggles, the many bitter scenes, the many many sorrows she and I went through together. Mine was a youth of adversity, a season of very sore trials, on which from my present calm I can look back with thankfulness for the good lessons that it taught me. We are too apt to grumble at the little crooks in our own lot, and not to be sufficiently grateful for being spared the serious distresses in our neighbours. My poor mother's years of difficulty, this poor Mrs. Moggridge unable to procure the necessaries for her family, or even to stop for a few weeks their more clamorous creditors except by the help of these debasing raffles, and cheerful Mrs. Wright with an idiot daughter and a half idiot husband; there is no need to go on, the world is full enough of misery, we have but to open our eyes to see it.

Mr. White and I had a long conversation during our walk upon the statisticks of crime – no less a subject; he is rather of the evangelical sect in church matters and he is amazed to find that in this dancing, singing country where the priest keeps the conscience and reflexion to the mass of the people is unknown, crime is but as one to ten, compared with England, proving, said I, that the English are too ignorant in matters of religion as in other things to be trusted out of the leading strings of priestly management; this struck him and we talked on – neither of us recollected the Irish, clever, pretty well informed and priest-ridden to the full as many crimes as the English. Mr. White lectured me on the novel-reading permitted at Mr. Gardiner's. It is not good as an occupation certainly, over-exciting and enfeebling the mind and indisposing it for better food; but a good novel now and then is a good auxiliary in education. There is a good *morale* running through our modern novels and I have no objection to them now and then.

The girls are quite happy at home, as merry as little crickets and they never pout when denied a visit though they very much enjoy the change as is natural to all young things, more particularly when so much made of as they are. Still it a'n't good for them to *dissipate* too often. So they must settle now after these holidays and I will exert myself to the utmost to enliven their home. Old people are apt to forget that their quiet notions of comfort are unsuitable to the gay spirits of youth, and they permit a dulness to settle over the hearth which destroys the cheerfulness of *home* to their children. If I were but a little stronger – able to be but half as active as in my youth. But it can never be again. I am failing, there is no concealing it, and though better in milder weather, better this winter than I have been for many, I can still only consider it as a reprieve depending for its duration on freedom from cold, fatigue, anxiety, and disturbance. And who in this suffering world can calculate on such exemption. I will do nothing imprudent of myself. God will order all for the best.

30. A letter from Mrs. Valpy from Florence where she very much counsels us to follow them. She gives particulars of expenses there with many useful directions in case we think of Italy and I shall copy them all here into my journal that they may be at hand if wanted.

31. Mrs. Valpy says an excellent house in Florence taken for six months would be fifty piastres a month.

A piastre is four and sixpence; there are ten paoli to a piastre. Thus in round numbers a house in the town of Florence would be about £100 a year, a carriage the same; three of the best masters £50; the house expenses with wages £200; washing, dress and amusements, say £150 more; altogether much about what we live at here, both places being about £100 a year cheaper than Pau. So here is a subject of contemplation for the Colonels. Colonel Litchfield is keen for Italy, has always been, on account of the climate and Janey's voice. Colonel Smith likes the climate here as it agrees so well with all of us; the expense and the trouble of moving and the distance of Florence from home, influence both him and me to remain where we are. So we will amuse ourselves with talking for the present and leave the event to chance. We shall go to Paris, I think, in the Spring. We may find it possible to stay there: we may or we may not; we may go on through Switzerland to Italy, or we may return home – to L'Hermitage de Bellevue, I mean, for to Baltiboys we are not to go for another year. Colonel Smith has written both to John Robinson and Mr. Darker to say so. I therefore care little where we pass our exile, wherever the girls can improve most will please me best.

1845

Richard Parkes Bonington. *The Clock-Tower* (Rouen). 1824.

WEDNESDAY, JANUARY 1. May be if we could foretell what a year is to bring forth we should not enter upon it quite so merrily. I recollect last year at Pau, laughing so with good Mr. Puyoo and his sugar plums, and then dear Mary's china cups, and all the fun we *tried* to make for the sake of the young spirits beside us. This year we made no attempt at a gaiety none could feel. We ate our Xmas and our New Year's dinner alone in both houses, and though the little girls sat up to drink their spiced wine after midnight in celebration of hogmanae it was a form without life for there was hardly a smile with it.

5. Sunday. Hal took us a long walk to the Cemetery, to dear Mary's grave. I had not seen it since the neat iron railing was put up. Instead of the high shapeless mound a long narrow slip of turf slightly raised marks the body, all round is an edge of gravel, without a weed, a little rim of mould inside the stone enclosure which supports the railing, creeping plants are planted in it and trained up the railing, neatly tied, not a withered leaf, the whole as if daily looked after. I am sure he does it himself – I am sure that when he takes those early walks alone, it is there he goes, to her grave to tend it. No head stone there as yet, what need is there of one, yet I suppose he will put one. Dear Mr. Gardiner, I did him injustice this time last year when I thought he would soon forget her; his grief is too quiet not to be deep; he don't try to show it, he is cheerful and busy and interested about every thing that happens. But her memory is ever with him, she lives yet to him. The little garden before the windows which she had called hers and was to beautify, he keeps like a show bed, his own hands rake and weed and cover and tie, his spring bulbs are planted, watched, as if her eyes could see them. Is not this better too than striving to cheat grief by repressing memory. Dearest Mary, I don't grieve for you, the sufferings of your beautiful form were too dreadful for me to wish you here, and your singleness of heart will gain you admittance there where the pure are promised an abiding place. It is for myself I grieve, for dearly I loved you, loved, admired and comprehended you.

8. The Bishop of Worcester has delivered a charge to his clergy, the good sense of which ought really to set these most

absurd Puseyite tomfooleries at rest.[1] He is Pepys, brother to Lord Cottenham, and ought to be the next Archbishop if preferment went by rational reasons. He is quite prepared, I should think for a further reform, which in the course of a few years the advancing world will find to be necessary, reform in the ceremonies, reform in the articles, above all, reform in the *constitution* of the *Church*, that collection of *dignitaries* whose riches and whose state, and whose uselessness would rather astonish the simple Apostles. The Christian religion! Its founder would not know it.

We have hired a man with a cart and horse from the farmer below at three fr. a day, and we employed them all yesterday in carrying in the wood for which we have to pay a small duty at the Bureau d'Octroi [Town Dues Office]. Jack managed this part of the business, he was in such a fuss the whole day, it put him in mind, he said, of Baltiboys, he went in and out, ate his dinner in a hurry, looked after the fires Abel had lighted in all the rooms there, bustled up and down, and was so tired at night he was asleep almost before he laid his head down.

The Colonels dined out again t'other day, a stupid bachelor's party, plenty of wine, no talent and cards, they were the first to leave after twelve o'clock, the rest all stayed gambling and drinking; I don't think they will try an Avranches dinner party soon again. What a horrid set of British have congregated here. That little vile doctor got more than tipsy, quite overcome, and only two days before he had had a fit in the streets, he will go off in one of them if he don't become more prudent.

16. Maison Frault, au Palet. Here we really are and very comfortable, nice warm house, well finished, plenty of accommodation and *conveniences* not elsewhere met with. We moved Monday, during the rain and had some trouble

---

1. Henry Pepys (1783–1860) was Bishop of Worcester for nearly twenty years but according to the D.N.B. he only spoke twice in the Lords and then on 'ecclesiastical questions of small importance'. His brother, the first Earl of Cottenham, was Lord Chancellor in the Whig Ministries of 1836–1843 and 1846–1850.

to keep our tempers between the showers with our too bustling housekeeper, her too dawdling assistants, the slowness of Madame Hallais' men and the imperturbability of the farmer with his wagon. Kind Mr. Gardiner took the Colonels home to dinner. We got a bit of boiled beef amongst us and we found some brandy for the weary men. All Tuesday the farmer and his wagon were creeping along the lane again, only yesterday had we any thing like what we most wanted round us. Now we must have a thorough cleaning, an inspection by Mr. Godin of a few '*dégradations*' [wear and tear] as Mr. des Mares calls them, and in a day or two more we shall feel quite at home. Hal took all the trouble of moving the wine which really was a trouble and an expense too for it had all to pay duty again as if it never had entered the town before. Our friend Bellais however, cheated the *Octroi* in a way that would have frightened us to death had we known it, he moved two quantities on the permit meant for one only, but as nobody found it out it was no matter, two or three of the excise officers were prowling about all day too. Mr. des Mares has been in a grand bustle upon this occasion; the French do make such an overwhelming fuss about every little occurrence in life.

Janey Gardiner has heard from Miss Hart from her new residence, it appears likely to suit her. I hope she may suit it, I think she may, as Mr. Boultbee directs all himself, the rising, the eating, the walking, the studying, the retiring, the whole employment of the day; he gave a sketch of the dispositions of the daughters and the kind of management each required, something new to Miss Hart who hitherto made all bend to herself. She is made very comfortable, is very kindly treated, but is quite controuled, a fortunate thing for her. She likes Mr. Boultbee very much, she will soon make him out to be a lover and as long as he don't discover this it will all do very well, he may be blind a long time, for ever, if he has wit enough, unless the elder daughters think fit to undeceive him, when as wearied as I was of her imaginary conquests over Spanish refugees, French proprietors, old Indian Colonels, and young English clergymen etc., etc.

Governesses seem to have a mania for fancying themselves captivating, poor Miss Elphick, [see *Memoirs*] who was something the shape of a beer barrel was always the victim of

some dream of this sort, and she carried her folly a great deal
further for she used to request private interviews to ask the
astonished conquerers of her virgin heart their intentions. So
that these scenes were really beyond anything humiliating to
all her friends in their senses. Governesses are badly brought
up, or they are from a bad class, or they are improperly brought
forward or something, for they all behave ill, and they are all
unhappy. I like a good *Bonne* and masters, those by way of
ladies with most vulgar feelings are intolerable.

19. Yesterday we were sitting round the fire, the girls and I having
just had a very pleasant visit from Mrs. Plunket, who talked
of Ireland and all the nice people there, when a Monsieur
Tillout or some such name was announced and in entered
a little man with an immense pacquet of papers, an *Etat
de lieu* [inventory] a *procès verbal* [minutes of a meeting], and
what not, all duly signed and sealed and typed up with tape
which he begged permission first to shew and then to read
according to instructions received from Monsieur des Mares,
who had required him to compare the actual condition of the
Hermitage with the state in which it was in May last year.

Look I could not help, but read I declined as a matter in
which I had no concern and still less curiosity; the poor man
was much perplexed.

I explained to him how utterly irresponsible we considered
ourselves, that he might rely upon finding the garden in proper
order and any thing we had destroyed replaced, beyond that
nothing, and though at first he talked big of immense damage,
crops destroyed, walls injured, wood lost, locks hurt (the
French laws requiring this and the French laws obliging that,
etc., etc.,) he descended a little upon finding that . . . we had
never received an *Etat de lieu* (and) were honestly intending
to make good all our own deficiencies. It is singular added
I that Monsieur des Mares should have allowed us to take
possession without a remark of any kind upon the property,
and most singular of all that before our term is out he should
tease me in this ungentlemanly way about a place we shall
leave better than we found it. This was all very grand, but as
we do not understand French law, and as one of its articles
seems to be a determination in every way to cheat the British,
I wrote a few lines to Mr. Hickey . . .

The meanness of our landlord is a bye word here. Colonel Smith heard from some of the people about that the old extortioner had laid his damages at 300 francs. I saw 100 at the end of a thick roll of papers, and if he would take that and his Hermitage together, we should be well quit of him, he would plant the artichokes for nothing, repair the bolts for little and jingle our poor crowns down into his deep pocket, while we will join in the refrain usual after his name, 'C'est l'homme le plus méchant, l'homme le plus indigne, l'homme le plus disgracieux de ce pays'.

24. Most curious divisions come to light in the Irish Roman Catholic church. The most *respectable* among her clergy avowing themselves quite hostile to the Repeal Agitation, which it seems the Pope is equally anxious to discourage, having so long ago as '39 written to advise the Priests not to intermeddle with political matters as subjects quite beyond their province, but to confine themselves to the proper objects of their Christian ministry, the care of the morals of their flocks and the healing of divisions among them, etc. This letter never met the eye of the public for in those days of Whig rule, Clergy and people fancied the ball at their foot and that their manikin Mr. O'Connell would continue to terrify the Government into whatever measures he proposed. But in these times of vigorous management, they find that with every disposition to remedy real evils, the bridle is held tight over their unconstitutional attempts to endanger the Protestant faith and the integrity of the Empire. So this second letter comes in good time to assist the determination of the wise to withdraw themselves from an agitation virtually at an end though still made the mischievous means of exciting and impoverishing the people.

The great body of the ignorant priesthood cling to the ambitions of 'John Tuam'[1] and with soft words of the Pope incline

1. John MacHale (1791–1881) became Archbishop of Tuam in 1834 and during his long pontificate he was renowned as the most uncompromisingly nationalistic of the Irish Bishops. Conciliation Hall was the headquarters of the Repeal movement in Dublin and Derrynane was Daniel O'Connell's ancestral estate in Kerry.

to throw his power overboard, while in the Conciliation Hall two or three lay members openly refuse to acknowledge his jurisdiction. O'Connell himself is evidently in a 'fix', as his very long letters after the manner of Oliver Cromwell and nearly as incomprehensible, prove pretty clearly. He announces very big intentions to-day, abandons them to-morrow, sulks at Derrynane, where he manufactures all these papers, while the Repeal rent is falling to nothing. A great many priests are coming over to the Established Church.

In Germany another reformation is beginning. In the Pope's own States a revolution is impending, they seem determined there to deprive him of his temporal power which his Cardinals abuse most grossly. Undeterred by the ill-success of the many revolts suddenly broke out and as suddenly suppressed within the last dozen years, they are but waiting this good old Pope's death to organise another, the expatriated Italians now in France, England and Greece keeping up a close correspondence in the meanwhile. Fifty years will make a great change in the world.

31. Such an idle week, I have done nothing, never left my room till eleven o'clock, hardly stirred out, written nothing, read only *feuilletons*, worked none, taught Johnny but half, and let the girls manage themselves. I had my cough to get rid of which is gone, my headaches to cure which are better, and a touch of sciatica in the left hip and leg which really was painful to lameness; rhubarb and colocynth[1] and cold water have nearly conquered this rheumatick attack, but what a poor wretch I am, much more worn out than any one thinks of, sadly useless, so different from the once active 'busy bee', neither strength nor spirits left, spirits which I had hoped would never desert me. Mary had much more courage. The lessons of those dear children are sometimes wearisome to me, particularly the everlasting musick, it nearly distracts me. The want of exercise makes these feelings worse and we can't take it for there has been a fall of snow and the whole place is a plunge.

1. This is a purgative drug derived from the Bitter Apple.

FRIDAY, FEBRUARY 7. Mr. Moggridge was sitting for about two hours with us yesterday morning, a clever, intelligent, well informed, gentlemanly agreeable man, active in mind and body in spite of very miserable health, busy as a bee in the improvement of the French, buying Leicester sheep to sell to them again, taking land, getting them good horses, establishing races, trying to teach them agriculture etc., and his own affairs in the most deranged condition. How queer is human nature!

John Robinson not quite settled yet with those nice tenants of the Colonel's. When the time came for Pat Quin to give him up the land he had ruined, according to previous agreement, forty pounds in hand and arrears forgiven, not a bit would he move, he had been offered more by another man, – Tom Kelly, and there went the respectable set, Quin and a crew to give over the possession, Kelly and ditto to receive possession, all in the gray of the morning, and Kelly puts his excellent brother-in-law, Healy, into the remains of the wretched cabin to keep possession, the man we had so much trouble to bribe off the property some years ago. The Colonel is furious, he won't sanction any of these arrangements, he wants the land himself, he wishes to get rid of his worthless tenants at every opportunity, so he has refused to agree to all this under scheming, though Kelly saved Mr. Robinson much trouble with Quin who has a spite against the Colonel and therefore hated yielding his land to him. I wish he and all belonging to him would take themselves off out of the country. I shall never feel quite safe while any of the name stay in it, they are such a wicked race, full of revenge and fury, and idle and reckless. How we tried to improve this man, how much kindness was thrown away on him and his, they are bad people.

8. I have been reading ever so many books new and old in these my sick days being fit for little better than a chair at the side of the fire, though said fire and almost every other comfort is prohibited by the doctor, cold food, cold drinks and cold rooms, a dreadful régime to one starving of cold. 'The Desultory Man' is full of pretty stories and gives a faithfully interesting account of Pau and the beautiful Pyrénnées, 'Gilbert Gurney', wittily written but not in my

way, 'Barnabys in America',[1] decidedly bad, it must be a gross caricature of the worst style of Americans, and for the party Barnaby it has sunk too entirely into a mere swindling gang of the most vulgar description to be any longer the very least degree amusing. 'Bishop Heber's Journal'[2] nearly as interesting as when I first read it, from the ease and simplicity with which it is written and the pleasure I find in turning my thoughts back to that fine part of the world where I have still so much to interest me and where I was so happy. I could but run it through hurriedly, so short a time is allowed by the Club for works which have not been in circulation before, that unless one devoted every waking hour to a closely printed double columned volume the two days don't suffice.

'Madame de Sévigné's letters' I have gone through again with undiminished relish. And Mrs. Plunket lent me a new work in three parts or volumes which has quite fascinated me: 'Ireland and its rulers', by a Mr. Madden of the Munster Circuit.[3] I have read nothing so clever I don't know the day when, brilliant, eloquent in many parts, energetick all through, and Irish to the core, full of the faults it condemns as of the genius innate. Coarse, ungrammatical, full of provincialisms, the style is really fine and the matter excellent; he deals his blows right round on all sides in good earnest, so must expect as little mercy as he gives, for all that the truth is in him and it will tell in time. It is new to deal with the living as if they were dead and to describe the characters of existing great men with all their blemishes attached to their names at full length.

1. Theodore Hook wrote 'Gilbert Burney' (1835); 'Barnabys in America' (1843) was one of Frances Trollope's most popular creations.
2. Reginald Heber, who was born in 1783, became Bishop of Calcutta at the age of thirty-two. He died just before E.G. arrived in India but his widow's endeavours ensured that he is remembered not just as a hymn-writer ('From Greenland's icy mountains') but also for his Travel Journals and his sermons.
3. The full title is 'Ireland and its Rulers since 1839' and, to illustrate how well stocked the Book Club was, its three volumes were published in 1843/4.

There is a great fair on the green before the house to-day – a crowd, no more. Nothing picturesque in the appearance of the people, nor anything attractive in their merchandise. It was far prettier in the South. A fair at Pau, even a market was a sight worth going out to see, the beauty of the dresses, the variety, the air of well doing about the people, the quantity of horses, ponies, odd carts, and the eagerness of action in every group, combined with the fine old town and its magnificent environs altogether formed an assemblage hardly surpassed by the religious festivals at Bombay. But here, on this bleak hill, in this shabby town of narrow streets, a mob of heavy dirty people clumping about with the air of 'moutons qui rêvent', no activity among the men, no beauty among the women, no look of health, no look of youth, nothing to relieve the mass but the white towering Normandy cap, in itself a monster; a fair here is a dull spectacle.

No people can have good complexions who live on such wretched fare as do the peasants hereabouts. Two meals a day of sour bread steeped in soup made of cabbage stalks or leaves, pease *cods*, and suchlike rubbish boiled in water with a spoonful of lard, in the interim, bread and cider for those who can afford it, the poor children get no better, potatoes and buttermilk is royal fare compared with this; then their ignorance is so entire that intellect they have none, no expression except of cunning ever crosses their stupid countenance, they are more Bretons than Normans here, and from very remote times, a Breton, a Bas Breton in particular, has ranked very little above the brute creation. We made a good exchange in our little island, the daring Norman and the firm Saxon for the poor British, the most degraded of the Celtick race who seem to have sunk still lower when driven from their own land to the shores of the stranger where they have been left to vegetate ever since without intermixture, or care, or education, part of France yet not French, their fine soil hardly cultivated, all neglected like themselves.

13. We have had a very interesting letter from Jane, of an old date, a sort of journal . . . her chief pleasure had been Charles Kemble's readings, most of which she had attended. He is admirable, old, broken down, feeble on the limbs, the Kemble voice yet remains capable of expressing all the accomplished

actor feels as he exquisitely modulates it to suit the various characters of Shakespeare's plays.[1] They met him twice at dinner and he had dined with them and they all got on charmingly. Now I will confess, honestly, after reading of this intellectual treat, recollecting the sort of society Jane habitually lives in, the splendour of her house, the style in which she keeps it, the income she is mistress of, so much larger than any wants, for a few minutes I grieved, not that she had so much but that we had not more. Our purse so much too light for our habits, our children requiring so much of it, but then we have those children, worth all the sacrifices we make for them, all the luxuries we deny ourselves for their sakes. If they but turn out well, and I think they will though I may not live to see it, their father and I will bear every privation, they will render his old age happy, ornament his dwelling beyond all the works of art, so my reprehensible discontent departed.

14. We have in our Irish paper of to-day the Queen's speech, of course she has to congratulate the country upon everything. She hints at the advisability of continuing the income tax, and of reducing some other duties, and she directs attention to the state of education etc., in Ireland. But there will be a great movement within and without when the great measures mentioned by Sir Robert Peel as in contemplation, come to be debated. Encreasing the grant to the Papist College of Maynooth, founding Universities open to all religions, and such like necessary means of better educating the mass of a great nation, will throw the Protestant bigots into a fury. None are to know right from wrong except as taught by them. Those who eat fish on Fridays must have no fellowship with those who profane the day of *rest* by turning it into a day of mortifications. All those Calvinists make me sick.

1. Charles Kemble (1775–1854) came from the distinguished theatrical family whose Edinburgh ventures had so enchanted E.G. as a girl. His last appearance on stage was in 1840 and in the last decade of his life, despite his deafness, he gave readings from Shakespeare.

16. Sunday. The R.C. Archbishop of Dublin, Dr. Murray[1] is to be a Cardinal and to reside at Rome, a sure guarantee of everything wise and gentle and Christian in the future management of his church in Ireland. Another of its Bishops has put down the unseemly practice of making the chapels political cabinets. A great petition signing was going forward under the superintendance of the priest, which his superiour not only stopt, but ascended the Altar and preached against, the congregation murmured, when he requested those to retire who were inclined to disturb him, so more than half left the chapel, of those who remained to hear his discourse, some immediately scored out their names from the petition. More priests in the South have come over to our reformed Church.

21. My poor, sweet Janey Gardiner came down yesterday. Dear child she opened her heavy heart, said how dull she found herself, her father all kindness is still not the companion her young lively mind requires, her brothers though very dear to her tease her and leave her. She misses her mother, she regrets her sister. Bitterly she cried. This is just what I hoped she would arrive at, now she can be consoled and gently directed and she will hourly improve in goodness and happiness. How wise it was to have patience, to let time do its work. To have her come to me as her best friend instead of being looked on as a lecturing aunt.

23. No post from either Dublin or London to us. Mr. Gardiner's *Scotsman* talks of snow ever so many feet deep all over England, having stopt the trains, still his papers come. Once or twice they were a day later that was all. We have no news therefore for though Colonel Smith reads the papers every day at the Club he seldom finds anything in them. I never knew a man who did. We have had no books this week, seen very few people for the

1. Daniel Murray's wise counsels guided his church during his near thirty years as Archbishop of Dublin down to his death in 1852. E.G. respected and admired him; before leaving for France she had corresponded with him about what she regarded as the unacceptable behaviour of her arch-enemy, the local priest, Father Germaine.

dirty roads and the bitter wind prevent people walking out, so I have nothing to say to my journal this Sunday morning. It was a bright idea the plan of keeping one. It fixes so many otherwise passing thoughts, connects events, impresses facts and it stands me in the stead of conversation, the mind would rust for want of it; and then though looking back on all it tells may awaken a little melancholy, it will be interesting by and bye to live over again these busy years. I often regret not having earlier begun this useful habit. I have kept journals occasionally when away from home in particular, for my mother and my Aunts, but they were short-lived, not written for myself, but to describe occurrences that would amuse them, they had not the private interest of this gossip with and for myself which I indulge in for the purpose of recalling the memory of their mother to my dear children when they will be old enough to understand the moral of my comments upon life, and when they will probably make a better use of my written thoughts than young people generally do of the same words spoken.

24. A note from Lord Milltown to Colonel Smith begging help in the disposal of the poor Italian boy for whom he much wishes a Cadetship.[1] Hal fears the ability to serve his noble friend will not equal his wishes, he knows but two of the directors and if they don't incline to give their good things they have such a ready excuse in the numerous applications they are assailed by, the many promises already given etc., that unless it be for their own interest they don't in general oblige. This poor young man too is almost twenty-one. He has been the cause of many disagreeable scenes at Russborough and he was foolishly brought up. I hope Hal may succeed.

26. Marquis of Westminster dead, the richest man, at least the richest landed proprietor in England. Long ago his income was counted as a thousand pounds a day. Such overgrown wealth must surely have cares with it to over-balance all enjoyment. 'Give me neither poverty nor riches', said the wise man; and he was right according to all experience. I am

1. Colonel Smith's aristocratic neighbour continually over-estimated the influence he could bring upon the Directors of the East India Company, in this instance to provide an opening for his natural son.

sure I hope my children may be a little richer than myself, not very much, but just so much as to preclude the necessity of so much self denial and so much carefulness and so much anxiety as a small income necessitates – of less consequence where there is little refinement, but with habits, tastes and feelings produced by a youth of affluence there are many little annoyances to bear on descending to a working day world, and I should just wish my girls to be saved this. As for Jack, his future depends on himself. Every man is the carver of his own fortunes. Educate him, set him afloat and it is his own fault if he don't rise to the top of his line. Opportunity is never wanting to those who are ready to seize it. I don't believe in good or ill *fortune*, good or bad *success* there is, according as it is merited. I am afraid Jack is both indolent and irritable, two faults almost inimical to success. I will do my best while I live to correct this disposition and I do not believe I shall fail for he is affectionate, reasonable, and don't want for talent.

None of our children have what I call energy. When we were young if we had anything we wished to do, up we jumped ever so early in the morning and we worked with just the zeal that makes a great character; these children are never interested about anything, never sufficiently roused to dream of making the least exertion. They do everything they are told, are particularly conscientious, but in a dawdling way, as if it were an unpleasant duty, I can't understand them. We were merrier, more eager, certainly naughtier than they are; so the good and the evil must be taken together. They don't take after their father either, for he, like a Frenchman, puts his whole soul into anything he has to do, does it at once, thoroughly, decidedly, as if it were of consequence and he himself alive. I can't make out the apathy of the children unless they are copying what ill health has of late years made me. I sometimes think that good Jane Cooper in her love of order did too much for them herself rather than be worried by training them to act without her. Annie is a little more awake than her sister.

27. Colonel Smith and I spent the greater part of this day in Mr. Loire's painting room, this is Hal's second sitting only and his picture is finished. An admirable likeness and a pleasing

one. A gentlemanly, agreeable-looking elderly man, with his active air and in his best humour, with a lively expression in the countenance and a sparkle of fun in the eye; he has hit him to perfection. What a pity he should have succeeded so ill with me. They say he don't do women as well as men, and he says women are more difficult to do, and that I am a particularly troublesome subject from the regularity and the delicacy of the features and the perpetual variety of the expression. Some painters would catch all that, but Mr. Loire has not that talent, so I am frightful, cold and hard and harassed, a perfect contrast to my brisk, happy-looking husband, he makes quite a pretty picture.

28. We have been reading Dickens' 'Chimes', his Carol for this Xmas, not so good as the last, but written for the same purpose and in the same style, good as a whole, many parts very affecting, the moral perfectly true. It is with the ignorant poor as with children. A want of charity in judging of them according to our own position instead of theirs produces a harshness of feeling towards them and a severity in dealing with them which hardens their natures, fosters every evil feeling and produces in many cases the crimes for which we punish them. If the spirit of Love called gentleness by some and Christianity by us would but be encouraged in our hearts so that it might be the directing spring of all our actions, what a world of happiness this would be. It was a rule with my father, the most perfect gentleman I ever met with, to address his inferiours with exactly the same courtesy he used to his equals, the consequence was his manner improved theirs, inspired them with a self respect that in some sort raised their feelings above a low dependance of behaviour miscalled humility. How often in Ireland have I burned with shame at the insulting tone of the vulgar *gentleman* to the humble but far better bred labourer who forced to indure in silence felt his heart swell into curses deep and lasting – dear children remember this.

SATURDAY, MARCH 1. Quickly the months fly even in this dull place. We are so busy within that we are independent of the very disagreeable weather without, the total want of interest in the town or neighbourhood, and the want of society we care about. If there were one dry walk we should be more comfortable, but there is not one, and as there is a great deal of rain and a very great deal of mud, walking out during two thirds of the year is a most wretched necessity, for me often an impossibility, and exercise being essential to the maintenance of at best the very indifferent health I can ever hope to enjoy, I feel the privation of it a good deal. If I can just rub on for another year here while the girls are laying foundations on which by after attention they can themselves raise their progress in the different arts to any height they like I shall be quite satisfied, for with care I may not become materially worse for some few years. If the heart be affected, which, I myself feel sure it is, this may make the more care necessary. I can't command all the means certainly, but all depending on myself shall be faithfully attended to. If George Robinson can't come over to look after me I shall write fully to him and guide myself by his advice. Children motherless is so melancholy, none can supply a mother's place. One precaution I am taking, I am endeavouring to prepare the girls to do without me, in fifty little ways, at every opportunity, storing up in them facts and reflexions that will be of use here-after and I have told them how uncertain is my life, how much may depend on their conduct, – their father's comfort, their brother's whole happiness, the improvement of our poor people, and they will have my books and my journal.

2. We paid visits yesterday, Papa, Annie and I. Annie says she likes going from house to house to see the different styles in which they are managed and to hear the different opinions of all the people. So Annie reflects and compares already.

It is a warm house, very comfortable and very cheerful and we congratulate ourselves daily that nobody relieved us of it. Just now some people in search of a large house would be glad to rent it for six months but the Colonels don't seem to have any wish to leave it, Colonel Smith don't even wish to go to Paris, he inclines rather to stay quietly out our time here and then take Paris on our way home. Colonel Litchfield has, however, set his heart on moving, starts here and there every now and then being essential to the existence of a man who allows all his faculties to stagnate so completely while at rest: his life here is curious.

Colonel Smith looks like his son and he really is six years

older. But he is so active he will never either be ill or old now that he has a certain palliative for the asthma, one hitherto unfailing without his ever having had to encrease the dose. On the contrary the dose remaining the same he never has to repeat it during the twenty-four hours, a couple of pipes at night relieves his breathing from every embarrassment. He walks with the little girls, goes to the reading-room, plays his game at Billiards, changes our books and reads them all, and by the help of a protracted toilette in the morning, a long dinner and good sleep after it he gets merrily through the day, although I cannot but think a man of his country tastes and active habits must find life in Avranches sadly tedious.

5. I forget what day I and my journal last conversed but I know I have had no head since for talking or thinking having had again to send for the little doctor who half killed me but has certainly done me good for I was better yesterday, not quite so well to-day. I can't get out in this nasty dirty place, and if I could I could not walk for my legs refuse to move, I don't sleep well either and I can't eat so I am in a happy way. The little man tells me it is all the liver, it could not well be worse. It seems to have been an unhealthy winter, many deaths among the old. Lord Mornington, eighty-three, Sir Somebody Buxton, Mr. Wilberforce's successor in philanthropick 'agitations', and Sydney Smith.[1] Mr. Gardiner regrets him much, he was their neighbour at Bindon, always very kind to them and always very agreeable, living in the very prettiest possible style, in a beautifully ornamented cottage, with good society round him. All of his writings that I know are excellent, both as to matter and manner, Lord Jeffrey will feel the loss of this his earliest friend. How often has he mentioned him and two or three more even more celebrated amongst whom originated the great work of our time, the awakening of the intellect, the

1. William Wellesley-Pole, third Earl of Mornington, was brother to the Duke of Wellington. William Wilberforce's successor was Sir Thomas Fowell Buxton Bart. Lord Jeffrey and Sydney Smith were two of the leading lights in the Edinburgh political and intellectual society she witnessed as a girl and describes so well in the Memoirs.

directing of the talent of our day by means of their wonderful *Edinburgh Review*, begun with little anticipation of all it was to effect; more as a means of furthering individual interest than with any idea of the moral revolution it produced. Lord Jeffrey has often told us and one fine summer's day that we were wandering along Corstorphine hill gazing from the rich fields below to the lovely firth beyond, he related more particularly some of the passages of his young days, and the famous supper among the rest in his poor lodgings up I know not how many pair of stairs in the old town of Edinburgh at which he, Lord Brougham, Sydney Smith, and two more stars whose names I am sorry I have forgotten originated the famous work which not only immortalised its projectors but advanced as if by enchantment the feelings of all their contemporaries; full of errour, rash, presumptuous, keen, it is with all its faults a mine of wisdom, as any one will find who will open an early volume and compare what was hazarded then with what is received now.

9. Mr. Gardiner gave me a letter from brother William, curious of course, plenty of allusions to himself, and not unwise strictures upon the scheme of remaining at Avranches which he thinks useless for the boys and improper for Janey, he advises Edinburgh as a residence, a folly to my mind. Who on earth would live there that was not forced. Colonel Smith seems thinking of leaving Avranches, Mr. Fraser gives up Baltiboys in May, without a tenant there it would be inconvenient for us to pay rent here, and with the exception of the good and cheap masters there are no advantages to be gained by a longer residence, for we pay more for everything we buy than we do at home, excepting wine, and the climate is extremely severe.

The East wind is blowing now in the most cutting manner, the cold is piercing and so harsh that no delicate person can stand it. I suffer much from it, no such violent cough as at home but still a cough, and I should say in other respects I feel more really ill than I have ever done, this may be that my complaint has progressed and that I must expect an increasing debility to accompany its progress but in that case I should say it has reached a point that makes such a climate as this quite unfit for me. Tom Kelly gave up Quin's farm very peaceably, fine mild weather in Ireland as yet but the east winds will not fail to set in immediately there as elsewhere.

We have had nothing to read all this week but trash, – tales, Travels and Magazines all on a par for stupidity, there are no Debates either, nothing to oppose, nothing to lament. Sir Robert Peel is another Louis XIV – everything. These prosperous times are not half so interesting as the troubled ones, or may be I feel too listless to occupy myself with news.

16. We are looking over two amusing books of Finemore Cooper's, one on France, the other on England, full of much truth, brimful of much nonsense, and written in a lively agreeable manner. The irritability of the Americans concerning everything English is really a kind of lunacy, they are all *raw* on the subject. Every cap is made for them, so great is their vanity, so entirely are they occupied with themselves that they always feel offended and insulted and hurt and annoyed and so on when nobody is thinking of them. And if they were to *think* they would feel that a *new* people without an aristocracy of any sort, with nothing to look up to, cannot be polished in mind or manner and therefore should not feel surprised at being suffered rather than courted by those who are. No wonder they feel themselves disliked everywhere. Their pretension is so great, their manner so coarse, their feelings so vulgar, they cannot fail to be extremely disagreeable in well bred society. Much sterling worth and some talent must be shown by an American before the prejudice his absurdities create against him can be got over. I have not seen many, but they were of the best – and odious. There is nothing like travelling for opening the mind. To find people full of themselves everywhere, either not thinking of us or despising us, to see customs we venerate derided, habits we approve unknown, to hear conflicting opinions, contemplate strange usages, etc, etc., is the best practical education man can get from his kind. We are all to the end the slaves of prejudices, but they may be greatly lessened by a good rub against those of the rest of the world.

21. Busy with Dickens' notes on America, not exactly good as a book of travels but charming from the sentiments sprinkled through it – of the puritanism in Boston – 'Wherever religion

is resorted to as a strong drink, and as an escape from the dull monotonous round of home, those of its ministers who pepper the highest will be the surest to please. They who strew the Eternal path with the greatest amount of brimstone, and who most ruthlessly tread down the flowers and leaves that grow by the wayside will be voted the most righteous etc.' Except Burns to the righteous overmuch I know nothing more truly Christian. He went to visit the factories at Lowell[1] and was charmed of course, young bright girls healthy and happy and well dressed, with large savings and every means of improvement and intellectual amusement provided for them was something new to one who had learned what factory labour was at Manchester, and if, as he says, a large class will choose to think their essays and their pianoforte and their parasols above their *station* he asks, 'what their station is. It is their station to work and they *do* work, twelve hours a day, and pretty tight work too. Are we quite sure that we in England have not formed our ideas of the *Stations* of working people from accustoming ourselves to the contemplation of that Class as *they are* and not as they *might be*'.

22. Mr. Gardiner has been sitting half an hour with us this morning, laughing with us at the craze among the children for Baltiboys, the three girls are like creatures possessed. We should all prefer home and be at home were it not for these same children, it is their improvement keeps us here, and if this climate does not injure me here another year we shall stay.

30. This was a very fine day, a few spring bonnets appeared among the French in the Jardin des Plantes though they looked rather premature. Vegetation is of course backward everywhere, but at the best of seasons the garden and the farm in France are weeks behind any part of Great Britain. The people seem to have no idea of assisting nature, *forcing* is unknown. There are new potatoes already in London, I don't believe they are planted here yet. Chickens there are none,

1. The previous year E.G. had read with great interest a book called 'A Mind Amongst The Spindles' which had as its subtitle 'A Miscellany Wholly Composed by the Factory Girls of an American City.'

not any early luxury, the market is beginning to be very bare, so Lent will be kept for many years, only the women keep it, still half the population not consuming meat leaves a better supply at this scarce season than the men could otherwise have, the women and the *poor* starve for six weeks on salt cod faithfully, but they grumble. Hal had a warm letter of thanks from Lord Milltown, as grateful as if success had attended the application, he catches at the idea of a mercantile clerk and entreats further advice and assistance, a clue to the proper steps to take. We know as little as he does of the way to approach the Merchant princes of England but we will make enquiries of those who do.[1]

WEDNESDAY, APRIL 2. The Colonels are off this beautiful morning to St. Malo, much against the grain when it came to the point, though they have been looking forward to this expedition for weeks with anxiety. They set out by diligence at 9 o'clock and were to arrive about four. We have been busy ever since their departure with the stay maker who will really make us all look like different creatures and probably much advantage our health as the shape and the fit are so perfect, there is no pressure anywhere. She has recommended a dressmaker who will prove, I feel sure, greatly superiour to those we have hitherto tried. How exact these French people are, how particular in everything they have to do, and what a regular profession the art of dress is. Certainly they do understand it, that we must allow, though their taste in colours is not chaste enough to please the perfectly educated taste of our refinement. An Englishwoman of rank dressing à la Française is very nearly equal to an Irishwoman in matters of toilette, the greatest praise that can be bestowed on this department of education.

Little Jack comes happy home from school, he is anxious to have his lessons perfect so it is plain he feels it would not do to be idle; he has not many and they are:- English, reading and spelling, French ditto, a little grammar, writing and cyphering, and these two days of trial he has gone but once, from ten till near one. Little Colin Jones came home with him yesterday and remained to dine with us; a fine, intelligent, well-disposed

1. See 24.2.1845.

child not the least aristocratick looking; a shabby, undersized bit thing with no appearance in air or manner of a gentleman's son, but an amiable little boy. That wicked little Harry Laurell I won't have here again if I can help it, vulgar little animal, swearing like a trooper.

6. Saturday morning yesterday, I was getting up, rather later than usual, when in burst Annie in a passion of tears – 'Mama, Dr. Robinson is downstairs' – I burst out crying too, Janey came up quite hysterical, we could hardly believe it, but there he was. He had left Blesinton the Saturday before, a day in Dublin, crossed by the evening packet and on to Liverpool and London Monday, down to Southampton, staid a day, on to Jersey, and he walked in to Dr. Eckford's much to his surprise two days before the letter he had written to announce himself, which says but little for the regulations of our post office. The steamboat not yet coming to Granville he had to come over by St. Malo, the Colonels therefore just missed him, starting themselves a few hours before he arrived there. We had a happy breakfast, and then all seemed hurry, running here and running there, so much to say, so much to see, and old Mde. Hallais to send to for furniture for the spare room which the girls had just quitted. At dinner we had Mr. Gardiner, his three children came to tea with Henry and Edward Moggridge who had dined with them. So the evening was merry indeed, a little playing, a little singing and an immensity of dancing, Dr. George taking the lead, inventing figures he fancied he could teach to the delight of the younger dancers who imagined that they learned them, and who at any rate persevered in the difficulties till my fingers could hardly move, they were all in high spirits without being the least boisterous.

7. Yesterday and to-day I have got up at six o'clock, walked half an hour in the garden, then read or wrote till breakfast. I hope it will agree with me as I enjoy the early morning much this fine weather. I have left the Doctor cleaning Janey's teeth which much want care, Annie's splendid set require nothing; he seems pleased with their improvement in appearance, satisfied that their education is progressing, therefore disinclined to take us home just yet, he thinks their manner just what it used to be, their affections quite unchanged, but he observes a gossipping turn they never

had, an acquaintance with their neighbours' concerns they had always been kept from, and a slight spirit of ridicule affected for any person or thing not such as they please to consider orthodox, which they never had dreamed of feeling in their more childish days. I shall remember this and apply the remedy silently, not that it can be effectual till that monkey their cousin is separated from them. Her head is filled with folly, she is in constant want of excitement, idle and was reared to be supercilious, and encouraged to amuse herself and those around her by laughing at every body.

We have heard plenty of gossip from the doctor himself nevertheless, news of everybody, not half told yet. We are to find Ireland much shot ahead, a rapid improvement in this short time that will be very delightful to look on. Our people are pretty comfortable but they much want us back amongst them. My draining has answered beyond expectation small as the scale of experiment was, it has given such an energy to the farmers that they are in high spirits and Hal having now a little ready money he can continue to lend on the same terms to any who are anxious to borrow, thus benefitting his property, encreasing his income, and best of all raising the condition of all depending on him. I am deep in a pile of pamphlets sent me over by Mr. Moore on the subject of National Education, but here comes breakfast.

11. Mr. Hickey paid me an interesting visit to-day, for he brought a pamphlet[1] he is writing on the state of the Irish poor, clever and kind and very judicious, he encouraged comments being in search of facts so that we had a long conversation upon subjects to which we have both paid great attention.

12. Mr. Hickey came again to read the alterations he had made in his Essay. We talked over the national schools now so flourishing that 'tis loss of time to deplore the folly which nevertheless has much crippled their usefulness, a set of the very ignorant and of course very bigotted pastors and people will still struggle against liberal sentiments, their number is happily decreasing as knowledge is spreading, many of our

1. 'The Labouring Classes in Ireland: an Inquiry as to what beneficial changes may be effected in their condition' was published in 1846.

clergy have come down from their stilts and are now willing to accept the plan of education they never had any valid reason for refusing, it was an insane principle of intolerance, a feeling of tyrannous bigotry, a love of power, an uncharitable aversion to all different from themselves, however, it is so nearly over as to be almost innocuous, the Tresham Gregg sect[1] is becoming so laughable as to bid fair to be soon forgotten.

13. Sunday, a dismal day, cold rainy dreary. How fortunate for me that on the last day of our dear good Dr. George's visit Avranches shewed her climate in some way approaching to the truth, had he not staid that day he would have left us persuaded that we lived in Paradise and that though the climate was a little too exciting for me this evil was counterbalanced by its steady soft clear dry air. The cutting wind upon the platform first roused him to believe our report of the inclemency of the weather here. He said from the first it would never do for me in the winter, but that sudden change experienced by himself convinced him that it is unsuitable to me at any time. Too variable, too harsh, subjecting me to the chance of colds which I am not strong enough to bear with impunity. The air also increases the action of the heart too much.

He examined me very particularly and finds the complaint to be in the *womb* and the best surgical advice necessary, the lower bowels are apathetick, something wrong with the duodenum, the liver torpid in a degree, considerable irritation everywhere, the nervous system deranged; the heart affected by sympathy, no organick disease anywhere. It is a state of very miserable ill health without any hope of speedy recovery but it is capable of great general improvement by extreme care, and the most formidable derangement, the complaint in the womb, may be cured under proper management in time. But for three or four years I must make up my mind to be a regular invalid, living by rule, a most disagreeable rule, for between medicines and lotions and frictions and bathings and minutes of exercise and hours of repose these years are to pass away, in the hope of what, comfortable *old age*. Were it not for the use the old

1. One of the most vociferously evangelical Dublin ministers who, for E.G., encapsulated the intolerant bigotry she associated with his creed.

head and the patient temper and the anxious affection of a
mother, will all be of to the children, who could go through
such a series of penances for such a reward! And I am to give
up all trouble, lay aside all care, suffer no fatigue, be saved
every annoyance, be cherished, nursed, tended, made much
of. Little book, if I dared write the truth in you, 'Impossible'
would be the answer to all these prescriptions. We must do
the best we can, hope the best, and bear all.

Well then it being settled that we are to leave this, the
question is where are we to go. Home say I, the comforts of
home, the interests of home, the support of kind hearts and
clever heads at home, are all necessary when health prevents
our seeking active occupation.. Our Wicklow hills may be too
cold, too damp for a delicate frame to bear the winter in,
though I doubt the outer air signifying much in such a house
as ours, but we could winter in Dublin, Kingstown, or even
Cork if really necessary. I think we should be very happy in
Dublin with so many pleasant acquaintance as we have there
and the power of enlarging our society as we pleased. Colonel
Litchfield is quite for this scheme, and Hal has his Club and
both could hunt and could run down to Baltiboys at any
moment they had nothing better to do. The girls might have
one master always, and a daily Governess for them and Jack
till Jane Cooper is again at liberty to come and take charge
of them. It would be too much happiness so I won't fix my
heart upon it.

George says we shall be very much pleased with the progress
our own locality has made, plantations very much grown,
fields in much better order, cabins with an air of greater
comfort, people more decent in appearance, a spirit of quiet
industry succeeding the restless beggary of other days. Richard
Hornidge has done so much, improved land, labourers, all
belonging to him, Mr. Owen as spirited an agriculturist as
Mr. Gore without the evangelical cant which hindered his
usefulness.[1] All getting forward but old John Hornidge who
grubs on in the old way suspecting, sparing, scraping, penny
wise and pound foolish, barely making a profit of a pound upon

1. These were the Agents .to Lord Downshire, the
largest landed proprietor in Co. Wicklow.

his weed-choked, undrained, ill-fenced fields, yet laughing at the outlay of three pounds which returns the improver six pounds. Quantities of fun, the gossipping doctor entertained us with far more than it would be proper to set down here where I am as it is too apt to criticise my neighbours even without an ill intention in my thoughts. It is a bad habit to talk of the *motes*, see them I cannot help, nature having endowed me with lively powers of observation. Look for them I never do, and talk of them might better be omitted.

But I am going, really in earnest, to exclaim upon the oddity of my mother and my sister Jane, who beg I won't remind my father of his debt to me, owing these fifteen years, *because* he is paying off everybody else this year! By the end of this year he and William will have paid off the debt as compromised with the Creditors at large. William 30,000 my father rather more than 20,000. But there is a class of private friends whom they propose to pay in full which will take 8,000 more – Uncle Ralph, Mrs. Cooper, etc., very right, but why not me, the smallness of the sum don't make any difference surely.

I don't intend to give up my claim they may depend upon it, why should I, they none of them deny themselves anything, they made no particular haste to pay these debts. They set aside a portion of their very handsome incomes to accumulate for this purpose retaining more than sufficient to live surrounded by luxuries, and Jane could herself in her own case allow my father to pay for her passage home – £300, she then being rich for a single woman and he then with a heavier debt upon him, yet she entreats me not to ask for the price of my *own* pianoforte given me by my dear Aunt Bourne, which as it had been made for India with all the expensive additions proper for the climate, I left with him to be sold intending its price to replace it at home. He told me through my mother that he should like to buy it himself, he did not, he sold it for £120, and she wrote to say that the money was supporting them for the moment and whenever they were rich should be repaid. So it shall be without a doubt if asking will bring it. I don't want any interest, I don't want the full amount even, I only want a good grandpianoforte as my kind Aunt meant I should always have. If they were generous I would care less, honest even, but they are not. It is quite out of sight out of mind with my father, he has quite forgotten that I ever helped him in any way, he never sent one rupee to Mr. Gardiner during all that long illness of poor Mary's – and there is William occupied exclusively with himself, and offering to Mr. Gardiner as an inducement to go and live in Edinburgh the *loan* of £*100* towards the military education, outfit, and Commission! of Tommy. In a novel all this would be said to be overcharged, I am not going to say a word about their absurdities to any of them. I shall take it very quiet, but I shall get my pianoforte nevertheless, ask for it at any rate.

16. We got an *Edinburgh Review* from our Library, and I have been interested again in Mr. Dickens' Chimes, in the life of Lord Eldon,[1] and very much indeed in an article on Agricultural Chemistry. A new profession will arise, two new ones perhaps, to take the place of those advancing knowledge will soon render unnecessary, there must be the chemical and geological *Tutor* to assist the farmer in analysing his soils and adapting his manures, and there must be a farming professor attached to the Colleges which also must be multiplied to receive the greater number of students the spread of education will very soon have ready to fill them with. A class of farmers also will rise from the ranks of those now preparing for Law, Medicine, Arms, etc., which will by and bye be a profession of itself requiring skill, talents, capital, much beyond the attainment of the peasant race for some generations to come. Fifty years will make wonderful changes in this world of ours. Twenty will do something, and we *must* grow in *worth* as we grow in knowledge. As the mind opens the heart too expands. Truth takes the place of Errour and the result must be an amount of happiness hardly to be imagined by us of these barbarous times, for so my grandchildren will not fail to reckon them. I never get into these reflexions without longing to be home among our own poor people whom I cannot but fear are standing still for want

---

1. John Scott, first Earl of Eldon, was Lord Chancellor from 1807 to 1827 and, as one of the most resolute opponents to change of any kind when E.G. was a young woman, he might stand as a symbol of the forces of reaction obstructing the path of progress.

of the helping hand. So much is to do in that wild country. The Doctor said we were much wanted though we shall find much progress made particularly by some of our neighbours who are quite making up by present zeal for former apathy.

18. Last night Mr. Gardiner sent me some Hock which I had appeared to like at his house and a kind note followed the present this morning. He is in a great fright lest the second reading of the Maynooth Bill[1] should cost our great statesman his life, there being quite fanaticism enough stirring to direct a bullet through a head so far beyond their own narrow bigotry, there is hardly a fear of the Bill passing, the old Whigs will all rally round Sir Robert, Mr. Gladstone votes with him!! – he has a strong party. But there is an immense number of evangelicals, old tories, and DISSENTERS screaming 'no popery' at the top of their cracked voices, making great demonstrations in the way of meetings and petitions, but they don't seem to be responded to by the country generally. There is too much good sense abroad, the offspring of daily encreasing enlightenment for such bugbears to frighten an age like the present. The fanaticks will make a little turmoil though and do mischief of course for a while but in the end good will come of it. We are reading the Vicar of Wrexhill again. How admirably that clever Mrs. Trollope hits off the *cant* of the *serious* set – Eating and drinking for the glory of the Lord, the Saviour's grace helping us to walk up hill, the prospect of the heavenly Jerusalem enabling us to bear comfort and riches and happiness in some pleasant nook on earth. Mr. and Mrs. Valpy, Mr. and Mrs. Connor, Mr. and Mrs. Kerr, the good Duchess of Gordon, Mrs. Macpherson etc., all seem to have had the essence of their spiritual communings extracted for the pages of this witty caricature. Will the world ever grow wise, the hope in the melancholy case of these puritanical insanities is that the children disgusted with the bondage of their youth will throw off their parents' folly on coming into contact with reality. These people live so completely in a world of their own that they have not an idea of the world as it is, and the false pride they carry with them into it makes

1. The complexities of the Maynooth legislation are explained in the Introduction.

the lessons of *truth* it teaches, harder to learn. So the reform won't take place in a day.

19. Mr. Hickey is furnishing me with sundry little works in some of which he has himself assisted, published by Knight for the improvement of the middle and lower orders and of the higher too, I may say, as they admirably introduce us to our duties towards our dependants. It seems to be the fashion of the day to attend to these, long may it last, it has not been introduced too soon.

We were really all shocked to see in yesterday's paper the announcement of the sudden death of the Marquis of Downshire, he was at Blesinton with his agent, Mr. Owen, and had ridden with him one morning over some of his mountain property and called at Kippure. Returning, Mr. Owen passed on before for some purpose when looking back he perceived the Marquis on the ground, the mare he had fallen from trampling on him, he was quite insensible, sighed once heavily and expired. Only fifty-seven, last year his second son Lord William was killed by a vicious horse as suddenly. He was not a man one could like. His silly pomposity, vanity, meanness, hardness as a landlord and want of politeness as a gentleman made him always quite uninteresting to me. But these sort of tragical ends always affect one, his death will probably occasion many changes in and about Blesinton. It is very fortunate for George that the attendance of a Doctor was rendered unnecessary, for he could not possibly have got home by the day this unfortunate accident occurred.

20. I had a letter from Ogle Moore, the beginning about the school which is at last taken into connexion with the Board, the supplies have been sent down, the master to have a salary of £15, Mr. Moore don't quite like him. Miss Gardiner has hardly any pupils at all and of course has lost heart, having set out with but little. She is sadly indolent, always required looking after, and latterly got into the Protestant cant of the ignorant people round her from which moment her usefulness began to diminish. I shall, I think, dismiss her, content myself with a sewing mistress and put all the children under the master.

Mr. Moore says Lord Downshire's death was apoplexy; he gives a very fair character of the man and seems to think that with all his faults we may miss him. It is difficult for the rich and the noble who hear but the voice of flattery, know no wants, and feel almost unlimited power, to act fairly by their less elevated brethren. It must be a clear head and a truly Christian heart to withstand the temptations of high station. To produce Louis Philippes, our Princes must be educated in adversity, yet a *revolution* is a fearful price for one generation to pay for the benefit of the next.

22. Four or five nights the debate on the second reading of the Maynooth Bill is dragging on, every individual member appearing to think it necessary to give a recordable opinion upon the subject. There is a vast amount of sectarian pride still existing amongst even the well educated, more far than I had expected, quite enough to make a good commotion these quiet times when there is so very little else to animadvert upon. Yet the fate of the measure is, I suppose, secure. The minister is much too cautious to have hazarded so great a measure without the certainty of carrying it, his first majority was very large. Debates change no man's vote, nor his opinion either, and nearly all the influential members are on the side of liberality, or we might call it justice. Young England[1] divided, Lord John Manners with the Government, Mr. D'Israeli, of course against them, and he made another of his brilliant *Peel*ippicks on the occasion, much amusing the house whose spirit wanted rousing these dull matter of fact days, it will put it into good humour the having a clever string of sarcasms to laugh at. He asked for place it seems, was disappointed and so 'have at him' was the revenge. A very harmless one for no one believes him in earnest and the immoveable object of all this clamour hardly appears to hear it.

23. The second reading of the Maynooth Bill passed by a very much larger majority than the first was – 147. The petitioning continues, but on analysing these modes of exciting clamour they are demonstrated to be fully five sixths

1. This was the loose political group Benjamin Disraeli had founded to try to return to rule by an enlightened aristocracy; by this time, it is arguable that hatred for the Prime Minister (who, of course, E.G. revered) was a greater motivating force.

of them emanations from the Methodists, and methodistical evangelists, etc., therefore of no importance as exhibiting the feeling of the country at large, the hubbub will soon subside and a few years will quickly prove how wise has been the measure as a means of tranquillising for the present and educating for the future the mass of the Irish. The Queen really pays her visit to the Emerald Isle this summer and she is to be received with rapture! ditto her minister!!

THURSDAY, MAY. 1. Waked at five by the cannon for Louis Philippe and not being able to sleep again took Lady Blessington's France into bed with me which led me on and on and on till very near nine o'clock so that I half dressed hurriedly and got no little walk in the garden. Dr. Eckford after breakfast sowed a quantity of seeds for me and we might have busied ourselves longer had not a slight shower sent us in. The National Guard paraded the town, M. Loire in the Band playing the cymbals, the Mayor, Juge de Paix and sous préfêt dressed up in cocked hats guarded in the midst, the radical or disaffected citizens spoiled the show, for unwilling to put themselves to the expense of uniforms they fasten their swords over their ordinary clothes and look shabby enough, though as a body they all appear to be above the average height, really a fine set of men.

2. I am not in low spirits about myself, not at all, God orders everything for the best. No mother, I suppose, could contemplate leaving a family of young people to struggle through the dangerous spring of life alone, without anxiety. Nor can a wife, who feels a kind husband's dependance on her care for his daily comfort, be supposed to think quite calmly of the possibility of his declining years passing gloomily, deprived of her companionship; otherwise I am quite indifferent. When they call my spirits low it is that my body is suffering, I am restless, irritable, easily fatigued, soon overcome, all in consequence of the peculiar disease I am labouring under which affects the nerves very considerably, those belonging to the brain with the rest. I am done up to-day rather, owing to the hubbub of last night. The fire-works tho' wretched, lasted above two hours, and all our windows on that side of the house and the terrace on the top were crowded with

visitors. Many of the things were connected by strings with our balcony, and directed in their explosions by the Mayor who with a large party occupied a good share of the leads.

16. Jersey is given up. Colonel Smith would not go when he found that I was nervous about the small-pox, and indeed it would not have been right to take two delicate girls from a healthy place like this to a bad climate filled with the infection of the most fatal and loathsome of diseases, and vaccination seems hardly to be a preservative now. Whether the virus be worn out, too much diluted in its passage from one human subject to another without returning sufficiently often to the cow, or whether it requires renewing frequently, as every seven or ten years or so, or whether from some want of care in the performance of the operation, something however must be wrong for small-pox has been raging almost as of old in the south of England and in Jersey and numbers who had been vaccinated in infancy have suffered from the worst form of this horrid disease, a kind of typhus being its accompaniment, and many have died.

18. We were also quite amused with a paragraph from the *New York Herald*, considered a vile paper in its own country yet speaking with the voice of a large proportion of the vulgar of the land. Alluding to their new President's ill judged vaunts about the disputed Oregon Territory, and the firm notice taken of this by our ministry, this paper regrets the necessity it foresees of giving us a good 'drubbing'. The Americans would if possible avoid anything so painful as this sort of family dissensions but events beyond their control render it imperative on them to 'lick us well' and so we are 'in for it' if only to prove the advance of democratical over monarchical principles.

20. The little doctor dined with us yesterday after vaccinating the children; he got quite tipsy and was very disagreeable. Annie prepared first for the operation by doing simply what she was bid and when it was over there was an end; Janey declared first of all nothing should induce her to submit to it, but she did, as all these stout speaking people do and very quietly, but she refused to go in to dinner with her sleeve tyed up and when assured no one would mind it she burst into hystericks and was let to run away upstairs where I was sorry her Papa

took the trouble to follow her with wine which of course she refused in her heroicks. I begged of every one to leave her to recover herself which of course she did all the quicker for being unnoticed, so she joined us at tea as if nothing had happened. I suppose it was nervous timidity, but these sort of scenes are so very ridiculous and so very troublesome and render a woman so useless that they must be discouraged by every means even should it be necessary to have recourse to my father's pail of cold water. Johnny was very grave, bared his arm quite composedly and as we were putting on his jacket again we found him near fainting, quite blind, quite colourless, it was a good half hour before he recovered and he could not touch his dinner. This was both fear and resolution, what curious children. I have had another kind little note from Jane forwarding an equally kind letter from Mrs. Macpherson. I am much interested in my morning readings, as I do not get up when I wake these cold rainy days I apply to Mr. Kohl, a clever German to help me to wile away the hours till breakfast and we are just now travelling very amusingly together through Bohemia, Hungary, Servia, etc.

25. Sunday, the Fête Dieu and up to this hour a rainy morning but it seems now inclined to clear which will be a great joy to the crowds collecting to see the Procession. As it moves through the town *twice* I shall try and get to the evening exhibition. A crowd of priests, incense boys, flower girls, musick, torches etc, carry a triumphal car highly ornamented in which sits a little box containing God Almighty, who notwithstanding all precautions wearies so much of the motion that he has to be set down to rest at stated intervals where for his amusement preparation has been made to cheer his resting places by a display in a sort of booth of the embroidery, laces, cachemires and jewels of the neighbouring Ladies. The maids are very much afraid that the show will be very meagre to day on account of the weather the ladies probably not inclining to expose their toilette treasures to the damp. Mr. Gardiner with whom we drank tea last night says this is the Roman fête to Ceres, to propitiate her for the summer growth – that these customs all remained when the mode of worship was changed, the people caring little in whose honour they kept their holiday. The statues of the ancient Gods remained too,

and as St. John, St. Paul, Joseph, Mary etc, these fine pieces of sculpture have continued to receive the adorations offered to them first as Apollo, Pan, Neptune, Venus. Food for thought here. Is it all fiction with but one great Truth?

27. Going out last night we came upon the close of the procession which it seems is to walk the town every evening during the week. I suppose there was more display on Sunday bad as the weather was for it appeared but a poor affair, not many priests and no crowd to speak of an all chiefly women most of them of the lower ranks. The first thing we saw was a large dark banner embroidered and fringed with gold, the pole supporting it held by a priest whose occupation was at certain intervals to lower it when the crowd all kneeled and to raise it when it was proper for them to rise. Behind this came four priests all in yellow and covered with fine lace each holding in his hand a little child in pink carrying a basket from which it scattered flowers before an immense gilt crucifix carried by another priest; the ark surmounted by plumes of white followed, borne on poles as in Jewish days and surrounded by a crowd of yellow priests chaunting very agreeable, young priests bearing censers were stationed all along the line throwing perfume into the air, and as the pageant slowly vanished into the church the fine organ resounded through the stillness.

It sounds very shocking to explain the mystery but it is all intended as a tangible illustration of the Trinity. The banner is the directing Holy spirit pointing out the gold Crucifix as the Son leading to the Father in the Ark behind. Altogether nothing better than the images and tinsel trumpery of the Hindus, not so striking in point of numbers and much about as low in point of feeling, only the ignorant in either case taking part in the absurdity. The humiliating part to me is the Priesthood, men of mature years, of strength, and of intellect lending themselves to a mummery which here in France their fellow men despise. They are taken young which excuses them, sent as Samuel into the Temple before they know to what wretchedness this dedication dooms them; taught little, their minds narrowed rather than enlarged and when some glimmerings of truth begin to dawn upon the brightest, the barrier has been long rivetted between them and the world and they have nothing left but to bow the head in silence.

I never meet a priest without feeling the profoundest pity. It cannot last long now, this barbarously unnatural severance of one class of men from every gentle feeling of their kind.

29. There has been the most ridiculous pantomime at Tara. The *martyrs* escorted there by a crowd of ragamuffins, mass actually celebrated near the grave of the old rebels, speeches made, huzzas shouted, and then the miserable ghost of the monster meetings of heretofore dispersed. Some patriots have receded, others have objected to certain sentiments, divisions are many, ardour cooled, the rent never beyond £400 weekly, not by any means sufficient for the expenses. It is all over. Railroads and Agricultural improvements are the present fury, for the opposing sects cannot get up an opposition to the new Education measures. There are plenty of little meetings, plenty of meagrely signed petitions, sound and fury sufficient to startle *asses*, but there it ends. One drawback to these tranquil times is their total want of interest. Sir Robert Peel like the French despot enacts 'L'état c'est moi', and we all sit by satisfied.

SUNDAY, JUNE. 1. This day week having been so rainy the Procession in honour of the fête Dieu was renewed to-day. An Exposoir or Reposoir, [a wayside or temporary altar] for the maids seem to call these halting places indifferently by either name, was begun yesterday on the Palet just in front of us. Four large cider hogsheads supported a platform of boards we saw last night as we came back from our close stroll through all the narrow streets of the hot town; this morning an immensity of hammering during the night was accounted for by the appearance of just such a sort of houdah as is sometimes set on a twelfth cake. A lady of the neighbourhood with all her household had been hard at work while we were sleeping hanging old carpets, old curtains, sheets, tablecloths and muslin toilette covers over the ugly planks built up into this absurdity. Wreaths of flowers and garlands of leaves festooned these pretty draperies, a double row of common flowers in pots, and a couple of dozen of branches stuck into the ground behind them formed an avenue of approach. Before eight the Banner, the Crucifix, and the plumed ark, four priests in gold brocade and half a dozen others more plainly decorated, eight or ten boys throwing up the censers, three or four children in pink muslin, two little girls in blue carrying a basket between them, and a crowd of about fifty country women with very few men among them, came in sight; the chaunting was indifferent, the bobs and bows tiresome. For about ten minutes this sort of mummery went on and then all moved on again to repeat the same ceremonies at the next station. The two French maids were in raptures. I would have been pleased if I could, but really it was not possible.

Margaret Fyfe was excited by it, out of all sense, John Knox could not have been more, violent; no terms were hard enough to express her horrour at such awful idolatry, the comfortable feeling that all participators in such sins would be damned everlastingly was the only solace her perturbed spirit could receive; and then came such a string of Calvinistick arrogance as made me quite grave, for she is a mild specimen of the religion taught to her nation. We talk of the Irish Catholicks forgetting the Scotch puritans – which is the most Christian in feeling would be a puzzle for the learned. 'Margaret', said I at last, 'did it ever strike you that your views upon these subjects may not be quite correct?' Another storm made up of amazement added to horrour, so I went on – 'Your presbyterian division of the reformed Church is but a small sect among the Protestants; not above one part out of six think as you have been taught to think. The protestants form but a small portion of the Christians, who again are nothing near so numerous as the Mohammedans, and all these together don't amount to *half* the Pagans. Reflect on this, don't believe in the monstrous notion that God made this beautiful world and filled it with living souls all destined to eternal perdition with the exception of a mere handful of a very peculiar people who appear to me to be entirely wanting in the chief of Christian virtues – Humility.' She burst out crying and it is possible she may think again with the eyes of her understanding wider opened. But it is very plain the Scotch priesthood are sadly in want of a more liberal education; probably this late schism among them may be the means of great improvement. The bigoted are gone out and perhaps the more enlightened may come in. The national arrogance is so extraordinary they actually glory in their ignorance holding as dust all who differ from them.

2. It was very close yesterday, our second summer evening, but very pleasant sitting in the Jardin des Plantes; the walks were full of Bourgeois French, very quiet in their behaviour, well dressed, nice looking, wandering with their children under the trees. We fell in with the Moggridges and passed a very pleasant hour with them. I am reading at the recommendation of the pious Mr. Gardiner and of the sedate Colonel Litchfield four volumes full of as much profligacy as ever met my eye – Letters from all the wits of the Age, the beginning of the reign of George III, to George Selwyn. It is little more than a gossip concerning every possible vice in every existing family, health destroyed, fortunes wasted, time lost, talents misemployed, morals laughed at, a melancholy picture commented on in so lively a manner that one is drawn on from one frivolous page to another so much does one become interested in the daily conversation of names so celebrated. How well I remember the wickedest of the set, the memorable Duke of Queensberry[1] sitting like a dried mummy with a parasol over his head in a corner of the balcony of his house in Piccadilly near a flight of steps which descended to the street. Were any of them happy in this vile life of theirs. Through all their sparkling fun I can see, far from it. God knows whether the great world of our own day be much better. They appear more *decent* at any rate, the women especially.

8. The journal is not going on very well just now. I have hardly been quite so strong this week as I hoped to be and have been unable to get up early in the morning. Then there are Jack's lessons to prepare for Mrs. Macleod, he comes to me as soon as he is up at seven and we work away at spelling and reading till eight, when instead of getting up to write I lay still and read my wicked book which is so amusing that much as the people disgust me I can't help admiring their talents.

1. That this was how he spent his last years at 138 Piccadilly was known to the author of the article in the D.N.B. who, after cataloguing his lifetime of misdemeanours, described how 'latterly he spent the greater part of the day at the corner of the bow window, or when the weather was fine, above the porch'.

After breakfast and my little walk I write the recollections of my life[1] which I began to do on my birthday to please the girls who eagerly listen to the story of their mother's youth, now as a pleasing tale, by and bye it will be out of a wish to feel acquainted with people and places I shall not be at hand to introduce them to. This effort of memory amuses me extremely. I live again my early years, among those who made the first impressions on my mind, many of them gone where I am perhaps slowly but very surely following, and I recall places very dear to my imagination which were I now to see I should probably from the changes made in them, know no more. I am glad I thought of this way of occupying my quiet day, a part of it at least, the hour or two thus employed steals easily away, the pleasure of talking over these bygone times with my children attaches us the more to one another as we become more confidential in our intercourse, we make the tale profitable too by the comments we engraft upon it, and best of all it encreases my content with the present, the contrast between my maiden days and married life being to all rational feelings so much in favour of the latter.

11. I have just been reading to Colonel Smith out of Tait's Magazine from Mrs. Norton's 'Child of the Isles'. Her aim is that of Mr. Dickens in his 'Carols', an aim now thank God for the blessed change taken in earnest by many; the poetry such parts as the reviewer has given is enchanting. Poor Mrs. Norton, her 'Autumn' in the highlands which she describes from the recollection of her early married days at Castle Menzies, is touchingly beautiful, poor thing she was more sinned against than sinning, her punishment just, no doubt, is but the fulfilment of the natural law which visits the crimes of the parents upon the children.[2]

1. This is her first mention of the project which she completed eight years later and which was first published in 1898 under the title 'Memoirs of a Highland Lady'.
2. Caroline Norton, poetess, and her strange husband were involved in a notorious trial in 1836 in which an action was taken out against the P.M., Lord Melbourne.

15. Sunday. The Colonels really went off yesterday by Diligence to St. Malo where they would remain to-day and start by the steamer to-morrow, for Southampton. I shall set about all my preparations in earnest to-morrow, for we may be off now at short warning, the sooner the better I believe.

17. These queer French, how they do try to encrease their francs by little nasty overcharges in all their accounts, so general that it quite proves the peculiar dishonesty of the people, they will cheat but they will not steal, and idle as they are they will work well for stray money. I told Bellais to get me a woman to weed the garden, I would give her thirty sous for the job, so he set to work himself at seven o'clock last night and had half the walks cleaned by nine.

22. Jersey. Not a moment have I had for my journal since the evening of the 17th when I made my last entry just before going to bed. Wednesday old Mr. Poe came to me and said that Colonel Home had arrived with all his family, was horrour struck with the hotel de Bretagne, quite at sea about lodgings, and in short disposed to close with an offer he had formerly in his ignorance despised. He would take our lease off our hands and buy all our odds and ends of furniture, only he must come in directly as his multitude of boxes were to arrive from St. Malo on Friday and he must have a place to put them in. I told Mr. Poe he should have an answer before the evening after I had consulted with Mr. Gardiner. He though bitterly lamenting our departure advised my closing with this offer. Since go we must in a fortnight better to take the first opportunity of getting rid of the house, and he entreated of me to take up my abode with him till Colonel Smith's proceedings should be arranged. In my own mind I determined on following Hal by the Granville steamer of Friday week, in the meanwhile thankfully accepting Mr. Gardiner's kind offer.

So Colonel Home was introduced to the house and to me and seemed to be a gentlemanlike man, very tall and thin with a narrow head and contracted forehead and a wide mouth full of big teeth; he would have been very easy to deal with but he appeared to be afraid of committing himself without the sanction of Mrs. Home's approval. So in the afternoon she came – a sort of decent looking housekeeper, fat and plain without manner or air or dress above such station, and to perfect the resemblance, she was evidently such a bargain maker as a cook at market. While she was maundering on with this objection and the other idea and a set of hopes already promising disappointment I reflected on the best method of dealing with a person so very wise in her own conceit, so when her very drawling lecture was concluded I told her that I wanted to get away & was therefore prepared to make some sacrifice in disposing of the remainder of our term – that I should only require the last quarter's rent due on the 1st of July (in advance) to be paid to Mr. Godin, that the hire of the furniture having been paid they should have the use of it for nothing, that it was the custom for the incoming tenant to buy all the little extras left by the outgoing at the valuation of Mme. Hallais, and that I could give up possession on Friday, that my brother-in-law, Mr. Gardiner, would act for me and they might chose a friend to act for them in these arrangements which would save our mutual delicacy. It was thus settled, and then this dawdling body who seemed a good sort of woman too, told me she was doubly connected with my family, having been a Fraser, and niece to old Mrs. Charles Grant the mother of Lord Glenelg,[1] and her sister being married to Felix Raper, my father's second cousin now commanding the artillery at Dumdum.

I feel still in a sort of maze so bustling has been my life since last Monday, for not wishing to be hurried and so fatigued I began then the preparations for removal, and our methodical ways keep us always so orderly in all our affairs that there really was little to do. We had bought nothing we could do without. We gave away all our rubbish as we were done with it rather than carry a load of rags back, and paying our little bills monthly we never have more accounts to call in than can be arranged in an hour. The principal thing was the transfer of the house, but the troublesome part of

1. Charles Grant, Baron Glenelg (1778–1866), as
President of the Board of Trade in the 1820s was
much involved in the fortunes of the East India
Company, and, as the Memoirs make clear, of those
of his extended clan.

that business dear kind Mr. Gardiner has taken off me. Mr. Hickey insisted on selling all the wine. The Colonels had bidden me give it away but Mr. Hickey would not let me. I therefore made small presents of a few dozens each, to him, Mr. Macleod, Mr. Gardiner and the Doctor, and the rest was disposed of, most of it during the day, though the money would take another to gather it. We had a great deal of fun in our bustle one way or other, and every one was so kind. I never liked the place so well as when I was leaving it. There were a few small bottles of the champaign Mr. Gardiner had hoped would have been good for me which I did not think he would like to see again, so I gave them to Mr. Hickey who thinking the French revenue had had enough of our money for its troublesome permits determined to cheat it of more, so he packed a bottle into each coat pocket, carefully as he thought, and went marching off across the palet with the two leaded necks sticking out in full view. Annie called him back and succeeded better in hiding them.

30. The last day of the month of June. When I end July we shall be at home, our dear home after nearly two years absence. What changes we shall find, some improvements, a few things perhaps gone wrong. We must not expect all to be right, it will be therefore wise to prepare ourselves for a little vexation by laying in a little stock of patience to meet it.

I was not out all yesterday and I think my prudence has been rewarded for I am considerably more comfortable to-day, feeling perfectly well too, head up to anything. The girls went twice to church accompanied in the evening by their father and Jack, and we passed a very quiet day, no one interfering with us. I made up a packet of scraps for my aunt Bourne like those of old which used to travel between us. What a pleasure is the penny postage, how delightful in so many respects to be in our own country again where for moderate people like ourselves living is, I am almost sure, quite as cheap as abroad; the necessaries are the same, taking one thing with the other, the luxuries certainly make a difference, they are considerably cheaper abroad, but we habitually indulge in so few of them that the difference is not so great to us. And there is a freedom of action at home the loss of which is extremely annoying upon the Continent. Still one could be happy anywhere, lucky that I think so, for I foresee that we shall very soon migrate again.

Colonel Smith will never stay quiet at home unless he is allowed to pull the house down to have the pleasure of improving upon it in the next edition, his head is full of alterations already, so that if he can he will keep us in a mess all winter. The moment he has a penny saved he seems to be in a fever till he has it buried in stone or lime, or iron pipes, no indeed, now it is glass pipes; all those of iron are to be taken up to be replaced by this new crotchet and the ground torn in every direction accordingly. I shall be extravagant too, get hold of the money first and spend it in what I have hitherto out of folly done without. My dear Colonel, Beware of me.

SUNDAY, JULY 13th. Dublin. I don't know what it was put me out of conceit with my journal but here are ten blank days in which I have either been too idle or too busy to enter a word in it. Our voyages and our restings and our arrival here have all been pleasant as travels could be, and I have born them well, yet somehow felt too unsettled to sit down to think of them. I have never been alone for one instant till just now that Hal has taken all the children off to Christ Church Cathedral, the girls being most anxious to hear the choir again now that they can better understand its merits. It is quite a relief to me to be by myself, I feel rested already. We have seen only the small circle of our intimate friends not having yet announced our arrival to the few greater acquaintance we can boast of in the more fashionable parts of the town.

And of humbler friends, Hannah twice to see her boy [Jack] and bring him country eggs and fresh butter and a bouquet as big as himself. She is in a most comfortable place with kind people, getting good wages, well dressed and happy, Marianne also in a good service, neat and tidy. Poor Sarah, her two babies and James, he is in a place he is likely to keep all his days with £25 a year and many perquisites; he has Sarah in neat lodgings almost in the country and being able to pay for them she seems inclined on her part to be idle under the excuse of attending to her sickly baby, whom she won't be long in making an end of she manages it so improperly. I will help her if she will help herself, not otherwise. She is a good creature but so foolish, so little able of herself to bustle through this busy life that I doubt her ever doing more than just drudging on in discontented poverty. Mr. and Mrs. Ogle Moore spared me half an hour of their short half day and met me with the kindness of relations.

And now how does dear old Dublin look after our absence? – beautiful – less misery in it than I ever saw before, its splendid streets thronged with busy crowds, walking, driving, moving as if alive, shops swarming like beehives, women dressed, I was going to say better than French women, but as well certainly, the same good taste in shape and colour and material, and their straw bonnets and their ribbons superior. After the vulgar shewy taste of the English the Irish women do look so nice.

Hal went down to Baltiboys on Friday by the Mail and returned by Mr. Kilbee's early car yesterday bringing word that the country was looking beautiful, but that Mr. Darker would not be ready for us before the end of the week. We have arrived in the rainy season and very showery it has been since we came, this delayed the masons. All his scraps of news I will not yet touch on, when we get home will be time enough. Paddy the gardener came up for seeds and brought us some unripe cherries, he visited his wife too, I suppose, for the old absurdity has got himself married to a dirty creature who was cook to Mr. Fraser and is living in town here with her sister till Paddy can find her a house.

14. All came home last night well pleased with their dinner party. It was the usual set. To-day the first person we saw was George Robinson, the next Richard Hornidge who came to offer us apartments at Tulfarris till the workmen were out of our own house. Lady Milltown too sent us word by the Doctor that she hoped we would make use of Russborough – it is very kind, more than we deserve for we were unsociable neighbours.

16. After dinner Hal and I walked out alone, he wanted to shew me a low phaeton he had been all the morning hunting out. They fancy, he and the doctor, that I get cold in the car. We saw several and I think both fixed on the same which will be ready in about ten days. We also looked at some mirrours and find that for twelve pounds we shall get one quite fit for the chimney piece of our little drawing-room or book-room as we mean to call it. We have saved money enough to make a thousand little improvements.

27. Sunday. Another long rest to my journal, I have indeed been

too busy to fill it, all the daylight almost having been occupied in a thousand active employments. So many people and things to see, so much to hear, so much to arrange, it seemed as if there never would be time to do all, and any little spare half hour there was I had letters to write, some on business which could not be delayed, others to friends who had a right to be early remembered.

We came home in a comfortable open carriage hired for the occasion on Thursday the 17th. It being market day in Blesinton, several familiar faces peered through the crowd and Mr. Dizest set the joy bells a ringing. The day was fine the drive very pleasant, the more so as the same indications of encreasing comfort which we had remarked throughout Dublin were fully more apparent in the country. Neater houses, tidier people, even a garden or two and flowers in some. The young plantations seem to be thriving everywhere and no where better than around us.

Baltiboys looks beautiful, quite sheltered, flourishing trees, clean fields, good fences, – it is quite pleasant to return to a place in such good order. The house has suffered very little from our tenants during these two years, upstairs hardly at all. We should have done as much mischief ourselves as they have done. Below it is rather more serious; the kitchen range boiler, steamer, hot plate etc. having been injured and dirt and neglect having destroyed the 'battery'. Ten pounds however, or less will repair all so that we have every reason to be satisfied. Mrs. White, Paddy's young wife, must be a horrour, the dirtiest creature existing, for though old Peggy and her daughter Mary were near a week scrubbing and scouring it will require fully another before we have the kitchen department any thing like decently clean.

Yet it is surprising how nearly we are settled already. We had to change most of the furniture to suit ourselves to our former ways, to unpack both what we brought and what we left, so we have been very busy. We have had many visitors too of all degrees and complaints and slanders and accusations to listen to, to sift, to turn a deaf ear to, for most unpleasant quarrelling has been going on, jealousies, envying and every sort of evil speaking, with much illwill to those in authority on account of Quin's farm for one thing and for some follies and much virtue for other things. All will come right now we are back. Steadiness, just arbitration, and the sifting of every slander will soon restore peace when the people see no good will come of their malice. Poor Tom Darker, honest and faithful as he is he had his failings; he is full of prejudices and he lets these prejudices interfere with his actions, unconsciously, I believe, but the effect is the same. Still he must be supported, he had done no positive injury to anyone, and though in strict justice so much favour to one family to the exclusion of every other be to be regretted where all want assistance, it must be allowed that these Hylands are more actively industrious than the general run of the labourers hereabouts. Unluckily the Priest has thought fit to meddle not only with our servants but with the school, not Mr. Germaine but a young Curate sent to assist him. He has gained little by his interference in either case and will probably retire from the Agitation now that the landlord is at hand. I am glad of the squabble, he has exasperated a strong faction among his parishioners, thus rather hastening the hour of freedom to all. No greater change has taken place than in the feelings of the people towards their priests.

It is a twelvemonth this very day since I heard my dear sister Mary's voice for the last time. It is all a dream. We are here again as we were before, these two years have passed as a vision of the night leaving only a weight of sorrow behind. Life can never be again to me what it was before this break amongst us. Sorrows and disappointments have not been spared to me more than to others, but amongst the many griefs of on the whole a happy life, I turned always in thought to the little band, unbroken yet, which played in long past days upon the sunny slope of the Doune hill together. God forbid I should repine at his decrees, we must all go where she had led the way, but I am lonely without her.

Index

Abercorn, Lord and Lady 44
Aberdeen, Lord 110
agriculture 10–11, 47, 98, 107–8, 139,
    160, 161, 181
Aire 138
Albigensians 117
Albret, Jeanne d' 59, 60
Algiers 79
Allan, Peggy and Robert 173
Alley, Mr (Blessington) 71, 76
Altyre 25
Angoulême 60
Antoine the cook 33, 37, 39
Argeles 121
Ashley, Lord 97, 98
Atholl, Duke of 181
Aumale, Duc d' 12

Bagnères 38
Baltiboys 26, 40, 44, 47, 64, 103, 184,
    193, 199, 204, 221, 226 reactions on
    return 245
Balzac, Honoré de 83, 173
Barèges 122
Barnes, Sir Edward and Lady 46
Bayonne 79, 114
Béarn and the Béarnais 32, 45, 49, 104,
    118, 132, 135
Bedford, Duchess of 44
Bedous 117
Bellini's 'Norma' 106
Betterham 121
Biaritz 35
Bickersteth, Edward 91
Black Prince 130
Blair Castle 175
Blakeney, Sir Edward 93
Blessington, Lady 232
Bordeaux 3–10, 134, 136
Bourne (Aunt Bourne) 163, 186,
    227, 242
Brest 138
Brougham, Lord 83, 219
Browne, Tom (Hal's cousin) 168
Buscalet, Rev. L.J. 30, 49, 112, 134
Buxton, Sir Thomas Fowell Bart. 218
Byrne, Michael (tenant) 166

Calvinism 237
Cambridge, University of 73
Campbell, Miss Emma 21, 30, 85
Campbell, Mr. and Mrs. 22, 30, 83, 105,
    her ball at Pau 85–6, 100

Canning, George, P.M. 117
Carey, Captain, R.N. 55–6, 84–5, 97
Carr (also Kerr), Rev. Mr. 30, 42, 56, 95,
    98, 229
Cauterêts 127
Cavan, Lord and Lady 47
Ceylon 51, 78, 93
Chambers, Robert and William 72
Chambord, Comte de (Henry V)
    163, 185
Charante 138–9
Charlemagne 132
Charles X of France 5
Cheltenham 126, 187
Church of Scotland 44
Church services 16, 24, 42, 48, 56, 61,
    95, 98, 112, 134, 242, Roman Catholic
    at Pau 57–8, 104–5
Churchill, General and Mrs. 93
Clark, Mr. (Bordeaux merchant) 5, 6, 7
Clarke, William of Dalnavert 88
Cobden, Richard 72
Cockburn, Mr. (banker) 39, 168
Cole, Lady Fanny 100
Cole, Mr. 46, 79, 97
Combe, George 43, 72
Commons (tenant) 135
Cooper, Jane 14, 15, 183, 215, 276
cost of living, see expenses
Costano, M. and Mme. 30
Cottenham, Earl of 204
Craig, James 166
Craig, William 133
Crane, Mr. and Mrs. 155
Crawford, William Sharman, M.P. 26
Cumming, Alexander of Logie 26
Cumming, Sir William Gordon, of
    Gordonstoun 26

Darker, William 161
Darker, Tom (steward) 26, 40, 98, 135,
    160, 186, 199, 244, 246
Dempsey, Brian (tenant) 64, 135,
    160, 177
Denmark, Prince of 127
Devon Commission 72
Dickens, Charles 196, 221
Disraeli, Benjamin 112, 231
Disruption (Church of Scotland) 43
Dodson, Paddy and Peggy
    (tenants) 103, 160, 244,
    245
Dorcas Society 48

Douglas, Colonel and Mrs. Percy 30, 41, 97
Downshire, Marquis of 230
Drysdale, Dr. and Mrs. 4, 6
Dublin 55, 65, 80, 82, 99, 147, 223, 226, 243, reactions to on return 244–5
Dublin University Magazine 183
Duoro, Marquis and Marchioness of 43

East India Company 13, 17, 75, 168, 191
Eaux Bonnes 111
Eaux Chaudes 113–4
Eckford, Dr. 147, 174, 178, 223, 232
Edinburgh 21, 71
Edinburgh Review 63, 71, 197, 219, 228
Eliot, Captain and Mrs. 97, 100–103
  his musical accomplishments 102
  lack of information *re* family from E.G.'s other sources 133
  reaction to Henry Eliot's accident 150
  reputed family connections to the Earl of St. Germans 104
Ellenborough, Lord 4, 51, 55, 93
Ellis, Mrs. 7, 24, 49, 51, 126
Elphick, Miss (former governess) 205–6
Elphinstone, Margaret Mercer (Countess Flahault) 108
Evening Chronicle 25
expenses 7, 8, 10, 16, 17, 19, 23, 33–4, 35, 36, 54, 57, 65, 69, 115, 119, 120, 131, 140, 145, 153, 155, 179, 194, 199

family finances 33–4, 186, 199
Fitzgerald, John 103, 160
Fitzgerald, Pat 64
Flahault, Auguste, Comte de 108
Foix, Gaston de 59
food (Bordeaux) 8, 10, 11, 31, 33
Fox, Mrs. 56–7, 101
Fox, Selina 56–7, 84–5
Fraser, Mr. (also Frazer) (Co. Wicklow) 40, 98, 103, 134, 166, 177, 219, 244
Fraser, Mr. (publisher) 87–8
Free Church of Scotland 44
French army 22, 29, 30, 40, 43, 54, 78–9
French customs 6–7
French fashions 9–10, 23, 29–30, 35, 54
Frere, John (cousin) 73
Frere, John Hookham (uncle) 73, 133
Frere, Mr. and Mrs. Bilton 47
Froissart, Jean 59, 139
Fyfe, Margaret 7, 11, 13, 19, 44, 143, 144, 145, 151, 164, 174, 177,
  her Calvinist reaction to religious procession 237

Gabas 113–14, 116

Gandalous 45
Gardiner, Miss (schoolmistress) 135, 163, 190, 230
Gavernie 124
Genlis, Comtesse de 83
George IV 108
Germaine, Father Arthur 183, 190, 246
Gladstanes, Mr. and Mrs. (Co. Wicklow) 103
Gladstone, William Ewart 229
Glen Ennich 124
Godin, M. (Juge de Paix, Avranches) 145, 241
Gordon, Duchess of 24, 96, 109, 118, 229
Gore, Henry (Lord Downshire's agent) 226
Gough, Field Marshal Sir Hugh 93
Graham, Sir James 97
Grant family
  father 51, 55, 89, 101, 149, 157, 173, 195, 216, 227
  mother 8, 55, 89, 156, 161, 166, 173, 195, 222
  brother John 3, 43, 55, 73, 156, 191, 195
  brother William 51, 156, 195, 219, 227, 228
  sister Jane 25, 43, 51, 65, 89, 133, 134, 150, 156, 157, 166, 167, 195, 211–12, 227, 234
  sister Mary 9, 12, 16, 17, 23, 24, 25, 30, 33, 35, 37, 38, 43, 46, 50, 58, 62, 66, 70, 71, 74, 79, 85, 88, 90
    criticism 27–9, 80–1
    servant problems 38, 46
    progressive stages of illness 18–19, 95, 107, 108–9, 133–4, 180, 203
    decision to move to Avranches 90
    and the Eliot affair 101, 102–3, 104, 106
    first appearance at Avranches 144–5
    deathbed 153–8
    portrait 186
  brother-in-law Thomas George Gardiner 9, 12, 16, 23, 24, 35, 39, 43, 47, 52, 72, 73, 84–5, 92, 94, 96, 109, 143, 149, 157, 160, 161, 166, 180, 203, 218, 219, 223, 228, 229, 234, 238, 240, 241, 242
    and Mary's death 156–66
    Avranches anxieties 134
    criticism *re* Janey and Mary 27–9, 61, 81, 107
    criticism of his politics 56
    criticism of his children's education 70, 118

reaction to dismissal of Miss
Hart 164–5
reaction to complaint by E.G. about
son's foul language 165
role in the Eliot affair 100, 101
niece Janey 23, 27, 35, 37, 41, 50, 61,
63–4, 70, 84, 96, 153, 156, 161, 167,
213, 224
'affair' with Henry Eliot 100–103,
106, 107
reactions in Avranches to his
accident 150
nephew Tommy 101, 109, 112, 122–3,
125, 156, 157, 159, 164, 174, 228
Grant, Charles, Baron Glenelg, 24
Grant, Elizabeth of Rothiemurchus (also
Mrs. Henry Smith, The Highland
Lady, E.G.)
advice to children 62, 77, 80, 212
and Baltiboys 26, 40, 44, 103
and French manners 8, 17, 27, 137,
144, 154, 158, 240
and her own health 31, 40, 41,
164, 225–6
and shopkeepers 27, 36, 145
books read 69, 72, 76, 83, 91, 108,
109, 112, 120, 153, 154, 160, 162,
173, 176, 183, 196–7, 209–10, 220,
228, 232, 239
contrast between French and English
servants 18, 33, 119–20, 151, 171,
192, 194
costume 97
criticisms of sister Mary 23, 27–8,
80–1, 110–11
description of houses
Avranches 142, 145–6
Pau 13
development of Mary's illness 18, 20,
107, 110–11, 133
education 27, 64, 73, 118, 176–7, 182,
183, 222, 224, 230
family finances 33–4, 65
fashions in France 9–10, 23, 46, 54,
58, 76, 104–5, 116, 129–30, 138–9,
142, 222
French shopkeepers 17, 172
French soldiers 22
her early writings 88
Indian memories 9, 11, 16, 130, 132,
138, 180, 235
landlord/tenant relations 26–7, 99, 160,
178, 209
need for social revolution 99–100, 112,
162, 228
opinions on French people 22–3, 116
proprieties of courtship 100
reflections on old age 180

relations with her husband 40, 64, 77,
150, 169, 173, 178, 179, 183–4, 193,
197, 232, 243
religion 16, 42, 43, 49, 56, 57–8, 62,
76, 91, 98, 99, 118–19, 132, 183,
187–8, 191, 193–4, 198, 204, 207–8,
212, 224–5, 230, 231–2, 234–7
repeal and Daniel O'Connell 41–2, 46,
47–8, 55–6, 57
and state trials 79–80
sentence 84, 86
verdict 126–7
judgement reversed 171–2
Sundays 16
views on Avranches 151
Bordeaux 13, 136–7
Pau 12, 20, 24, 65
views on British royal family 25, 26
views on French peasantry 31, 45,
104, 151–2
views on Miss Hart 15, 30–1, 40, 71
views on noise in Pau 21, 107

'E.G.' at Avranches
begins *Memoirs of a Highland Lady* 239
children's routine 181–2
criticisms of society 184–5
criticisms of the climate and society
192–3, 204
des Mares, M. the landlord's
ball 188–9
description of town 151
disapproval of Margaret Fyfe's
bigotry 237
dismissal of Miss Hart 164
Doctor Robinson's visit 223–26
English community 152
Florence and Avranches compared 199
French surgeon's report 160
house-hunting 145–6
markets 142–4
Mary's funeral 159
old Grant family debts 227
organisation of household 145, 151
Pau and Avranches compared 211
prejudices against Bretons 143,
187, 211
preparations for Mary's funeral 158–60
reflections on Mary 167

'E.G.' at Pau
Academy 52
advantages of Pau 26, 33, 64–5
castle 59–61
criticisms of society 30–1, 59, 65–6
daily routine 37
etiquette 69
factions and quarrels (mostly

medical) 47, 74–5, 79, 83, 91, 92,
95–7, 98
Janey's 'affair' with Henry Eliot
100–103, 104, 106, 133
lack of progress 58
local philanthropy 61
markets 34–5, 39, 53
Mrs Campbell's ball 85–6, 100
music and dancing 58–9, 102, 105,
111, 189
travels in the Pyrenees 112–119,
120–133
unreliable tradesmen 92
varied street life 32, 36, 41, 53
water problems 33

Grant, Sandy 147–8
Gregg, Rev. Mr. Tresham 225
Grey, Charles, Viscount Howick 87
Grey, Sir George 87
Guizot, François 97, 99

Hall, Basil (explorer) 150
Hart, Miss 3, 6, 8, 9, 10, 11, 24, 28, 35,
37, 38, 50, 69, 70, 72, 74, 85, 112, 123,
125, 129, 133, 140, 151, 159, 160, 164,
166, 173–4, 185, 186, 205
criticisms 14, 30–1, 140–1, 144
Hazelwood, Mr. (medical quack) 91, 92,
96, 98, 110
Heathfield, Lord 104
Heber, Reginald, Bishop of Calcutta, 210
Hedges, Rev. Mr. 81, 84, 98
Henry IV of France 12, 20, 59, 60, 121
Hickey, Rev. Mr. (Martin Doyle) 145,
146–7, 159, 225, 230, 242
Home, Colonel 240–1
Honfleur 90
Hornidge family (Co.. Wicklow) 9
Hornidge, John 226–7
Hornidge, Richard 161, 166, 226, 244
Hotel de la Charrente (Bordeaux) 7, 136
houses (descriptions) 13, 47, 49–50,
143–4, 188–9
Hunter Blair, Colonel and Mrs. 47, 49,
54–5, 102
Hunter Blair, Sir David 49

The Inspector, periodical 89
Ironside, Edward (uncle) 81

Jacques (Jacques Fort, manservant) 19,
33, 38, 39, 111–2, 119, 120, 135
Jeffrey, Lord Francis 63, 218
Jersey 174, 222–3
Joinville, Prince de 12, 26
Jones, Captain and Mrs. Stanhope 154
Jurançon 35

Kearns, George (tenant) 138
Kelly, Tom (tenant) 64, 209, 219
Kemble, Charles 211–2
Kent, Duchess of 127
Kerr, Rev. Mr, see Carr

La Croix, M. (the Pau shoemaker)
27, 36, 45
La Rochelle 139
Landseer, Edwin 44
Lavater (the phrenologist) 43
Le Gras, M. Antoine 23, 100
Leinster, Duke and Duchess of 118
libraries 99
Lingard, John 37
Litchfield, Colonel 8, 9, 11, 13, 14, 15,
20, 22, 29, 34, 41, 44, 48, 64, 65, 66,
69, 70, 77, 100, 102, 111, 112, 113,
115, 117, 120, 123, 128, 131, 133, 149,
150, 152, 159, 174, 178, 179, 192, 217,
226, 238
Literary Gazette 89
Lorient 138
Louis XIV 60, 220, 236
Louis XVI 141
Louis-Philippe 5, 25, 59, 60, 83, 99, 109,
162, 231, 232
Lourdes 121, 130
Louvie 112–13, 116
Lowe, Sir Hudson 77–8, 163
Lynch, Mrs. (mother's old maid) 102
Lyon, Captain 83, 92, 153

MacHale, John, R.C.Archbishop of
Tuam 207–8
MacKenzie, Peggy (former housekeeper)
44
Mackintosh, Sir James 149
Macpherson, James 'Ossian' (Belleville)
88, 152–3
Maguire, Mrs. (Naas) 9
Maharajpur, Battle of 93
Maistre, Comte Xavier de 153
Manners, Lord John 231
Marlborough, Duke of 43
Medlicott, Rev. Mr. 61
Melbourne, Lord, P.M. 239
Memoirs of a Highland Lady 239
Menzies Castle 239
Merrey, Miss (Blessington) 163
Milltown, Earl and Countess of 75, 146,
166, 214, 222, 244
Mont de Marsin 11
Mont St. Michel 152, 175–6
Montauban 4, 7, 61
Montpensier, Duc de 11, 12, 20, 60
Moore, Rev. Mr. 72, 98, 103, 163, 183,
190, 230, 244

Morning Herald 45
Mortagne 139
Murphy, Francis Stock, M.P. 87
Murray, Daniel, R.C. Cardinal
  Archbishop of Dublin 213

Naas (Co. Kildare) 9
Nantes 138–9, 141
Napier, Sir Charles 102, 141
Napoleon (Buonaparte) 41, 51, 55, 77,
  79, 83, 93, 162
Navarez, Marquesa de 21, 30, 65, 117
Need, Mrs. 63
Nemours, Duc de 12, 162
New York Herald 233
Newark, Lord 96
Nicholas Nickleby 91
nobility 99
Norton, Caroline 239

O'Connell, Daniel 47–8, 135, 172, 178,
  181, 182, 207–8, 236
  monster meetings 41–2
  prosecution 46
  trial; spell broken 55–6
  state trials 79–80, 82–3, 109
  verdict 84
  reactions 86
  sentence 126–7
  overturned 171–2
O'Connell, John 42, 46, 80
O'Meara, Barry Edward 77
Old Curiosity Shop 146
Oleron 116–7, 119
Oregon Dispute 233
Orleans, Duc d' 12, 30, 162
Osse 118
Owen, William (Lord Downshire's agent)
  226, 230
Oxford 8
Oxford Movement 16
Oxford, University of 73

passports 9, 10
Passy 28
Peel, Sir Robert 4, 81, 89, 109, 127, 194,
  212, 220, 229, 231, 236
Pennington, Colonel 77, 89
Pepys, Henry, Bishop of Worcester 204
Perronet, M. de 5
phrenology 42–3
Piper, Colonel and Mrs. 154
Planté (Gardiner's valet) 109, 143
Poe, Robert 145–6
Polignac, Jules and Armand 5
Pollard, Dr. 133, 146, 149, 153, 156, 157,
  159, 160, 166, 169, 184, 191, 218, 233
Pomaré, Queen 90

postage 35–6, 181, 242
press and newspapers 25, 45, 47, 50, 56,
  72, 73, 87, 88–9
Protestant Church in Ireland 99
Punjab 55
Pusey, Edward Bouverie 16
Puseyism, comments on 16, 20, 191,
  193, 204
Puyoos (Pau landlords), father and son
  14, 25, 32, 47, 50, 58, 69, 83, 86, 102,
  134, 141, 165, 203
  and the National Guard 50
  E.G.'s irritation 21–2, 49, 58
  admiration 52

Quarterly Review 73
Queensberry, Duke of 238
Quin, Pat (tenant) 135, 178, 193, 209,
  219, 245

railroads 99
reading rooms 99
Rennes 142
Repeal Movement (*see also* O'Connell)
  41–2, 44, 46
revolution 99
Richmond, Duke of 43
Riddell, Campbell 52, 78
Robertson, General 17
Robinson, Dr. George 26, 44, 47, 72, 75,
  98, 103, 166, 171, 174, 177, 184, 217,
  229, 230, 244
  visit to Avranches 223–26
Robinson, John (agent) 64, 161, 163, 178,
  186, 193, 199, 209
Rochefort 139
Ross-shire riots 43
Rothiemurchus (including the Doune)
  24, 37, 43, 89, 114, 128, 130, 139,
  156, 247
Russell, Lord John 87
Russia, Emperor of 127, 162
Ryan, James (tenant) 135, 177

St. André cathedral, Bordeaux 10
St. Germans, Earl of 104
St. Helena 77, 162–3
St. Jean de Luz 43, 122, 130–1
St. Sauveur 120, 133
Saintine, Xavier 153
Sarrance 118
Saunder's Magazine 99
Saxe-Coburg-Gotha, Ernest, Duke of 108
Saxony, King of 127
school at Baltiboys (see also Miss
  Gardiner) 64
Scotsman, The 25, 63, 71, 160, 213
Scott, Mr. (Pau tutor) 70, 90, 112, 176

self-improvement 99
servants 17, 18, 19, 33, 38
Sheil, Richard Lalor 80
Simpson, Mr. (Edinburgh) 63, 71, 72
Smith (Smythe) Dr. 19, 41, 70, 74–5, 79,
    91, 110–111, 155, 160
Smith Bouveries 154
Smith, Annie (E.G.'s daughter) 6, 61, 71,
    106, 112, 113, 140, 164, 171, 176, 182,
    189, 215, 216, 226, 233, 242
Smith, Colonel Henry 11, 29, 64, 72, 74,
    98, 137, 152, 155, 156, 157, 186, 215,
    216, 234
    arrangements for Mary's funeral
        158–166
    asthma 7–8, 14, 20, 31, 77, 113, 130,
        164, 168–9, 174, 177, 178, 181
    Bordeaux arrangements 7
    expedition to St. Malo 222
    health 20, 22, 40, 53
    ignorance of French 9, 11, 117
    nature of relationship with wife 40, 64,
        77, 150, 178, 179, 183–4, 193, 197,
        232, 243
    on French soldiers 22, 29
    opinion of Miss Hart 15, 30, 40
    role in niece's 'affair' 100
    travels in Pyrenees 112–119, 120–133
Smith, Jack/Johnny (E.G.'s son John) 15,
    19, 26, 40, 41, 44, 77, 80, 112, 140,
    164, 165, 171, 177, 184, 204, 215, 222,
    223, 226, 234, 238, 243
Smith, Janey (E.G.'s daughter) 27, 42,
    71, 85, 106, 112, 140, 164, 171, 176,
    182, 184, 189, 219, 223, 226, 233
Smith, Sidney/Sydney 218–9
soldiers (French) 22, 29, 30, 40, 43,
    54, 78–9
Souza, Botelho 108
Spurzheim (the phrenologist) 43
Stanhope, Hon. and Rev. Fitzroy 155

steeplechasing 106
Stratton (Straton), Captain 47, 100, 120,
    122, 126, 128, 130–1
suttlers 29–30, 38–9

Tahiti 8–9
Templars 132
Thiers, Adolphe 97
Tod's *Sunday School Teacher* 94
Todd and Burns (Dublin) 99
Travel:
    Bordeaux to Pau 10–12
    Pau to Avranches 135–42
    Southampton to Bordeaux 3–5
Trollope, Frances 69, 109, 210, 229
Tunbridge Wells 119
Turnbull, Mr. (son-in-law of Sir James
    Mackintosh) 149
Tynte, Mr. (Co. Wicklow) 90

Valpy, Mr. and Mrs. 3, 8, 13, 17, 20, 22,
    41, 47, 48, 49, 52, 59, 72, 134, 135,
    136, 199, 229
Valpy, Richard (headmaster) 3
Vendée, La 139
Versailles 60
Victoria, Queen 25, 26, 108, 174–5,
    180–1, 212, 231
Vivian, Mary-Anne 88

Wakley, Thomas 97
Waterloo 22, 53
Wellesley, Henry, Lord Cowley 36, 96
Wellesley-Pole, William, Earl of
    Mornington 218
West, Rev. Mr. 26, 47, 75, 103, 135, 161,
    166, 171
Wiseman, Sir William 149
Wordsworth, Dr. 73
Wouverman, Philip 103